V

2 CDN ARMD BDE

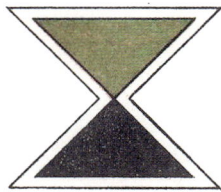

33 ARMD BDE

162 (INDEP) INF BDE

BEACH GPS

V

4 ARMD BDE

34 ARMD BDE

I CDN AGRA

AIRFIELD CONSTRUCTION GPS

N

V

6 (GDS) TANK BDE

4 CDO BDE

2 CDN AGRA

"R" FORCE

V

8 ARMD BDE

56 (INDEP) INF BDE

ROYAL NETHERLANDS BDE
(Prinses Irene)

I INDEP BELGIAN BDE GP

DIV

27 ARMD BDE

115 (INDEP) IN BDE

CZECH INDEP ARMD BDE GP

NETHERLANDS DIST.

CDN ARMD BDE

31 TK BDE

116 (INDEP) INF BDE

G.H.Q. LIAISON REGT

BRITISH FORCES IN GERMANY

THE LIVED EXPERIENCE

BRITISH FORCES IN GERMANY

THE LIVED EXPERIENCE

PETER JOHNSTON

First published in Great Britain in 2019 by
Profile Editions, an imprint of
PROFILE BOOKS LTD
29 Cloth Fair
London EC1A 7JQ
www.profileeditions.com

10 9 8 7 6 5 4 3 2 1

Printed and bound in Great Britain by Gomer
The moral right of the author has been asserted.

A CIP catalogue record for this book is available from
the British Library.

ISBN 978 1 78816 032 2

Design: TwoSheds Design
Project management: Neil Burkey

FSC MIX
Paper from
responsible sources
FSC® C114687

COVER: Colour Sergeant Taylor, his
wife and two children with their
purchases after a visit to the NAAFI
Families Shop in Berlin in 1949
(Imperial War Museum)

PREVIOUS: Soldiers of the 1st Battalion
The Royal Fusiliers receive
instruction on German geography
before their departure for Osnabrück
in June 1963 (Crown)

FOREWORD

The British have maintained a military presence in Germany since the end of the Second World War in 1945, when Britain's 2nd Army was nearly 800,000 strong. Indeed many would argue that the British presence goes back further but ceased in 1933. At the end of the Second World War our role was to police and administer occupied Germany, but the short-term plans of 1945 went on to change constantly, influenced by world events over the next seventy years. With this, our relationship with our Host Nation changed and developed: it went from our arrival as occupiers, growing into partners, and now sees us as firm friends and allies.

The story of British Forces in Germany is one to be celebrated and told – in all its variety. It is the tale not just of soldiers, airmen and their families, but of a way of life and of partnership with the Germans themselves. In addition to the obvious training and alliance benefits, a posting to Germany has offered many a good quality of life, and opportunities that they had never encountered before, ranging from sailing in the Baltic to skiing at Winterberg, to adventure training in the Harz Mountains and Bavaria. Life in the garrison towns has been great, with a strong sense of community, which has made postings to Germany much sought after and fondly remembered. It has been a place to experience, somewhere in which deep friendships have been forged, where marriages have been made and where many have chosen to make home permanently.

The rebasing of all of the final major Field Army Units from Germany follows a decision taken in the UK's *Strategic Defence and Security Review* in 2010. However, the reality is that the British military presence in Germany has reduced consistently since the end of the Second World War as our friendship with Germany has grown and our strategic partnership deepened. The major rebasing in 2019 represents the next chapter in this close and strong friendship and partnership. It also sets the conditions for the Future Defence Presence in Sennelager, which will further develop the interoperability between the British and German Armies and maintain fantastic training opportunities long into the future. As a result, it is more a case of 'Tschüss' than 'Auf Wiedersehen'.

As we prepare for the next chapter in our shared history with Germany, the aim of this book is to reflect and remember the lived experience of all those who have served with British Forces in Germany between 1945 and 2019. This will undoubtedly bring different memories and emotions to the people who have served, or know people who have served in Germany, particularly over various generations. I hope you agree that it is a fantastic account of the British Military's time in Germany to date and is a very enjoyable read, whether you have served here or not. It captures a constantly shifting but iconic time for the British Forces in Germany.

Brigadier Richard Clements
Commander British Forces Germany
23rd September 2019

OPPOSITE: **A Challenger tank from the Queen's Royal Hussars (Queen's Own and Royal Irish) firing on Range 7 of the Bergen-Hohne Ranges during annual firing camp, 2018. QRH were the longest-serving tank regiment in Germany, and the last to leave in 2019 when they left Athlone Barracks in Paderborn (Crown)**

CHAPTER
I

FROM WAR TO PEACE
1945-1948

THE LAST DAYS

Late on 23rd March 1945, Field Marshal Bernard Montgomery launched Operation PLUNDER, as part of a coordinated set of crossings to get across the Rhine and break into northern Germany. Supported by Operation VARSITY, the largest airborne operation in history to be conducted on a single day and in one location, the operation was a success. Nearly six years after the outbreak of the Second World War, the British were across the Rhine and advancing deep into Germany. This began a period of rapid, if difficult, advance for Montgomery's 21st Army Group.

The area west of the Rhine had been cleared in heavy fighting, in particular during the battles through the Reichswald forest and beyond that had seen towns like Kleve captured on 11th February 1945. The Germans were forced to retreat eastwards across the Rhine, blowing any bridge they could – and leaving 230,000 of their soldiers to be captured by the Allies.

One by one, towns in Germany began to fall to the advancing Allies. Osnabrück was captured on 4th April when the VII Corps of Field Marshal Montgomery's Second Army entered the city having faced little resistance. But other towns and cities proved harder targets. At the Battle of Rethem on 11th and 12th April, as the British advanced north from the Weser, the 53rd Welsh Division lost 230 men clearing the crossing of the River Aller. The advance continued. Celle in Lower Saxony was occupied by 15th Scottish Division on 12th April. Uelzen was captured on 18th April and Bremen on 25th April.

Among the towns being captured were Prisoner of War camps holding British prisoners, as well as those from other Allied countries. 7th Armoured Division liberated Stalags XIB and 357 near Fallingbostel – some of whose inmates had been captured at Arnhem, Among the POWs was the

Bernard Law Montgomery, 1st Viscount Montgomery of Alamein, by Frank Salisbury, 1945 (Private Collection, on loan to the National Portrait Gallery, London)

OPPOSITE: Men of 2nd Battalion Gordon Highlanders supported by tanks of 6th Guards Tank Brigade fight their way into Kleve, 11th February 1945 (NAM)

PREVIOUS SPREAD: A British 5.5-inch Breech Loading gun firing at targets across the Rhine on 24th March 1945, ahead of operations to get across the river (NAM)

indomitable RSM Lord, and others, soldiers of 51st Highland Division who had been forced to march from Thorn in Poland when the camp was relocated from there in September 1944. Hamburg eventually surrendered on 3rd May 1945.

Despite fierce fighting, day by day the Allies were advancing deeper into Germany, getting closer to Berlin and the heart of the Reich while the Soviet Union advanced from the east. Victory was within reach. The only question remaining was how much longer the Germans would continue to fight.

'If you do not agree to ... the surrender, then
I will go on with the war and I will be delighted to do so.'

Field Marshal Sir Bernard Law Montgomery to the German delegation, 4th May 1945

'STUNDE NULL'

As the advance across Germany had continued, more towns and cities fell to the advancing British and Canadians. The small city of Lüneburg in Lower Saxony, 50 kilometres southeast of Hamburg, had been captured on 18th April 1945. The headquarters of 21st Army Group had been established in the Villa Möllering in the village of Häcklingen. It was here that a German delegation arrived with an offer of surrender on 3rd May. Initially the Germans had wanted to negotiate a partial surrender of a small number of their forces, but their offer was rejected. Montgomery demanded a total, unconditional surrender of all forces on his northern and western flanks. When the Germans hesitated, Montgomery was unequivocal, and is reported to have said, 'If you do not agree to the ... surrender, then I will go on with the war and I will be delighted to do so.' This was agreed the next day, and on 4th May 1945 Montgomery accepted the unconditional surrender of the German forces in northwest Germany, the Netherlands, Denmark and Schleswig-Holstein.

But this did not end the Second World War in Europe. That only came with the signing of the German Instrument of Surrender, which took place first at Reims on 7th May, then again in the early hours of 9th May at Karlshorst in eastern Berlin, this time with representatives of the Soviet Union High Command present. Wednesday 8th May had been designated as Victory in Europe Day. Europe was – officially at least – at peace.

For Germany, it was 'Stunde Null', Hour Zero, marking the end of the Second World War and the beginning of a new era. As Montgomery said in his message to British and Canadian troops on that day, 'We have now won the German war. Let us now win the peace.' Yet how was this to be achieved? Montgomery had himself served in the original British Army of the Rhine, which had occupied

part of the Rhineland from 1919 to 1929 following the end of the First World War, and in part viewed the rise of Nazism and the Second World War as the result of the failure to adequately enforce total defeat on the Germans. He was not going to allow history to repeat itself, which is why he – and the governments of the victorious Allies – were so adamant that Germany needed to sign an unconditional surrender and accept total defeat, both militarily and politically.

The Allies had decided at Yalta in February 1945, well before the end of the war, how the defeated Germany would be governed after its defeat. Like Austria, Germany would be divided into four Zones of Occupation, with each of the victorious powers taking responsibility in their Zone. This structure was established by the Berlin Declaration on 5th June 1945, which pronounced the end of the Third Reich and the replacement of all German civic and political

The German Surrender at Luneberg Heath, May 1945 by Terence Cuneo, 1969 (Estate of Terence Cuneo/ Private Collection/Bridgeman Images)

BELOW: The final edition of the *Cologne Post*, the newspaper of the original British Army of the Rhine. Montgomery was keen that the mistakes of the past would not be repeated after May 1945 [NAM]

RIGHT: A map belonging to Marjorie Buy, who served with the Auxiliary Territorial Service in VIII Corps' district of Germany in 1945, showing the country divided into four Zones of Occupation [NAM]

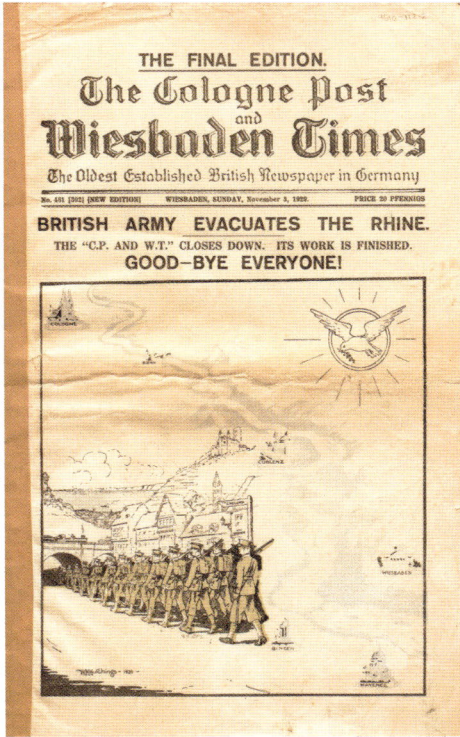

THE FINAL EDITION.

The Cologne Post
and
Wiesbaden Times
The Oldest Established British Newspaper in Germany

BRITISH ARMY EVACUATES THE RHINE.
THE "C.P. AND W.T." CLOSES DOWN. ITS WORK IS FINISHED.
GOOD—BYE EVERYONE!

authority by that of the Allies. They would be the sole political and legal authority in the defeated Germany. The Potsdam Conference of 17th July to 2nd August 1945 later formalised the goals of the four powers, that Germany should be demilitarised and de-Nazification should take place at all levels of society, and also confirmed the Zones of Occupation of Germany and Berlin. The four main powers would work together in the Berlin-based Allied Control Council, constituted on 30th August 1945, which would oversee matters relating to the country as a whole. In a matter of weeks the British had moved from conquerors to occupiers and governors.

To facilitate this, the conquering forces quickly evolved; 21st Army Group was dissolved in August 1945 and became the British Army of the Rhine [BAOR], with an administrative rather than a military role. It was headquartered in the spa town of Bad Oeynhausen in North Rhine-Westphalia.

The war-fighting machine that had battled its way from Normandy to Hamburg was turned into something quite different, and was tasked with a different responsibility. Similarly, the 2nd Tactical Air Force, another well-honed fighting force, was transformed by its new role. On 15th July 1945, a new organisation had been created, the British Air Forces of Occupation (BAFO), headquartered near BAOR at Bad Eilsen. BAFO was spread across 20 operational airfields in Germany and the Low Countries, with four Groups and 20 Wings. Their role was to support BAOR and carry out air policing. Together, the two organisations formed the backbone of the Military Government that took over political and civic responsibility for the British Zone in Germany.

In this, the British Military Government would be aided by the Control Commission Germany (British Element). The Control Commission, with its staff consisting of UK civil servants, Foreign Office appointees and demobilised military personnel, eventually took over the aspects of local government, including public safety, housing and transport, and entered an uneasy relationship with the military authorities, working parallel to them. It took some time to establish who was setting the policy for Germany, whether it was the War Office or the Foreign Office who held overall responsibility.

For the soldiers involved this meant a transformation in the routine that they had become accustomed to during wartime. A.C. Jenkins, who served with the Argyll and Sutherland Highlanders in the Second World War and later the York and Lancaster Regiment and Royal Army Service Corps, remembered this change:

'Our time there was spent, for the most part, apart from parades, in doing guard duties, because at that stage we'd come under the ... control, I suppose, of the Control Commission for Germany – also known as Complete Chaos in Germany. And all they seemed to want us to do was guard. Guard this, guard this, guard that, guard this, guard this cow dung, guard that food ... And in the end we were doing guard duties every other night. It got a bit wearing, in the end.'

But in addition to being guards and governors, the British would also have to be builders. The scale of this task cannot be underestimated. The Zone that the British took authority over had suffered some of the most severe damage in the fighting, and from May 1945 an enormous reconstruction and stabilisation programme needed to be initiated. Agriculture and industry were virtually non-existent in places. The infrastructure had been all but obliterated. There were shortages of all commodities, from food to fuel, clothes to cigarettes. Housing was also an enormous problem. In North Rhine-Westphalia, for example, even by April 1947 only 36 per cent of pre-war housing was left in a liveable condition, among which 92 per cent of the pre-war German population was trying to live.

Efforts to re-establish the German economy put even more pressure on this situation. There had been some debate about whether such an economic rebuild should even take place. The Soviets had suffered appallingly in the Second World War and there was a desire to inflict punitive measures on the defeated Germans in the aftermath of the war. Some of the more vindictive ideas suggested in the Allied Control Council included flooding all the German mines and reducing the country to an agrarian state without any heavy industry that could again be used for war – to ensure the Germans were never capable of waging war again.

Demilitarisation, however, occurred at pace, and was a major role of the occupying forces. Each of BAFO's Groups, for example, had an Air Disarmament Wing. Their job was to carry out the search, identification and reporting of war material, along with the disarmament of the German aircraft industry, removing the potential for any future German militarisation. Five thousand potentially air-worthy craft had been discovered in the British Zone, some of which were taken back to the UK for testing along with a further 8,500 pieces of equipment. Explosives disposal also took place – a hazardous role. At its peak, 8,000 personnel in BAFO were dedicated to disarmament, and it was attacked so efficiently that the bulk of it had been completed by the middle of 1946.

In the division of Germany, the British had assumed responsibility for the economic heart of Germany. This was where efforts had to be targeted if crises were to avoided in the provision of fuel and food before the onset of winter at the end of 1945. The British administrators, both those working in the Military Government and in the Control Commission, were not extensively trained for the task of rebuilding Germany. It

TOP: **Formation badge for the Control Commission Germany, 1945 [NAM]**

BELOW: **Enamelled sweetheart brooch decorated with the emblem of XXX Corps, 1942. They had fought their way from North Africa and Sicily to Normandy, and then through north-west Europe and into Germany. They were one of three British corps to transition from war-fighting to occupation in the immediate aftermath of the war [NAM]**

became a case of simply improvising and doing as they saw best in their particular areas of responsibility. To that end, several operations were launched that aimed to pull Germany up again, and prevent mass civil unrest boiling over into open revolt. Operation BARLEYCORN, masterminded by Major General Gerald Templer, saw thousands of the former German POWs who had been captured and detained in the British Zone released between June and September 1945, in order to work the land and bring in the harvest. Operation COALSCUTTLE saw a further 30,000 released to work in the coal mines of the Ruhr, but it was not enough to bring output back up to pre-war production levels. Life would be hard for the Germans in the years to come. These were the people who were going to become the Army's new neighbours, even subjects.

LIVING EVIDENCE

As well as living alongside the local Germans, the British had to deal with the legacy of the Nazi crimes, the evidence of which certainly influenced attitudes to the local people in the aftermath of the war. The most infamous of these came from the discovery of the concentration camp at Bergen-Belsen.

In early April 1945, General Sir Evelyn Barker's VIII Corps

were advancing north-eastwards across Germany towards the Baltic. Word had reached them that the Germans were looking to call a local truce. On 12th April, a German emissary was brought into the advancing Corps HQ to negotiate the terms. Among the British troops closest to this area were the soldiers of the 11th Armoured Division. They had crossed the Weser on 5th April with 270 tanks and were closing on Lüneburg, aiming for the River Elbe and advancing across the woodland and heather of the Lüneburg Heath. But they had been

LEFT: An aerial view from c.1945 shows the level of destruction in Berlin (Panoramio Creative Commons)

RIGHT: German prisoners of war moving through Elmshorn in Schleswig-Holstein to be demobilised as farm workers as part of Operation BARLEYCORN in 1945 (NAM)

BELOW: How *Soldier Magazine* reported on the discovery of the Belsen concentration camp (Crown)

HERE IS THE EVIDENCE

On the left is the Monster of Belsen, S. S. Commander Josef Kramer. This well-fed sadist knows that whatever is in store for him he will not have the flesh slowly cut from his bones by the knife of starvation — the fate of the victims you see below.

fighting hard, and heavy losses meant that whole battalions had been withdrawn from the division and replaced.

On their line of march lay a camp at a place called Belsen. The German envoy explained the presence of a camp where diseases such as typhus were endemic. His plan was to declare it an open area, and so not engage in any fighting that would risk allowing the inmates to escape and spread disease to soldiers of both sides as well as local civilians. Early reconnaissance groups (including SAS and Reconnaissance groups from 20 Armoured Brigade under Brigadier Roscoe Harvey) had verified the presence of the camp. The truce was accepted, and on 12th April a 48-square-kilometre exclusion zone was placed around the camp, and the area was declared neutral. No shots would be fired in its vicinity. The Germans, and the Hungarians they were employing, would remain only to guard the camp until the British arrived, after which they would be allowed to march back to their own lines with their weapons.

On 15th April, three days after the truce, and with strong German resistance still being met in the area around the neutral zone, the first British troops entered the camp. These were Gunners from 63 Anti-Tank Regiment Royal Artillery under the command of Lieutenant Colonel Richard Taylor MC, part of the Corps Commander's Artillery Group. Together with a loudspeaker truck from the Intelligence Corps commanded by Lieutenant Derrick Sington, a journalist in civilian life, they made their way down roads that led away from nearby villages and deep into the woods. They were utterly unprepared for what they found.

There were more than 60,000 emaciated prisoners in desperate need of sustenance and medical attention. Worse still, 13,000 corpses lay around the camp, unburied and rotting. It was unlike anything any of the British soldiers had ever seen. In his radio report from the camp that day the veteran BBC journalist Richard Dimbleby, who had been accompanying the troops, said simply, 'This day at Belsen was the most horrible of my life.'

Despite still being at war, the British took on the humanitarian crisis. Emergency medical aid was

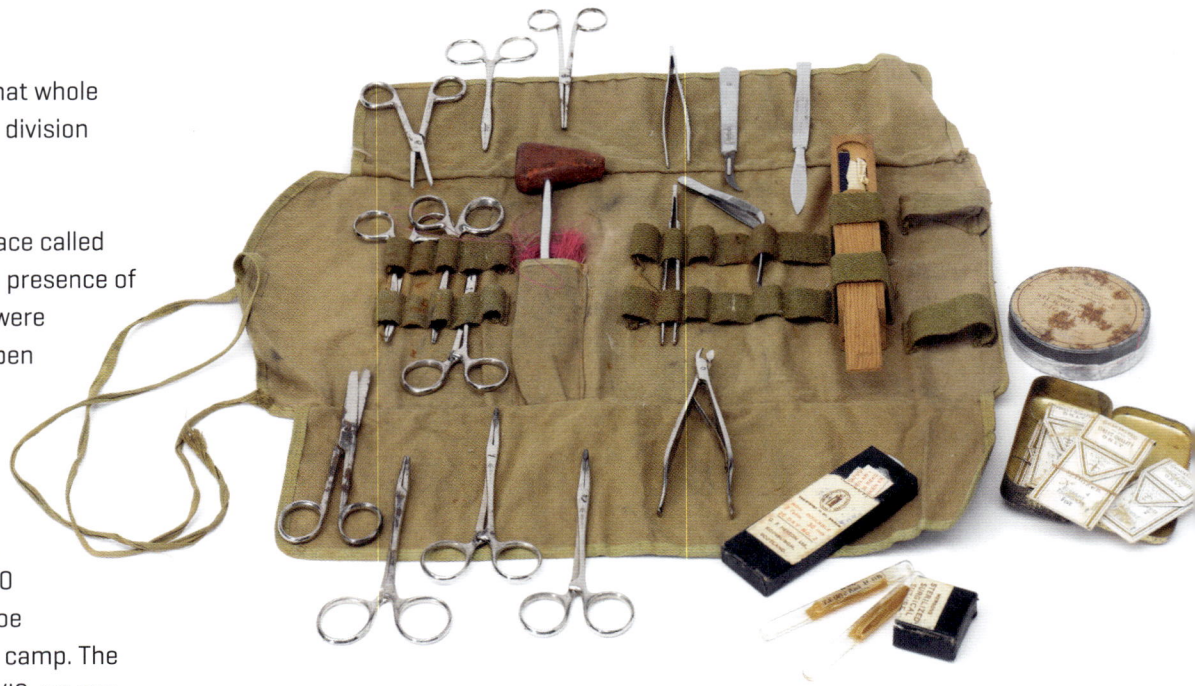

The medical kit of belonging to Major John Russell Grant Grice, Royal Army Medical Corps, 1939–1945. Grice was one of the first British medical officers to enter Belsen and begin administering aid (NAM)

organised under the direction of Brigadier Glyn Hughes, and attempts were made to clean up the camp by burying bodies and implementing a form of quarantine to prevent the further spread of disease among the weakened population. Aiding the living was also a major task. By the end of 16th April, 27 water carts had been provided, along with enough food for an evening meal, all delivered by VIII Corps. But it was not simply a case of handing out the food. In fact, the Army rations had a negative effect on the weakened prisoners, who could not cope with the more complex food. The prisoners' health needed to be monitored, and their diets steadily improved; a special gastric diet for those on the verge of starvation was implemented, adapted from the experience of the Bengal Famine in 1943. Limited amounts of milk, sugar and water were given to the former internees, either by the medical volunteers who had arrived on 29th April, or by those internees strong enough to feed themselves. Despite these efforts, a further 14,000 people died after the camp had been liberated.

The internees who survived were stabilised, deloused and moved to the nearby panzer training barracks at Bergen-Hohne. The Round House there, which would become so significant for the British after the war, was used as a hospital. In Hohne camp (as it became known to the British in subsequent decades), where some of the prisoners had been kept before Bergen's liberation, the internees were registered, given medical attention by the British, reclothed and made ready for repatriation. Within four

Bergen-Belsen concentration camp,
April 1945, taken from a watchtower
[IWM]

weeks, 28,900 people had been moved. Throughout this time, the Army also had to organise the burial of all the bodies of those prisoners who had died of disease or starvation – 15,000 in total. The Hungarians and SS guards were still on the site, and other German prisoners of war, were made to help. Local civilians were also forced by the British to come to the camp and see it for themselves.

On 21st May 1945, once the last prisoners had been moved and the last casualty buried, the camp accommodation huts were burned to the ground. Outside the camp, the British put up a sign to mark the scale of what had been done.

Belsen was not a death camp like those the Red Army would discover in their advance from the east, but the scale of the atrocity still horrified all those who saw or heard about it. Owen Smart was part of the transport support for 21st Army Group. He recalls:

'In the last week of April 1945 we were sent out on a detail and all I knew as a platoon sergeant [was] that my part of the platoon would go to this place called Belsen. We were told it was a matter of clearing up. Before we entered the camp I had never heard of Bergen-Belsen. I knew nothing of what had been going on. We heard about atrocities, which are bantered backwards and forwards, but we didn't realise really what it was, and then it was just after that, that all the rest of it came about, other camps just like Belsen. But to me the name Belsen after that was shocking. I didn't see anything of the inmates in the prison really. I saw a few, possibly the remainders of those that were fit enough to be put into a hospital – the camp was made up as a hospital, but I didn't see many of the actual people. They had been taken away, or the remains of them. That was awful ... There's no doubt that after seeing something like what had gone on in Belsen, it does stay in your mind and never goes away.'

Word of the camp quickly spread around the wider Army. It was the first concentration camp encountered by the

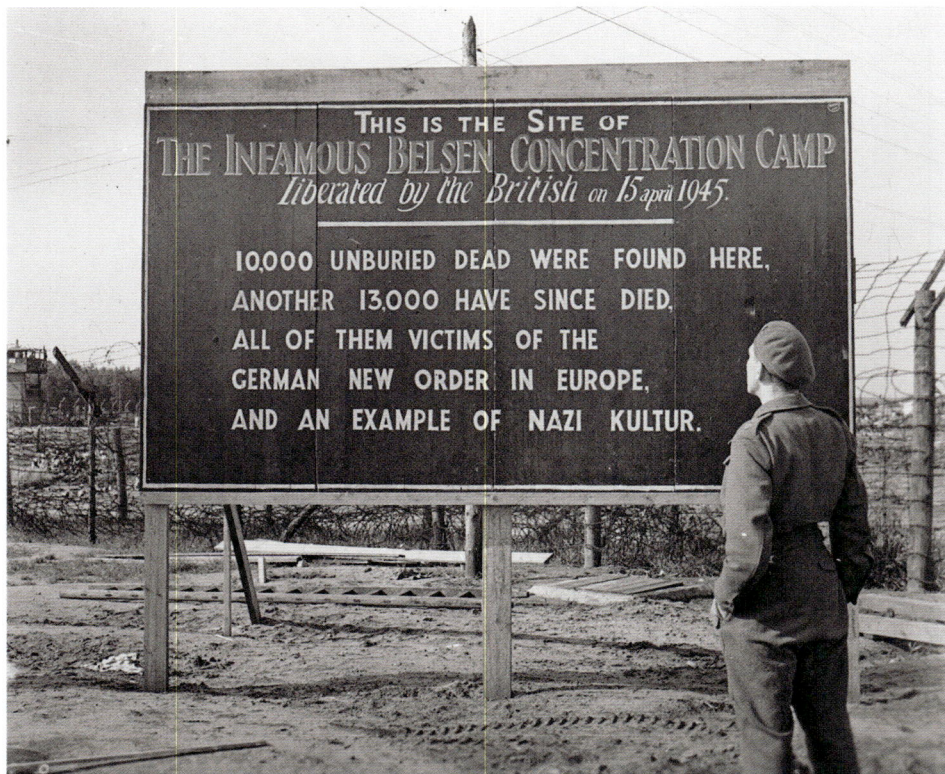

British and instantly influenced opinions and attitudes to the local German people. While many of the advancing soldiers had expressed sympathy for the plight of ordinary Germans as they moved through the shattered towns and cities, Belsen led to a hardening of feeling. There was enormous doubt that the locals could have not known what was happening there, despite their protestations to the contrary. At a time when British soldiers were increasingly coming into contact with local Germans, it undoubtedly affected interaction. Furthermore, given the long-term garrisoning of Bergen-Hohne camp and nearby Fallingbostel, the horror of Belsen was always part of the British experience of life in Germany.

AMONG A DEFEATED PEOPLE

In 1946, the British Crown Film Unit produced a short documentary entitled *A Defeated People*, which was shown in cinemas and aimed to tell people in the UK why the British Army was committing to occupying Germany, and the scale of the challenge it was facing. As the film's narrator made clear, for the British, 'we can't wash our hands of the Germans because we can't afford to let that

new life flow in any direction it wants'. Indeed, 'we have an interest in Germany that is purely selfish. We cannot live next to a disease-ridden neighbour. And we must prevent not only starvation and epidemics but also diseases of the mind, new brands of fascism from springing up.'

The film showed the level of destruction in Germany, the piles of rubble and the pitiful state the German people were in – scenes that, despite the damage of the Blitz on British cities, few people in Britain could fully comprehend without seeing it for themselves. Albert Winstanley, who arrived with his Royal Army Medical Corps unit in Germany immediately after the war and was part of the reconstruction effort, captured his first impressions of Hamburg thus:

'I shall never forget that experience of entering Hamburg in our transport, for almost as far as the eye could see, it was just devastation. What had obviously once been lovely buildings were now just ruins, shattered walls, great tumbles of stone, and a population seemingly staggering about like tired zombies. I remember the stench, too, as hundreds of bodies remained, still awaiting burial.'

The impact this tremendous destruction, and the

LEFT: British soldiers watch as the last hut in Belsen is burned to the ground, 2nd May 1945 [NAM]

ABOVE: A British soldier in front of the sign erected outside of the Belsen camp [IWM]

damage inflicted on infrastructure, had on the local German people was something that struck the British occupying soldiers. Jenkins, serving in the occupation forces, recalled that the local civilians had,

'No fuel, no food, only what we gave them, and you know, some of them were really desperate. I mean they'd be picking up bits of coal from the coal trains that fell off the trains and all that. In fact when we were up at this, guarding a coal depot, we were under instructions to, if we saw any civilians around there, to shoot without asking any questions. I think the CCG [Control Commission Germany] were trying to regulate the supply of food, such as it was, throughout Germany.'

Douglas Godfrey-Cass had joined the Blues in 1945 as a 15-year-old Trooper, and thought he would see the end of the war, but did not get to Germany until the immediate aftermath. For him,

'It was awful, they had nothing. One of the terrible things that people never knew was that it was cold, and they had no fire, they had no nothing. All they could burn was wood, and if there were no trees anywhere there was no wood. So the Guards Armoured Division went up into the hills themselves, and they cut down trees and gave the chopped wood to the Germans because they had nothing at all to live. They had no food, they had nothing ... It was pathetic.'

Increasingly, it became clear that Germany was at risk of collapsing into social unrest that could lead to a revolution that would only benefit the Soviet Union. Germany therefore needed to be built back up. It would be a long-term process to bring a new Germany out of the ashes of the old. But it was something that the military authorities were prepared to commit the Army to and increasingly, as relations with the Soviet Union quickly cooled in the aftermath of victory, something British politicians recognised the value in as well. As the narrator of *A Defeated People* told viewers: 'Much as we hate it, we shall stay in Germany until we have real guarantees that the next generation will grow up a sane and Christian people. A Germany of light and life, and freedom. A Germany that respects truth, and tolerance, and justice.'

But what of the citizens of this new Germany? The German people presented one of the greatest challenges to the occupying powers. It was widely acknowledged that the Germans were guilty of starting the war and should be punished for that. The first trials held by the Allies had been by the British, who had begun to investigate what had happened at Belsen virtually immediately after the liberation of the camp. A British military tribunal tried 44 men and women who had worked at Belsen in Lüneburg between 17th September and 17th November 1945. More than a hundred international journalists reported on the progress of the trial and broadcast the evidence to the wider world. Eleven of the defendants were sentenced to death, including the camp commandant, Josef Kramer, head of the female guards, Elisabeth Volkenrath, and the last of the camp doctors, Fritz Klein. They were executed in Hamelin in December 1945. The Nuremberg tribunals that began on 20th November 1945 tried, among others, 24 of the most important political and military leaders of the Third Reich, exposing to the world their role in the Holocaust and wider war crimes. German guilt was proclaimed as the horrors of Nazism were dissected in the glare of the world's media.

De-Nazification was a stated aim of the occupation, and the Military Government embarked on a process of sifting out those who had held positions of authority in the previous regime, and to find those attempting to bury their past. For example, Germans applying for employment with the occupation forces had to fill in a questionnaire, or a *Fragebogen*, that asked them details about their past. This was then examined, and the

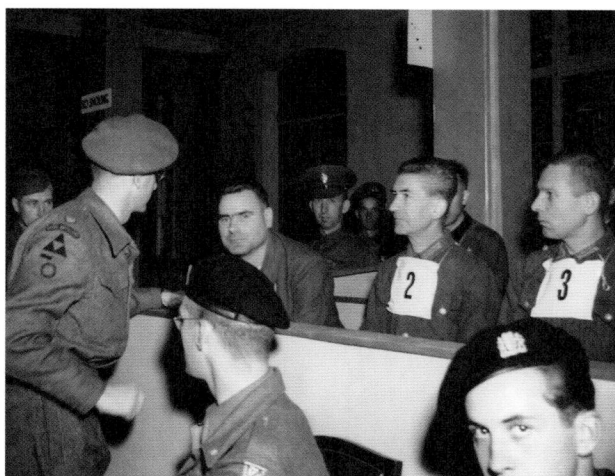

Major T.C.M. Winwood, Josef Kramer's Defence Counsel, speaking to him at the courtroom in Lüneburg, 19th September 1945 (IWM)

applicant questioned. Different categories of offender were identified, and in some cases pragmatic decisions made about the value of somebody's experience to reconstruction and stabilisation projects regardless of their past as a former Nazi Party member.

For those who were suspected of greater crimes or complicity in the previous regime, however, there was a process of internment. The Army guarded internment camps, which sometimes included holding families together while enquiries were made. There were nine camps in the British Zone, including at the previous POW camp at Stalag XIB/357 near Fallingbostel.

Another way in which the British could help rebuild Germany was through providing employment for the local Germans in their zone, contributing to economic recovery, the re-establishment of social order, and ultimately a piece of normality. There was a huge market of unemployed Germans, both men and women, seeking jobs. All civilian labour working with the British was organised by the Pioneer Civil Labour Unit (PCLU), the successor to the Administrative Unit Civil Labour (ACLU) that had employed civilian workers in the period since the D-Day invasion. After the fighting had ended in Germany and peace returned the British Forces went into a static role and could become major employers.

On entering Germany the Western Allies found two further sources of labour. In one category were members of the former German Army, in the other members of eastern European lands who had been captured by the Germans and whose homelands were now under communist governments to which they had no wish to return. This second category – mainly Yugoslavs, Estonians, Balts and Poles – were formed into the Civil Mixed Watchman Service (CMWS), which was tasked with guard duties. Initially 7,000 strong, they were issued with a rifle and 20 rounds of ammunition to be carried on duty. They were forbidden to wear badges of any former army, and instead were issued with a British Battle Dress, dyed blue. The Civilian Mixed Labour Organisation (CMLO), also issued with a blue uniform, was formed in March 1947, and performed primarily logistic tasks rather than guard duties. Initial approval was given for a force of 8,500 made up into 3 Post Operating Unit, responsible for postal services across

the Zone, as well as a railway construction unit and eight labour units. In 1959, HQ BAOR decided to amalgamate the CMWS with the CMLO, and formed the Mixed Service Organisation, better known by its acronym, MSO, or their nickname of 'Mojos'. They would become an enduring part of the British presence in the Zone.

Another source of labour were the Service Groups (Dienstgruppen), which were made up of Surrendered Enemy Personnel (SEP) – those combatants who had not actually been taken prisoner before the end of hostilities, but had laid down their arms after the surrender. The Allied Forces found it necessary to employ substantial numbers of these men rather than allow them to be discharged and sent home. In the late summer of 1947 these groups were given the opportunity to enlist in the newly formed German Civil Labour Organisation (GCLO). They were given British Battle Dress, dyed green, and were paid as civilians with inducements such as accommodation in barracks, food at heavy work scale and a separation allowance for married men. By the end of 1947, the GCLO had grown to 55,000 men, including 15,000 skilled workers, 17,000 drivers and mechanics, and 23,000 general labourers.

A late 1940s watercolour of a German internee leaving the Civilian Internment Camp in Oerbke, a former POW camp near Fallingbostel, after being de-Nazified (private collection of Hinrich Baumann)

Organising the payment of this enormous workforce was a challenge in and of itself. As a result, local German authorities, normally the Labour Exchanges (Arbeitsampter) were give the responsibility of paying civilian labour under the overall control of the PCLUs. In the area of Hamburg alone, in 1947, 60,000 civilians were employed, and in order to ease payment, the Lohnstellen – or pay offices – became an integral part of the German organisation. These offices would report the costs to the Office of Occupation Costs – later the Defence Costs Office (or AVL – Amt für Verteidigungslasten).

Yet people were on the move across the British Zone, a tide of humanity that created its own issues. Besides the damage to the physical infrastructure of Germany, complicating things even further for the new British administrators were the vast amounts of Displaced Persons after the surrender and additional refugees in the British Zone who had fled westwards from the advancing Red Army. There were 1.2 million refugees in Schleswig-Holstein alone in 1947. These refugees were housed wherever space could be found. This amazingly included the administration blocks at Bergen-Belsen, such was the need for physical structures. German POWs were also returning from the UK and Commonwealth at a rate of more than 15,000 per month, putting an ever increasing pressure on food, fuel and housing, all of which were in short supply.

The British Army did what they could to ease these issues, but inevitably they also exacerbated them. As the British Army of the Rhine (BAOR) established itself in the Zone, and the various corps established their areas of responsibility, it needed to be housed. The only way it could establish itself was through the requisition of buildings required for administration and accommodation. There were nearly 800,000 British and Commonwealth soldiers in Germany at this time, and they needed to be fed and housed. While there were many modern Heer and Luftwaffe barracks available (introducing the term *Kaserne* to the British soldier's lexicon), which were astounding in their quality to the ordinary soldier, many other offices and accommodation were requisitioned directly from the local population. When it came to establishing the headquarters for BAOR, the entire centre of the spa town of Bad Oeynhausen

LEFT: Cromwell and A30 Challenger tanks of the 8th Hussars, part of 7th Armoured Division, outside the severely damaged train station in Hamburg, 5th May 1945 (NAM)

BELOW: A souvenir cigarette case and lighter engraved with a map of the British Zone of occupied Germany (IWM)

was taken over. Montgomery's headquarters was located in the Hotel Königshof, barbed wire was erected around the perimeter and the local residents – apart from those locally employed – were prohibited from entering. The British took the central park, the Kurpark, the Kaiserpalais, and all the buildings and established a fully working town for the military community. The Wandelhalle, for example, the elegant colonnaded promenade and attached buildings as part of the spa, was turned into the Navy, Army and Air Force Institutes (NAAFI). The process of occupation was being repeated across the British Zone. Seventy homes in the already severely damaged city of Osnabrück were requisitioned for military use. The British laid down roots in Hamburg, Minden, Menden, Dortmund, Celle, Wolfenbüttel, Hameln and many other areas besides. This was going to be a long-term occupation.

Yet even while they were enforcing the terms of the surrender on the Germans, and dismantling some German heavy industry to either sell as reparations or prevent it being converted to warlike purposes in future, the British were also trying

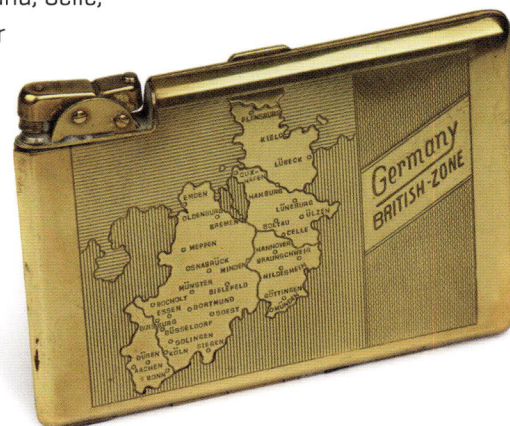

to rebuild their zone economically. Through combined military and civilian efforts, which saw the Army cooperating and supporting the Control Commission's programmes, German businesses were revived and rebuilt. The most famous of these was Volkswagen, which was revived under the direction of Major Ivan Hirst of the Royal Electrical and Mechanical Engineers. With a workforce made up predominately of Displaced Persons, the factory at Wolfsburg was re-established and rebuilt, and the Army were a major market for the newly produced vehicles as soon as they began coming off the production line in January 1946. Cars were sourced for soldiers and for the messes, but also for international clients such as the US forces and International YMCA, with 4,370 produced in the first six months of 1946, mostly for BAOR use. By July 1947, there were discussions about exporting them to the UK domestic market, and in September 1947, there were even discussions about exporting to Austria for use by the Control Commission there. In December 1947, the 20,000th Volkswagen built since the occupation began

left the factory. Yet it was not only as a customer that the British supported the recovery of the business. Production for Volkswagen, like any other industry, initially depended on allocation of raw materials by the controlling bodes within the Control Commission. Without their positive approach, it never would have been possible for Volkswagen and other businesses like the KWS grain factory, *Der Spiegel* magazine or even the Hannover Flughafen and the Deutsche Trade Fair Ground at Hannover to begin as commercial enterprises.

One area where the British occupying authorities were less successful was in their attempts to curb the black market in the Zone. Illicit deals and commerce was utterly rampant across the British area of control in the aftermath of the war. This was due to a shortage of food, the useless value of paper marks, a lack of transport for proper distribution for supplies, a lack of working German courts. But the implications of the occupation were also having an effect, with smuggling from neighbouring Holland and Luxembourg, from the

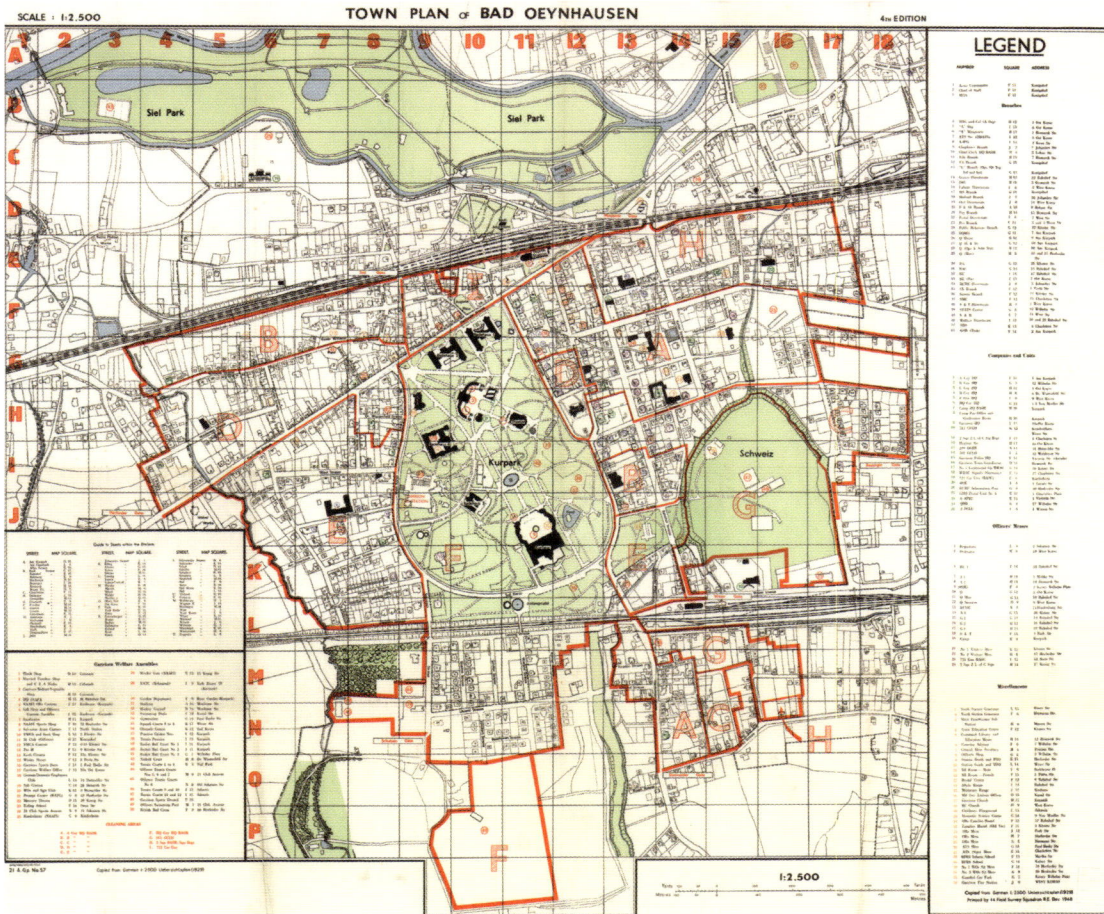

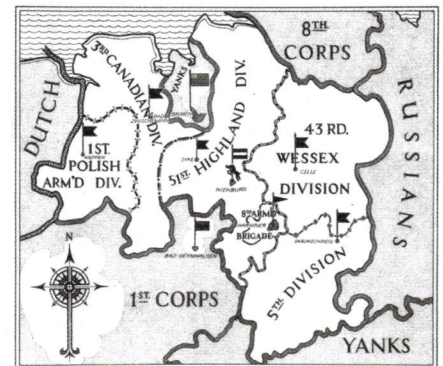

ABOVE: The XXX Corps area of responsibility, from a 1945 information pamphlet they produced and distributed to their soldiers explaining why they were occupying Germany (Crown)

LEFT: A 1945 map of Bad Oeynhausen detailing how the British had taken over and occupied the town (Bad Oeynhausen Stadtarchiv)

Ivan Hirst behind the wheel of the 1,000th Volkswagen to have been built since the end of the war. Hirst's efforts, and the investment and support of the Control Commission laid the foundations for a company that would at one stage become the largest car manufacturer in the world (Volkswagen A.G.)

French Zone and even reportedly by 'Belgian troops in Belgian Army lorries' contributed to the chaos.

In the absence of a functioning economy, cigarettes became the major currency. But anything could be used to barter with. Bernard Tamplin, who served in the BAOR as a National Serviceman between 1947 and 1949, was a willing participant:

'They couldn't get coffee for love nor money, and the Germans do like coffee. So when I went to England I used to come back loaded with 10 pounds of coffee beans. You could smell me coming. How I ever got through customs I'll never know. You could sell five pounds of beans for something else – I had two civilian suits made while I was in Germany. It was all on the black market. It was stuff we sold that we shouldn't have had. But that was the way life was ... Cigarettes were terribly short in Germany and their tobacco was awful, so they used to like English cigarettes. For 200 cigarettes you could get a suit. There was nothing in the German shops at all. It was all black market.'

Indeed, so pervasive was the black market that in the various towns and cities they operated brazenly like normal marketplaces, in full view of the authorities. On 1st August 1945, I Corps District personnel noted that in Essen, for example,

'The Market functions between 1000 hours and 1230 hours and from 1400 hours to 1600 hours. It would seem that it is under some organised control, for on certain days of the week the market area is empty and no business is done. In appearance it is like any ordinary market with people walking around stalls or doing business in a small way from a suitcase.'

In Hannover the 'main centre of activity is in front of the Main Station [afternoons only!]'. In Hamburg it was in the side streets north of the Reeperbahn, with about '200 persons to be fully occupied in the Black Market and making a good living out of it'. In Cologne it took place in front of the cathedral. A I Corps District observer noted that

LEFT: Two British Armed Forces Vouchers used in Germany by Sergeant A.R. Wilson, Durham Light Infantry and later Northamptonshire Regiment. They are from the second series, introduced to fight corruption and the black market (NAM)

RIGHT: A 1946 information pamphlet produced for families travelling to Germany as part of Operation UNION. It was a daunting journey for many, leaving behind family and friends in Britain to move to a foreign country that had so recently been an enemy (Peter Harrison)

'The Cologne market is patronised by a regrettably large number of Allied personnel of all ranks. On the day of the visit some 50 Allied officers and ORs were seen to be actively engaged in illegal transactions.

A troop-carrying vehicle was seen to arrive with a load of Canadian soldiers, ostensibly and probably officially to visit the Cathedral. Not one of these soldiers was seen to take any interest in the Cathedral. The driver who remained with the vehicle began to sell tots of whiskey to German customers.

No attempt was made by any of the offenders to conceal their activities. In another part of 'Market place' an Allied major was selling tobacco to anyone who wished to buy.'

It was virtually impossible for the Control Commission to stamp this out initially. In January 1946 it was noted that, 'if the flow of cigarettes, chocolate, tea, coffee, and preserves from Allied troops and DPs into the Black Market could be stopped it is certain that in many areas the Black Market would cease to exist'. It was particularly bad in Berlin, where the only way a business could keep open – on occasion with the tacit approval of the military authorities – was through engaging in the black market. The most highly organised black market gang in the British Zone was believed to be operated from within the DP camp at Bergen-Belsen. During February 1948, more than six million American cigarettes were seized in Niedersachsen on their way to Belsen, and a further 200,000 were discovered in the camp.

But the authorities did try to fight back. The Military Government, and soldiers from BAOR, were pressed into service. From 1946, combined British and German teams began actively pursuing black marketeers, instigating investigation, raids, roadblocks and checkpoints across the Zone. February 1948 saw one of the busiest months for anti-black market activity; there were 20,704 raids and investigations, a total of 4,288 arrests, 450 Military Government convictions and 3,683 German convictions leading to fines or imprisonment.

In March 1946, it was also decided that a special military voucher system was needed to try to curtail the black market. On 1st August 1946, the first series of 52.4 million British Armed Forces Special Vouchers (BAFSV), valued at just over £10 million, were printed and officially issued in Germany. The soldiers would be part paid in these, and they were the only accepted currency in the NAAFI canteens and various messes. However, the ingenuity of the local black market quickly reacted and absorbed these, and they entered wider circulation. In mid-1947 plans were made to issue a second series, and then immediately demonetise the first to limit the conversion of illicitly gained first-series vouchers. This scheme was carried out on 6th January 1948 and, combined with the beginnings of an economic recovery, helped break the back of the black market.

THE GERMANS AS NEIGHBOURS

To make Germany even more attractive for the British Army, and help support the long-term occupation, in 1946 it was decided to designate Germany as a home posting, so that the families of soldiers could travel out to the garrisons and stations. From August 1946, Operation UNION saw yet another influx of British personnel into the already struggling system of housing. The establishment of British islands in a German sea was well and truly under way. Another implication of Operation UNION was a need to provide schooling for the children of British Service personnel and those of the Control Commission staff. This required the hiring of teachers, and the sourcing of relevant buildings. Prince Rupert School was officially opened in a former German submarine base in Wilhelmshaven on Germany's North Sea coast on 7th September 1947, and King Alfred School in Plön, in Schleswig-Holstein, was opened on 11th May 1948 as the first boarding schools, but other schools were also established in other garrison areas. Within two years of the war's end there were 3,543 pupils being taught by 216 teachers in 85 schools across the British Zone.

While the local German population were, for the most part, accepting of the demands placed on them, the requisitioning of houses and furniture led to several flashpoints. There was conflict in Bielefeld, in Hamm the local council resigned in protest at requisitioning and at Essen the local Bürgermeister was threatened with being forcibly removed from his post by the Control Commission for his refusal to comply. Operation TRANSPLANT, which began in early 1947 and was aimed at finding accommodation for the Belgian military contingent inside the British Zone, exacerbated the problems further and resulted in greater conflict.

The policy of requisitioning was also attracting criticism at a higher level, both in and out of Germany. Josef Frings, the Archbishop of Cologne, wrote to Sir Sholto Douglas, Commander-in-Chief of the British Zone, to complain, and Douglas also had to field lengthy enquiries from John Hynd MP, Chancellor of the Duchy of Lancaster and Minister for Austria and Germany, in early 1947. Douglas wrote that 'the rules and regulations appear to me to be most reasonable. In fact it seems to me

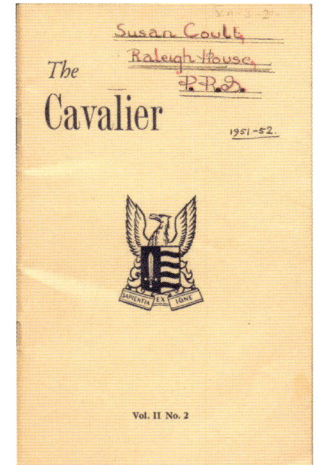

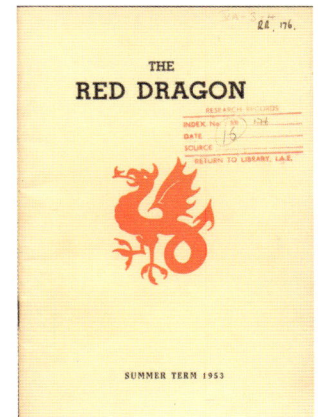

ABOVE: The covers of the school magazines produced by students at Prince Rupert and King Alfred Schools. The schools would continue to educate the children of service personnel for decades to come. Prince Rupert would eventually be moved to Rinteln and re-opened in September 1972. It closed in July 2014 (NAM)

LEFT: King Alfred School pupils used to arrive and depart from Plön railway station by school train, being based across the British Zone. Paul French, a former pupil, captured the scene in this painting (Paul French)

'You have a positive part to play in winning the peace by a definite code of behaviour.'

Field Marshal Sir Bernard Law Montgomery to the German delegation, 4th May 1945

that both the Services and CCG are conducting the requisitioning of houses and furniture with every possible consideration for the German population.'

The British were certainly constrained in how they could respond. Such civil disobedience and criticism created a real dilemma for the occupying forces. On the one hand, the British were the new authority and could not be seen to back down in the face of opposition. But, as was noted in a report about the Essen incident from the Regional Commissioner that was sent to Douglas, 'you will no doubt consider the grave repercussions both in Germany and in the UK which might result from the use by British troops of physical force particularly in relation to women and children'.

The impact requisitioning was having on the local Germans was certainly something that the soldiers occupying these houses were aware of. It could be acutely uncomfortable, even for the victors, as Captain William Stallybrass of the Intelligence Corps recalled:

'We were billeted in a village and we had taken over the whole village and surrounded it with barbed wire ... The inhabitants had been turned out and found accommodation elsewhere, locally. And the housewives were allowed in each day to clean their own houses for us. And we were, again, supposed to keep the barrier between them ... I remember being there at Christmas time, and the woman who owned her house and was cleaning for us came with her little daughter and put up Christmas decorations for us all ... It was an uneasy sort of time.'

This recollection touches upon another of the more striking aspects of the early occupation: the non-fraternisation rule.

In March 1945, HQ 21st Army Group had released a

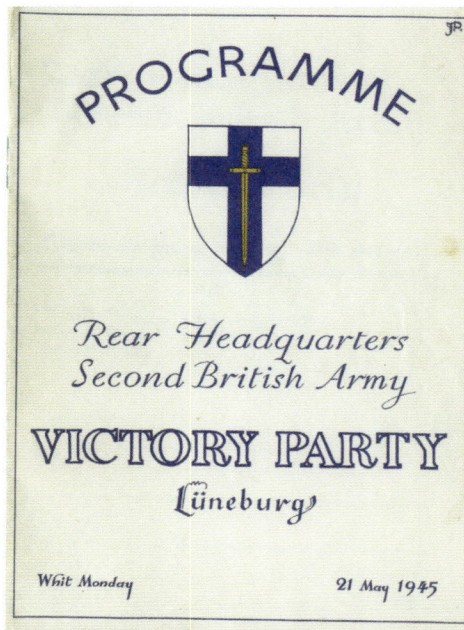

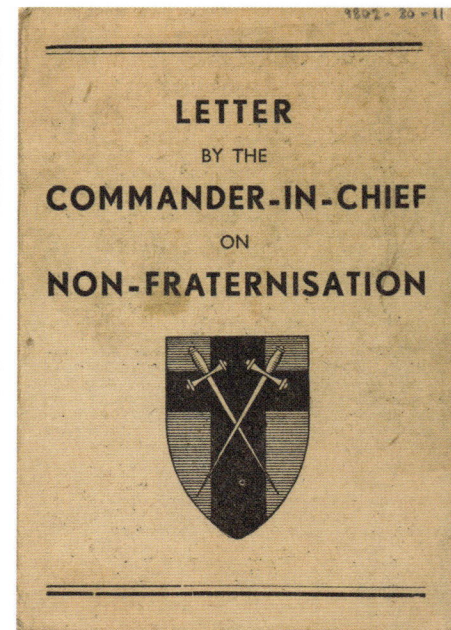

'Memorandum of Punishment for Fraternisation', and circulated it among all of the soldiers. It clearly laid out that there was to be no social fraternisation with the Germans of any kind, and emphasised that, 'no case, however trivial, will be allowed to pass without investigation'. In the same month, Montgomery issued a letter to all officers and men under his command laying out the reasons for the policy, and its conditions. The policy, he wrote, was bound up in helping to enforce the sense of defeat on the Germans:

'Twenty-seven years ago the Allies occupied Germany: but Germany has been at war ever since. Our Army took no revenge in 1918; it was more than considerate ... So accommodating were the occupying forces that the Germans came to believe we would never fight them again in any cause. From that moment to this their continued aggression has brought misery or death to millions.'

For Montgomery, 'peace does not exist merely because

LEFT: The programme from one of the smaller victory parades and parties held across the British Zone – this one by the Rear Headquarters of the British Second Army in Lüneburg on 21st July 1945 (Hans-Joachim Bold)

RIGHT: Field Marshal Montgomery's first letter laying out the conditions of the non-fraternisation policy, March 1945 (NAM)

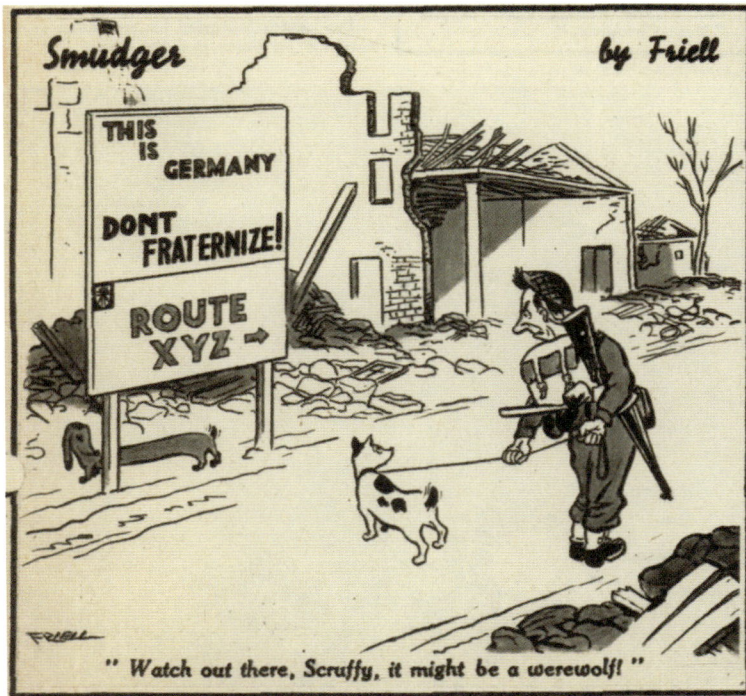

Smudger by Friell

THIS IS GERMANY
DON'T FRATERNIZE!
ROUTE XYZ →

" Watch out there, Scruffy, it might be a werewolf! "

of a surrender', and the non-fraternisation policy was vital in helping win the peace:

'You have a positive part to play in winning the peace by a definite code of behaviour. In streets, houses, cafés, cinemas, etc., you must keep clear of Germans, man, woman and child, unless you meet them in the course of duty. You must not walk out with them, or shake hands, or visit their homes, or make them gifts, or take gifts from them. You must not play games with them. In short, you must not fraternise with Germans at all.'

There was a clear sense of punishment in place for times when the policy was violated, based on a scale of offences. The official policy proclaimed that 'the most effective punishment for minor cases of fraternisation is forfeiture of pay'. This was anything from one to two weeks' pay for a first, modest offence, and up to 28 days' pay for a second offence. Examples of minor cases included 'ogling of women and girls', 'shaking hands with Germans' and the giving of 'small gifts to Germans, including children'. Examples of serious cases, which would be tried by courts martial, included 'associating with women or girls', 'drinking with Germans', 'playing games or sports with them' or 'attending German dances or social events'.

The non-fraternisation rules were very difficult for the British, particularly in regards to children. Albert Winstanley, based in Hamburg, remembered that time:

'I have one vivid memory of that non-fraternisation period. There was a kiddie's fairground with roundabouts and kids' merry-go-rounds. And there were our soldiers, all sitting astride the miniature horses, whilst the sad little German boys and girls looked on in envy. I recall that rather upset me at the time.'

Similarly, William Stallybrass commented on the practical difficulties the policy could have:

'It was quite tricky, in a way. I can remember for instance, we had a British sergeant of German descent – I mean, he had come from Germany, escaping from Hitler. And he found himself right next door from his own relatives. And he at once asked for a posting away. I mean, he couldn't cope with the non-fraternisation.'

Yet many of the British were working directly with the Germans in their duties as an occupying power, making the idea of non-fraternisation utterly impractical. Owen Smart, having moved with his unit to Paderborn in North Rhine-Westphalia in the middle of 1945, was involved in

LEFT: A 1945 cartoon from *Soldier Magazine* pokes fun at both the non-fraternisation rule and the idea of a resurgent German military waiting to strike back at the Allies (Crown)

RIGHT: Even Army-run enterprises relied on German workers. In Hannover the British took over a sausage factory – which employed local Germans – and produced 23,000 sausages a day (Crown)

preparing British quarters for the families of British servicemen who were coming out as part of Operation UNION. This involved sourcing and requisitioning furniture. To help him in this, he had been assigned a secretary, a local German girl. They fell in love, and Smart wanted to propose:

'And as a warrant officer at that time I had to go to my Brigadier to ask permission to marry, which I thought was just a routine matter. I was doing a pretty good job and they appreciated it, and there was certainly a commission in the near distant future. So when I got there I thought it was going to be like old pals, but when I walked in I heard, "What's this business about you wanting to marry a German woman?" I said, "Yes, certainly, sir." He said, "No. A German woman and a British officer is out of the question. Go away and think about it." I thought it would all be forgotten and a few weeks later I was called before him again. He said, "Smart, this can't continue" – and I was posted, and that was that. But he didn't win because my new unit was wonderful. My new CO was very helpful and sent the chief clerk to Hamburg to try to find the papers of my application for marriage. It had been put to the bottom of a pile, and that's the sort of thing that was going on. It was brought to the top and I was married on 16th October 1948. We spent many happy years in Nienburg ... They were wonderful times, a new beginning.'

British troops march past Winston Churchill and Field Marshal Montgomery during the British Victory Parade, held in Berlin on 21st July 1945

Regardless of the official orders, for pragmatic reasons or even just on the grounds of common decency, the non-fraternisation policy had been circumvented or simply ignored in many places. Montgomery was attuned to this, and the impact on morale that the orders were having. On 12th June 1945, the policy was revised and the orders on non-fraternisation no longer applied to small children. On 14th July, it was again revised and soldiers were then able to 'engage in conversation with adult Germans in the streets and in public places'. Montgomery was also a realist. The thousands of cases of venereal diseases that were being treated by the Royal Army Medical Corps and nursing staff were a clear indicator – while being a disciplinary issue – that the policy was being ignored and that British troops were complicit in spreading disease further. Tamplin, for example, was struck by the extent of venereal disease in the early years of the occupation:

'One of the worst things in Germany was VD. There's always venereal diseases where troops are going through. At one time I was driving ambulances, and we used to drive around all these clubs. The police would raid the place and every German girl there would be taken to Münster hospital and checked to see if they had VD, because it was rife. In the camps we used to have FFI – free from infection – and every week you queued up for inspection. It was quite embarrassing actually. You had a long line of troops and you'd drop your trousers, and a woman doctor would lift up your what's-your-name and have a look. There were always facilities for soldiers to collect what they wanted, but a lot of them didn't and VD was rife. You had to be very careful in those days.'

In September 1945, Montgomery's fourth and final letter on the topic of non-fraternisation cancelled all previous orders, and stated that instead the Armed Forces were called upon 'to conduct themselves with dignity, and to use their common sense, when dealing with the Germans'. The British could not successfully rebuild Germany if they continued to subjugate its people so harshly, and the new policy aimed to remove the inconsistencies and confusion surrounding the previous proclamations. Even so, Montgomery still placed a ban on soldiers being billeted with German families, or marrying Germans. It was not to be forgotten that the Germans had been 'twice our enemies in war during the last 30 years'.

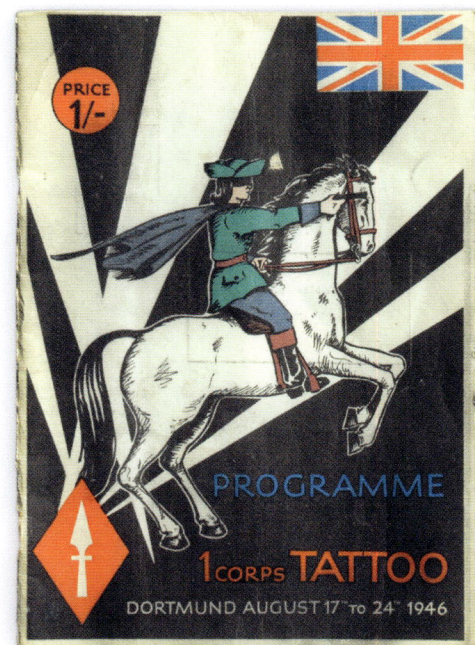

British Forces Germany spent the years immediately following the end of the Second World War adjusting to their new role, coping with demobilisation and slowly transforming itself from a war-fighting army of conquest into an army of occupation and government. But on the global scale, relations between the Allies were deteriorating rapidly. The dawn of the Cold War would lead to new challenges, and new experiences for the soldiers and their families based in Germany.

On 21st July 1945, the British had held a victory parade through the ruins of Berlin to commemorate and celebrate the end of the war. Countless other parades had been held by units in their small patches of occupied territory.

On 7th September 1945, there was another parade through Berlin, this time featuring all of the victorious allies. However, neither Montgomery nor the US General Dwight D. Eisenhower, the Supreme Allied Commander, attended. They were represented instead by their deputies. While seemingly insignificant, this gesture signified a deterioration in the relationship between the Allies. The differences in ideology between the West and the Soviet Union were becoming harder to ignore, and the partnership was growing more fractious. The increasing frostiness was unmissable; the slide towards a Cold War had begun.

ABOVE LEFT: A programme from the Berlin Victory Parade, held on 21st July 1945

ABOVE: A programme from the 1 Corps Searchlight Tatoo held at the racecourse in Dortmund between 17th and 24th August 1946. Montgomery's non-fraternisation rule would not last, and while events such as this were primarily for a British audience, Germans were allowed to come to specific performances.

CHAPTER II

FROM PEACE
TO COLD WAR
1948–1955

A NEW WAR

In the summer of 1949, Europe was at war again. Fierce fighting had taken place, and northern Germany was a battleground for heavy armour, infantry, artillery and aircraft. British forces and their allies were on the back foot. They had been forced into fighting a defensive battle, using the terrain and landscape of northern Germany to slow the advance of the enemy, while trying to mobilise their reserves and move them into the battle theatre via ports in Holland, northern Germany and Denmark. But soon they were back on the offensive. Fighting their way through Paderborn and Sennelager and across the River Alme alongside the Belgians, the British had the enemy on the run.

None of this had been real, however. It had all been an exercise, fought between the forces of the imaginary REDLAND and BLUELAND. Exercise AGILITY ONE and the follow-up AGILITY TWO, which saw 7 Belgian Independent Brigade and 2 British Infantry Division fighting defensive battles and then counter-attacking, were elaborate training plans aimed at testing the war-fighting capability of Britain and its allies.

Montgomery had talked about winning the peace in the aftermath of May 1945, but preparation for the next war was already under way. Increasingly, the British Army began exercising regularly, in large numbers, and, ever more creatively, in their occupation zone.

While the British had ended the Second World War on strained terms with some of their allies, in the aftermath of the peace there was hope that a new Europe could be built from the rubble of the old. But there were directly opposing visions as to how that should be done, and what a post-war Europe would look like.

In 1947, as part of their occupation, the British and the United States had unified their Zones to form the Bizone, an area of economic and political cooperation. On 1st June 1948, the French also joined their zone to this new entity. In March 1947, the Truman Doctrine had been announced by the United States, whereby they pledged to 'support free people who are resisting attempted subjugation by armed minorities or by outside pressures', effectively signalling support for any country resisting the further expansion of Communism. In June 1947, the European Recovery Plan was announced by US Secretary of State George Marshall. The Marshall Plan – which it became better known as – was designed ostensibly to support economic recovery in Western Europe by rebuilding the shattered economies, but also to shield further against Communist and Soviet expansion by delivering growth on a capitalist model. The world was effectively split into two opposing camps, between the capitalist-led West and the Soviet-dominated East. The divided Germany lay squarely between the two.

Throughout 1947 and early 1948, the Western Allies began to prepare a programme of currency reform that

The post-1952 unit flash for British troops in Berlin (NAM)

PREVIOUS: A British tank crew attracts the attention of local Germans during a pause in Exercise AGILITY, 1949 (NAM)

'I believe that we are committed to war with the Russians eventually.'

General Brian Robertson, Military Governor of the British Zone in Germany, September 1948

would introduce the Deutschmark into their Zones in western Germany and Berlin, and help deliver independent economic prosperity. This, it was hoped, would offset the threat of the rise of a Communist Party in their Zones. But they also recognised that their Zones of Occupation should be unified politically to form the basis of a new West Germany. In March 1948, the Soviets discovered this plan, and in response withdrew from the Allied Control Council, the cooperative body that had met regularly in Berlin since the end of the war in order to coordinate occupation policy between zones. With this pretence of cooperation and partnership removed, a confrontation between the former Allies seemed inevitable.

June 1948 saw the first overtly hostile acts between the former powers. The setting for the first major confrontation between the two opposing blocs was Berlin. Since the end of the war, the British – and other allied – presence in Germany had been precarious, deep as they were in the Soviet Zone and dependent on pre-agreed corridors of travel that enabled movement in and out of the city and the respective Zones of Occupation. West Berlin was truly an island in a Soviet sea, and it is often claimed that this was the inspiration behind the formation badge of British Troops Berlin, later Area Troops Berlin and the Berlin Infantry Brigade: a black circle completely surrounded by a red ring.

On 24th June 1948, following increased tension and agitation, the Soviets took the provocative step of blockading Berlin from the outside world. Trains, trucks and barges carrying goods and people in and out were all held outside the city. The Western Zones of Berlin were under siege.

There were only two options: either capitulate to Soviet political demands or embark on what was to become the largest civil-military air-supply mission ever undertaken. Armed road convoys could not be sent to

force the blockade for fear of provoking the Soviets and escalate the situation from a political confrontation to a military one. Therefore any resupply had to be via air.

Although the blockade was an extreme step, it was not entirely unexpected. Berlin's vulnerability had been recognised, and the British had contingency plans in place should something similar occur. However, the events of 1948 transformed the operation; as an interim report noted six months into the airlift, 'The operation, from being a modest affair, became overnight a first class political issue.' It was a test of the Allies' resolve in

The Allied position in Berlin was precarious, given the city's location deep inside the Soviet Zone of Germany. The alliance that had delivered victory began to fray almost immediately in the aftermath of May 1945. Here, a Soviet military patrol passes through the Charlottenburg Lock on the Spree-Oder waterway – part of the British Zone – under the eyes of British soldiers and civilian Berliners in 1948 (IWM)

An RAF Avro York being loaded at RAF Wunstorf during the Berlin Airlift (Heiner Wittrock)

Berlin, in Germany and in the wider defence of Europe. Yet it acquired an additional complication. Any operation would be aimed at supplying not only the Armed Forces of the Occupying Powers, but also the civilians under their charge. Civilian morale and public order needed to be maintained, and the Allies could not allow a wedge to be driven between them and the civilian population. The British already needed to supply 9,500 British personnel in West Berlin; as a result of the blockade there was an urgent need to provide for two million Germans as well.

The mission therefore became one where the objective was simple, even if the delivery was to be complex: 'To supply the island of Berlin with the necessities of life by air.'

The Berlin Airlift, or *Luftbrücke*, began on 26th June. It was an enormous operation. In order to avoid antagonising the Soviets further, or provoke them into more extreme steps, it was agreed that the three air corridors into Berlin from the West that had been identified by the quadripartite agreement at the end of the war would be the only ones used. No new ones would be established, even if it would have meant increasing capacity. This was self-limiting, but necessary.

During the 13 months from 26th June 1948 until 1st August 1949, more than 266,600 flights, carrying more than 2,223,000 tons of food, fuel and supplies, were made to Berlin by British and US aircraft. At its peak, one plane landed every 60 seconds at either Tempelhof, Gatow or Tegel. Even flying boats were used, which landed in the Havel See, and were then unloaded by barges. The Allies had estimated that 4,500 tons of supplies were required per day to keep the garrisons and civilians fed, clothed and heated. In the end they managed 5,579 tons on average.

At the same time as essential goods were being flown in to West Berlin, the outputs of the factories were being flown out. This was vital, to prevent economic disaster and mass unemployment, as well as the social unrest that would have accompanied it. Millions of pounds worth of goods – 'they may range from nails to dynamos' that had been produced in West Berlin were shipped out in this way and kept the Allied Zones economically afloat, a vital imperative given the fragile economic recovery that was in its nascent stages. Human cargo was also flown out, including sick children and hospital patients who required more complicated treatment than what was otherwise available in the

LEFT: Berlin children about to depart
Tegel airport on an RAF flight. As well
as essential food and supplies, the
RAF carried human cargo in and out
of Berlin, often including those in
need of medical treatment, or to
provide some respite outside of the
besieged city [Allied Museum Berlin]

RIGHT: An RAF Short Sunderland flying
boat on the Havel river. Twelve of
these aircraft provided additional
capacity during the Airlift [Allied
Museum Berlin]

besieged city. This helped the Western Allies win an important battle on the civilian morale front.

While the Soviets did not actively engage the Allied aircraft, they still hassled the crews. It wasn't uncommon for them to overfly the airfields or try to intimidate the pilots flying in and out of Berlin along the corridors. In April 1948, there had been a fatal mid-air collision between a Soviet Yak fighter and a British European Airways aircraft above the British airfield of Gatow, so the pilots and aircrew were aware of the risks this posed. Indeed, 18 RAF and 21 civilian airmen died in accidents throughout the airlift. Monty Zeid was completing his National Service with the RAF and worked on the transport of goods from the UK into Berlin:

'Not the most wonderful experience in the world ... We were flying with pallets full of coal, flour, various other bits and pieces ... The Russian MiGs used to play games with us. They'd fly off the port and starboard, then they'd bank away one after the other and make the plane rock. It was a good job those planes were well engineered otherwise they'd have fallen to pieces. And if you didn't have your cargo well strapped down it would go shunting all over the plane.'

With the battle lines between east and west now firmly drawn, the Western Allies escalated their diplomatic cooperation. The North Atlantic Treaty was signed on 4th April 1949, while the blockade was still taking place,

with the member states of the Western Union joining the United States, Canada, Portugal, Italy, Norway, Denmark and Iceland in a new alliance based on collective defence. This was enshrined in Article 5 of the treaty: 'An armed attack against one or more of them ... shall be considered an attack against them all.'

On 12th May 1949, the Soviets lifted the blockade of West Berlin and the phenomenal operation was drawn to a close the following month, though flights continued to bring in supplies to build stockpiles. It had revealed several things about the British – and wider Allied – presence in Germany. First, despite the success of the operation, the British were exposed, and some of their limitations revealed how much they had declined since the Second World War. Due to a shortage of both air and ground crews, for example, the Royal Air Force had to be augmented by personnel from training establishments, and then Royal Australian Air Force, South African Air Force and the Royal New Zealand Air Force. Second, the seeds of the partnership between the Western Allies and the Germans they governed were sown by the airlift. In Berlin in particular, while the British, French and Americans were still clearly governors, they were also protectors. But it was clear that the German people could no longer be mere participants as global politics was played out across the ruins of their country. Indeed, the final report produced by the British and Americans after the end of the airlift highlighted the crucial and essential role that German workers had played in loading and unloading the aircraft at places such as Celle, Fassberg and Wunstorf in

the Zone, and Gatow and Templehof in West Berlin. The German Civil Labour Organisation had been vital. In Berlin alone, 14 Independent Pioneer Civil Labour Unit, with a staff of 60 British officials, had marshalled 45,000 workers. It would take several years, but partnership with the Germans living under Western control became a more definite possibility as a result of the airlift.

Another form of cooperation between the British and a West Berliner gave rise to one of the most iconic dishes in German cuisine. Herta Heuwer was working as a shop assistant and living in the British sector in 1949 when she created currywurst using ketchup, Worcestershire sauce and curry powder – which legend has it she obtained from the NAAFI. Seventy years later, an estimated 800 million are eaten in Germany each year.

A NEW ARMY

The Berlin Airlift forced the British to confront the new political reality, and ask themselves some tough questions regarding their capabilities. The forces in Germany that would be confronting the increased political tension were very different from those that had ended the Second World War. The demobilisation of the British Armed Forces

following the end of the war had begun as early as June 1945, a process that had seen them drastically reduced in size, with fierce arguments raging in Parliament about how big the post-war forces should be, and where they should be deployed. Some 4.3 million men and women had returned to civilian life by the end of 1947. While there were still volunteers for the regulars, these were not going to fill the looming manpower crisis.

Wary of the global political landscape – including the independence and partition of India, which had seen Britain lose an irreplaceable source of manpower that had proven its essential value in two global wars in the 20th century – Parliament had approved the introduction of peacetime conscription in 1947. It was a deeply contentious and unpopular issue, but the Labour government was determined and committed to maintaining Britain's global outlook in the aftermath of the war. Peacetime conscription was the only way in which this could be achieved. National Service formally began in January 1949, with 174,000 young men being called up and pressed into uniform to complete a full 12 months of service. This was later extended to 18 months, then two years, due to the pressures of campaigns like Malaya and Korea. Thus, the late 1940s and early 1950s saw a transformation of the British

LEFT: West Germans queue in Herforder Strasse in Bielefeld after the introduction of the Deutschemark in June 1948 to draw their allowance of the new currency. The currency reform in the Western Zones had prompted the crisis in Berlin, but the response of the Western Allies had shown that they were willing to defend their Zones – and the people in them. This helped bring the occupiers and the occupied closer together (Stadtarchiv Bielefeld)

RIGHT: This NAAFI mobile canteen was the first vehicle, apart from press cars, to reach Berlin after the blockade was lifted. It is seen here having set up show at the Helmstedt barrier, waiting for the autobahn to be opened (NAM)

'We lived in great style in the Officers' Mess there.
I'd never seen anything like it in my life. You know, child of the war,
I think I'd eaten my first steak at the age of 17 … And then suddenly,
I was an officer in the 13th/18th with this wonderful Officer's Mess,
wonderful meals! Wine and everything.'

Lt Michael Sissons, 13th/18th Royal Hussars, 1953-55

Army from a lean, wartime fighting machine into a different force altogether.

Similarly, the British Air Force of Occupation was transformed on 1st September 1951, reverting to the Second Tactical Air Force, or 2TAF. It was no longer an air force of occupation, but on the front line in the new conflict. It had been receiving jet aircraft since 1948, and the Vampire and Meteor were superseded by the Venom from mid-1952. The pace of technological advancement in the Royal Air Force was, at this stage, unprecedented. New 'clutch' airfields were also opened to the west of the Rhine, including Wildenrath in January 1952, Geilenkirchen in March 1953, Brüggen in July 1953 and Laarbruch at the end of 1954. The RAF in Germany would also take their share of National Servicemen. In total, there would be 35 Squadrons under the command of 2TAF by 1955, a post-war peak.

The British Armed Forces would have global commitments, and as such National Servicemen were deployed across the world, from the UK to Korea, Malaya and Hong Kong. They would also be deployed to Germany, to the occupation forces there. In 1949, it was decided that manpower in the BAOR would be somewhere between 53,000 and 55,000 men. It was this force that would actively confront the rising Soviet threat.

Even after the Berlin blockade, a direct conflict with the Soviet Union was not considered likely before 1955 due to the catastrophic damage they had suffered in the Second World War. But it was possible. The changing geopolitical landscape made it obvious that new battle lines were being drawn, and that a new conflict was developing.

The advent of the Cold War would make Germany the centre of Army commitments for the next 40 years.

Yet integrating the new National Servicemen into the Army, and bringing the whole force up to standard, was going to be a challenge. It was clear that many of the lessons learned by the Army during the Second World War had been quickly forgotten, and huge amounts of experience and competence had been lost with demobilisation. On 2nd April 1947, Field Marshal The Viscount Montgomery of Alamein, the former chief of the 21st Army Group that had arrived in Germany as conquerors in 1945, but who was by this point the Chief of the Imperial General Staff, had sent a memorandum to all the commanding officers of Primary Training Centres entitled 'Responsibility of officers to look after their men: What is wrong today'. It was later sent to

Corporal Malcolm Barker of the Queen's Royal Regiment, 1952–1953. Barker was a National Serviceman who did his basic training with the Royal Sussex Regiment and then served in Germany with the Queen's Royal Regiment, 1952–1953. For much of the time he was a non-commissioned officer in charge of the officers' mess at Iserlohn (NAM)

From his armoured car in front of the ruins of the Reichstag, a military policeman of 247 (Berlin) Provost Company, 2 Regiment, Corps of Royal Military Police monitors Russian military and civilian pedestrians in the British sector of Berlin on May Day 1950 (IWM)

Corps Training Centres, Training Regiments and other units where young soldiers were handled. In it, he explicitly drew attention to the changes in the Army and the challenges of incorporating National Servicemen that the professional and regular officers needed to be aware of and adapt to. As he said, 'We have never before had National Service in Britain in. It is vital that we accept those responsibilities and carry them out.' In his call to action he wrote:

'We are dealing with a citizen Army. The young soldiers coming into the Army today are not volunteers; in many cases they regard their period of National Service as a necessary evil; they look at the Army through civilian eyes and are quite prepared to dislike it heartily; on the other hand a great many are prepared to like it.'

The National Service generation had been raised in the shadow of the Second World War, and for those posted to Germany there were conflicting emotions about what they were there to do, and the people they were going to

be living among. On the one hand, there was an excitement and trepidation in being posted to Germany, of going overseas. On the other, there was a curiosity about what it would be like to live amongst the Germans, who only a few years before had been bitter enemies.

Lt Michael Sissons, who served with the 13th/18th Royal Hussars as a Troop Commander from 1953 to 1955 for his National Service, explained this from his perspective: 'I came from a Yorkshire family which had been really crippled by the two world wars ... So I was really brought up by grieving women, and I hated the Germans. I hated them real bad, and so did everyone else in my family. And it was as simple as that.'

The travel to Germany was itself an adventure for the British personnel. Troop trains departed from London Liverpool Street and moved via Harwich to the Hook of Holland, and from there the National Servicemen would move to their various postings on colour-coded trains.

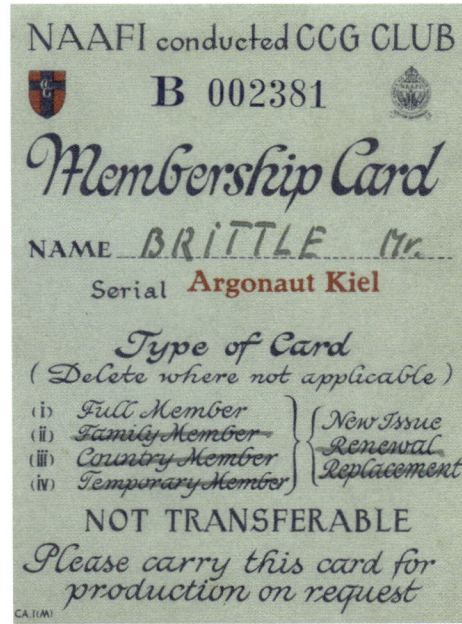

Their first introduction to Germany could be a shock. As Sissons recalled when he arrived just before Christmas 1953: 'I was decanted into Braunschweig station. The station, eight years after the war, still didn't have a roof ... And Braunschweig ... just consisted of neatly squared-off piles of rubble. There was scarcely a building standing still eight years after the war.' He was, however, quickly moved to Wolfenbüttel, which,

'Was untouched, not a bomb on it. We had the old Luftwaffe barracks on top of the hill just outside the town, and we had taken it over – of course, that had had fighter planes on it until the end of the war – and it was a very fine barracks. And we lived in great style in the Officers' Mess there. I'd never seen anything like it in my life. You know, child of the war, I think I'd eaten my first steak at the age of 17, hitchhiking in France, and it was probably horse meat anyway! And then suddenly, I was an officer in the 13th/18th with this wonderful Officers' Mess, wonderful meals! Wine and everything.'

The old German Army and Luftwaffe barracks, with their striking architecture and apparent luxury in comparison to what the soldiers had known in Britain during their basic training made an impression on many National Servicemen. The huge 'Hitler blocks' with double glazing and central heating amazed many of the civilian soldiers who had spent their short military careers to that point

in cramped barrack huts in the UK. Private Henry Deeks, who completed his National Service with the South Wales Borderers between 1952 and 1954, spoke for many when he said, 'Our barracks were wonderful, how well Hitler looked after his troops.' The food was good, and for many life seemed to be considerably better among their former enemy than in Britain.

Once among the German people, the British soldier then needed to adjust not only to a new way of life, but also living with an enhanced status in their German surroundings. Barry Smith, of the 1st Battalion Royal Fusiliers, recalled that there was an obvious need to maintain standards on behalf of the Army, and a clear desire to present a suitable image to the Germans as the occupying authority:

'When I got to Iserlohn, the discipline there was very rigid, in that we were in view, as it were, of the German public. And they immediately said, 'get another haircut. If you haven't had another haircut, get another one.' And our uniforms were literally taken from us and tailored – we were tailored like chocolate soldiers, in effect, at the pleats, the bagginess of the standard. Uniforms were just the same as the last war – they were all taken out. And we were very, very smart, to say the least ... I understood at that time that we had actually exceeded the Guards' regiment when it came to accomplishment for smartness at that time.'

While the non-fraternisation rules had been relaxed since the initial stages of the occupation, there was still a legacy of remaining separate from the local Germans. For Sissons, there was a clear attitude to the locals in his regiment: 'We were emphatically an army of occupation. Nobody had any idea of integrating with the Germans.' But for those looking to fill their spare time away from military duties with more than just socialising in the bar or enjoying the entertainments put on in the camps, the local towns could be a great attraction. Some soldiers found German girlfriends among the locals. Others took the opportunity to see more of Germany beyond the camp walls. Malcolm Barker, who completed his National Service with the Queen's Royal Regiment in Iserlohn between 1952 and 1953, for example, was so intrigued by the portrayal of German soldiers in the war films he watched in the Forces cinemas that he actively sought out more Germans, and even visited the homes of Wehrmacht generals that featured in books he read about the war and that he discovered were nearby.

However, the Army was not in Germany to socialise, or learn more about their neighbours. While initially it was stationed there to occupy, as the Soviet threat loomed larger, attention turned to the war that was to come. Preparation for this became the central component of most National Servicemen's lives.

ON THE GROUND

Training exercises became a major aspect of life for the Army in Germany, and began to shape the timetable and lived experience of service in BAOR and BAFO. The point of these was clear: they were not simply about giving the troops something to do, they were about preparing for when the next confrontation came, as was noted after AGILTY ONE and AGILITY TWO: 'The whole object is to raise the standard of battle fighting in the Rhine Army.' The AGILITY exercises were the largest undertaken since the end of the Second World War, and they were designed to test the Army's ability in all of the operations they expected to fight, including offensive and defensive.

Even after the establishment of the Northern Army Group, or NORTHAG, in November 1952, it was clear that the British forces in Germany would be heavily

outnumbered should the Soviet Union attack. However, it was believed that where they would be able to exert an advantage would be in professionalism and skill at arms – but this had to be drilled into the new recruits, many of whom were only short-term soldiers. But it was not only the ordinary soldiers who needed to improve their standards. The exercise's report recorded that 'poor junior leadership, incorrect use of ground and bad minor tactics were noticed at various times in the majority of units. It is realised that with the large number of NS men the strain on junior leadership is very great.'

TOP: Dempsey Barracks in Sennelager in 1953. The distinctive architecture, and comparative luxury, available in some garrisons amazed National Servicemen and regulars alike (NAM)

BELOW: In 1949 NORTHAG was established, moving in to HQ BAOR in Bad Oeynhausen (Stadtarchiv Bad Oeynhausen)

'We must produce an efficient, quick-thinking, hard-hitting Army. We can do that and we are on the way to doing it. We owe it to our country and we owe it to ourselves.'

Field Marshal William Slim, Chief of the Imperial General Staff, December 1950

Indeed, in the detailed critique of AGILITY ONE and TWO it was noted that, 'the exercises demonstrated the difficulty of training officers and NS [National Service] men for war'. As the Commander-in-Chief of the BAOR at that time, General Sir Charles Keightley, said, 'clear and straightforward battle drills are particularly important now that the Army consists so largely of National Service soldiers'.

The exercises provided valuable lessons regarding the provision of supplies and ammunition, how to maintain morale and the need for security. The exercise also saw the use of Centurion tanks, which were found to have performed well, though petrol consumption was discovered to be particularly heavy – they could not go more than 40 miles in a non-tactical move without refuelling. It was also pointed out in the evaluation that, 'in war men should either be fighting, moving or resting. There should be no "hanging about".'

As the exercise was diligently planned and critically reviewed, several lessons were taken forward into the following year. In AGILITY it had been found that a sense of realism was lacking, particular in relation to the threat of enemy air power:

'Infantry appeared to ignore the presence of aircraft on the grounds that it was probably their own. This was a very dangerous assumption and somehow everyone must be brought to realise the dangers of air attack and taught to take the necessary steps to minimise its effect ... The young men who now constitute the bulk of the Army and RAF, as well as many of the officers, have little idea of the devastating effect which air power can have ... a demonstration of the latest weapons, bombs

etc, should be arranged to educate them in this.'

Therefore, the major exercise the following year, BROADSIDE ONE and BROADSIDE TWO, held between 24th and 30th September 1950, saw the Army move and concentrate in the face of enemy air superiority, and operate on wider fronts. This was also the first occasion since the war that administrative units were exercised on a large scale, 'and many lessons which were forgotten were re-learnt'. Field Marshal Slim observed both elements of BROADSIDE as Chief of the Imperial General Staff, and in his summary he captured the renewed drive for increased professionalism across the entire Army: 'We must produce an efficient, quick-thinking, hard-hitting Army. We can do that and we are on the way to doing it. We owe it to our country and we owe it to ourselves.'

British soldiers taking part in a game of hockey at a local farm to pass the time during a break in Exercise GRAND REPULSE in September 1953. The exercise was held near Osnabrück, a joint effort by BAOR and the Netherlands Corps together with considerable air participation from the Allied Air Forces of Central Europe (NAM)

Centurion tanks moving up at the crossroads near Bispingen, West Germany, on Exercise INTERLOCK TWO in 1953. Centurions had first been used in action in Korea in 1950 with the 8th Hussars, and British armoured regiments in BAOR were equipped with them from 1952 to challenge and deter Soviet forces [NAM]

The exercises were explicitly international in their outlook. They were about interoperability, combining and collating military power, and saw the British training alongside their European allies. They also became increasingly ambitious and inventive; GRAND REPULSE, for example, ran from 19th to 23rd September 1953. The scenario saw the 'enemy', composed of the 2nd Infantry Division and a Danish contingent, making a landing in northern Germany on an imagined section of coast, and friendly forces consisting of a Dutch corps with a Dutch division, the British 11th Armoured Division and 27 Canadian Infantry Brigade Group.

The friendly forces advanced to contact, followed by a battle designed to destroy the enemy bridgehead. Both sides were uncontrolled, and Generals were free to manoeuvre their force as they saw fit, based on intelligence gathered by reconnaissance troops and aerial recce.

Such large-scale exercises provided opportunities to resolve doctrinal issues, as well as to explore operational

concepts and make advances in professional standards, particularly in regards to communication across wide battle fronts when brigades and divisions were in the field. Exercises, while simulations, provided the next best testing ground for identifying weaknesses and then trialling solutions. There were also exercises designed to mobilise reinforcements from the UK for the BAOR, who would be moved swiftly through the Lines of Communication Zone should they be required.

Detailed analysis took place of issues like the flow of information, all of which were designed to give British forces as much of an edge as possible, and enable them to exploit any advantage they might have. Communications was one area where the British believed that they could make up for their lack of numbers, and develop an advantage over the opposing Soviets. It meant that, despite being outnumbered, their increased professionalism could act as a force multiplier.

The scale of these exercises also increased. The 1954 EX BATTLE ROYAL was the largest set of military manoeuvres conducted since the Second World War. It involved 80,000 troops, drawn from six Division and Brigade Groups from the 4th Dutch Infantry Division and 6th British Armoured Brigade, plus Belgian and Canadian divisions and the British Parachute Group. Air elements of the 2nd Allied Tactical Air Force were also involved. The exercise also reflected the modern political and tactical landscape; the exercise was observed by high-ranking Germans and also involved a nuclear element for the first time, with a 280mm atomic cannon being used, and the 'flash' of an imagined nuclear blast being replicated.

These exercises were as much about convincing the soldiers of the possibility of war, as it was about raising the standard necessary to fight it. For Sissons,

'We had been led to believe that it was only a matter of time before the Russians came swarming across the border. And if you were Orderly Officer at Wolfenbüttel you were issued with a password which changed every day from Division, which I think was in Hannover. And if the phone went, and that password was uttered, it meant that the Russians were coming over the border on our watch, on our sector, and we'd better get out of there – and we had an hour to get out of there. The whole regiment had an hour, theoretically, to get out of Wolfenbüttel, and start heading west. And the idea was we would first try to make a stand on the River Leine … and then we would go back to the Weser, and then we would go back to the Rhine, and if there was anything left after that we'd go back to Antwerp! I mean that was the strategy. And that was still the strategy ten years after the war, spring of '55 when I went back to England.

The assumption had been there subliminally, I suppose ever since I'd been a small boy. And it had certainly only been reinforced by serving in Germany. You asked me whether it was "when" or "if": it was unquestionably "when". The assumption, which proved, thank God, to be incorrect was that it was "when".'

John Robert Arnold, who served with the Royal Army Service Corps in 1952 and then transferred to the Intelligence Corps before later becoming the Dean of Durham, shared these sentiments:

'I still think it was right to fight in 1939, and I think it would have been right to fight in the 1950s if the Red Army had started to move again, which I thought was the bit that we were being prepared for … We had been trained, in the spirit of 1939, that it was right for Britain to stand up to aggressors. And therefore we would have stood up to the Red Army if it had been an aggressor.'

Arnold did, however, spot an anachronism in the way the Army was being trained with the looming shadow of the nuclear development:

'It's very strange, you see, because the … war might have been an atomic one, and we were still, really, doing the kind of drill which we had in the Boer War. And even using the same weapons! I mean, our only weapon was the Lee-Enfield rifle. And I, until today, have never handled anything more sophisticated than a Bren gun. One really wonders what would've happened.'

Brian Davis, who had commissioned in to the Royal Artillery and was first posted to Germany in 1952, however, did not necessarily see war becoming a possibility without major political failure: 'Not really. There were too many politicians involved. It would have needed a major error on somebody's part. It would've been an error rather than an intent to do it. We were fully trained to do it, and we were busy deterring each

Soldiers of 33 Armoured Brigade on traffic control duty inside a radio truck, nicknamed the 'Gin Palace', near Reinsehlen on the Soltau-Lüneburg Training Area during Exercise ADAM'S APPLE, June 1953. British exercises always attracted curious local civilians [NAM]

Sporting medals and trophies from some of the earliest ski races organised by BAOR in 1948. Winterberg would become a familiar and favourite place for many BAOR soldiers in future decades. Garmisch was run by the US Army, and British personnel had a chance to visit with their families (Private Collection)

other, really. And we had to stay at that standard. Which we did, I guess.'

The idea of deterrence extended beyond the major exercises. There were duties such as border control, and the British actively patrolled the inner German border, the division between the British and Russian Zones. Between 1949 and 1952, 675,000 people had fled from the Soviet Zone into West Germany, and the Soviets had responded by increasingly militarising the border. In response, the Bundesgrenzschutz (the Federal Border Protection force) was created in 1952, though the British maintained the military responsibility for the border in their Zone. Working with the Bundesgrenzschutz brought the British into contact with Germans at a professional level, but as Sissons noted the recent past could still throw a shadow on the relationship:

'Our border workings were extremely professional ... We got to know the Bundesgrenzschutz very well, and to admire them and in some cases to like them ... I'll never forget an incident on the border, of one of the Bundesgrenzschutz reaching under the wire to pull through a young East German who had been mortally wounded, as it turned out, by machine-gun fire coming through. On the Eastern side there was a strip called the verfluchter streifen, "cursed strip", which ... was mined, and anybody who went on it was fair game for the ... [East German] Volkspolizei machineguns. And two of them had run through it, and ... one of them got through and survived, the other one didn't. But as he was coming through, this Bundesgrenzschutz chap pulled him under the wire, and his cuff rode up, and I saw his SS tattoo on his arm. It turned my blood to ice. I knew him, and I knew he had fought on the Russian front. He

didn't tell me he had been in the SS. So God knows what he'd got up to.'

The British had to be seen to be willing to fight in their sector of Germany. The continuous training served to underline that point, both to the British soldiers and the Russians, but also the civilians living under their occupation. Since 1948 there had been extensive debates between the commanders of BAOR, the Foreign Office and the Ministry of Defence regarding troop strength in the British Zone. In May 1948 the Chiefs of Staff had informed General Brian Robertson that the ceiling of manpower of the Rhine Army would be 50,000 as of 1st January 1949. Robertson had argued that such a reduction could be made only by cutting fighting units, which was unacceptable, and argued that BAOR should actually be increased. He made the case strongly that the Army was needed for internal security as much as external threat, particularly when it came to issues such as reparations, the establishment of new frontiers and the creation of the Ruhr Authority – the international body responsible for monitoring production in Germany's traditional industrial heartland. In 1949, it was recognised that a general strike was a real and present threat, one which the Army and RAF would need to counteract. The Army was already stretched, and such an event would test it further.

There was also a need to preserve fighting units for the integrity of the Western Union. Germans already viewed with some scepticism the idea that the British, Belgians, Dutch, French and Americans would stand and defend Germany should the need arise. Discussions over whether to pull troops out of BAOR to form a mobile reserve in the UK or redeploy them across the world were met with

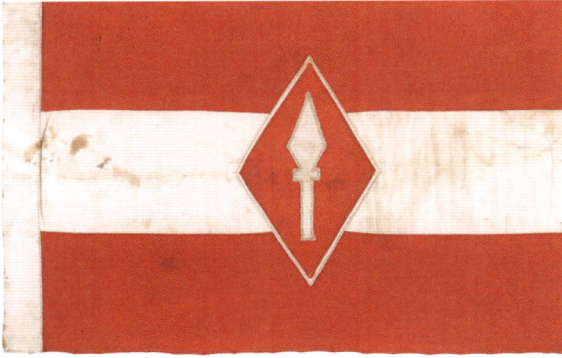

consternation in Hamburg. As a January 1949 Foreign Office report prepared for Sir Ivone Kirkpatrick, the British High Commissioner in Germany, noted: 'Withdrawal of a fighting unit would increase this distrust, cause a slump in morale, and encourage the timid to re-insure with the Communists.' Britain's military strength was clearly linked to its political prestige: 'To allow our military situation to appear obviously weak will speedily lead to the undermining of our political position as well.'

Thus, for British forces, everything was geared towards training and preparedness. Activities outside of military training were also geared towards maintaining a physical and mental edge. Sport was a natural extension of this. Even the adventure training opportunities that the forces developed, from sailing in the Baltic, to Nordic and downhill skiing competitions, organised by BAOR from as early as 1948 with the coordination of the Sports Board, were designed to mentally and physically strengthen soldiers. In turn, the opportunity to visit places like Winterberg, a winter sport resort in North Rhine-Westphalia, on an annual basis became an enjoyable aspect of life in the Rhine Army.

The British were still firmly in control in Germany, and improving the quality of their forces all the time. But the British Zone was clearly changing, and a new Germany was rising from the ashes of the past.

THE NEW GERMANY

The British Zone was still heavily marked by the experience of war. But among the wreckage and the rubble there was still an opportunity for all of the British soldiers and

airmen – both regular and conscript – who were stationed there to experience more of life. Initially, the centre of gravity in the British Zone was Hamburg. As Brian Davis noted of Hamburg on his first visit in 1952,

'They'd made a sort of start on Hamburg, but there was still a lot that was damaged. They got industrial structures going first, and the temporary structures that the people lived in … a lot were still there. There weren't a lot of housing estates there, they were too busy rebuilding factories and steel works and iron works, Volkswagen motorcars and … government offices.'

Hamburg, as well as being the centre of power in the British Zone, was also the centre of entertainment – both legal and illicit. Some described it as the biggest brothel in the world. It was also the headquarters of the British Forces Network Germany broadcasting service, which closed the distance between those stationed in Germany and their friends and family in Britain. Programming had quickly been adapted to include more for the spouses and children of those serving, which proved popular. A weekly segment, 'Sprechen sie Deutsche', aimed to encourage the families to pick up more of the language to help them in their day-to-day contacts with the Germans.

On 23rd May 1949, the Federal Republic of West Germany had been formally inaugurated, based around new states that the Allies had helped design, breaking

LEFT: A I Corps flag carried on the successful 1953 expedition to climb Mount Everest. The expedition was led by then-Colonel John Hunt [NAM]

ABOVE: A Hamburg street scene in 1953. The city was a magnet for soldiers on leave [NAM]

'If Western Germany is to be defended, it seems to us only fair and reasonable that the people of Western Germany should help in their own defence.'

Nye Bevin MP, 29th November 1950

up pre-war territories in some cases. Its first elections were held on 15th August, and Konrad Adenauer was elected Chancellor, a post he would hold until 1963. Adenauer believed not only in continuing the economic recovery of West Germany but also in closer integrating the Federal Republic with the occupying powers and the other Western European states in order to fight the oncoming Cold War. From 1951, the occupying powers relaxed political and economic rules on the western zones of Germany to further enable this.

As a result of the increased threat of the Soviet Union there was a renewed drive among the Western Allies to help Germany stand again on its own two feet. Previous fears about the threat of a resurgent Germany, while not entirely discarded, were placed to one side. As British MP Aidan Crawley noted in a 2nd March 1951 article entitled 'A German Contribution to Defence', in order to defend Britain against Soviet expansion and attack, it was clear a line had to be held as far east as possible. This meant in Germany. After all, 'Europe is dominated by the immense Soviet armament and if the clash comes Germany is the main battlefield.'

Yet this took the British and their Allies into new territory. It was increasingly difficult for Germany to be excluded from discussions about how to protect Western Europe at a political, strategic and tactical level given that it was clearly the front line in a new conflict, and the space in which the decisive action would occur. The new West Germans needed to play a more active part in defence. Brian Robertson had prophesised as much in September 1948, when he said, 'We cannot be choosers in such a conflict when it comes to allies. The Germans, the best fighters in Europe apart from ourselves, are basically anti-Russian – and anti-Communist in consequence.'

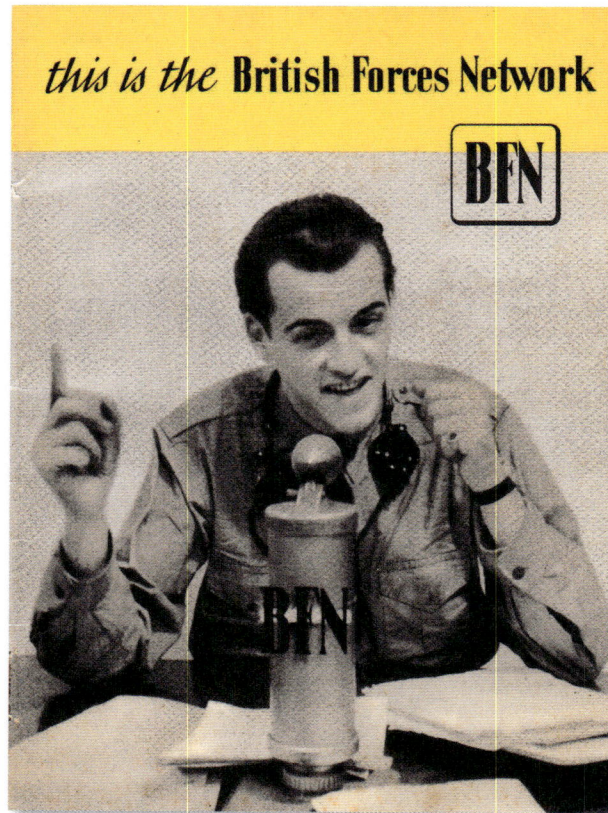

this is the **British Forces Network**

BFN

A promotion image for the British Forces Network of presenter Bill Kemp on a BFN microphone. Hamburg was also the base for BFN, which provided entertainment to the troops and a taste of home (Crown)

West Germany needed its own armed forces.

But creation of this organisation was obviously very difficult, politically as well as practically. A fear of Germany becoming militarised again was one of the major reasons why the British forces had committed to occupying the country in 1945. The terms of the surrender that the Allies had dictated to the defeated Germans actually prevented them from playing a role in mutual defence. A proposed solution was that the new West German military would only be made up of units integrated into Allied formations, and incapable of operating as an independent force. But this was dismissed as impractical and unworkable.

At the political level, the legacy of militarism had led to a deep resentment of and distrust of the military among the West German people. Furthermore, the renewed economic prosperity had created a climate whereby fewer people were willing to risk this through belligerent acts. While Adenauer was eager to provide a West German military contribution, he had a difficult task convincing his electorate, something London readily acknowledged while supporting his aims. General Sir Richard Gale, Commander-in-Chief BAOR and Commander NORTHAG noted in September 1955 that this was essential in overcoming the pervasive attitude of cynicism and defeatism that threatened to undermine the Western defence of Europe: 'The sooner the German armed forces, and particularly the army, come into being the better; because the army itself, if properly handled, will probably be the best propaganda against the defeatist attitude which is now to a greater or lesser extent undoubtedly prevalent.'

For Gale, there was a need for words to match actions. He believed that, 'NATO is the visible proof of the intention of the Free World to oppose aggression', but that 'to be effective, the intention to oppose aggression must be capable of being supported by deeds'. Diligent training, of actively practising how to fight wars on the ground they expected the war to be fought on, was a major part of this, and its impact extended beyond the soldiers of BAOR and the NORTHAG units. It extended to the Soviets, observing across the internal German border, but it also convinced the civilians of West Germany

– and Western Europe – that their armies were willing to fight to resist any potential aggression.

As of 29th September 1955, NORTHAG could deploy one Dutch division, four British divisions, one Canadian independent brigade and two Belgian divisions – seven and one-third divisions. Central Army Group could deploy five US divisions and four French divisions. Arranged against this were 22 Soviet divisions in East Germany (ten mechanised, four rifle, eight tank) supported by two artillery divisions and nine anti-aircraft divisions.

In Gale's opinion, while they were outnumbered, 'the Allied divisions are fit physically, well equipped in most of the essential items, and well trained … Bearing in mind the roles allotted to the divisions I do not think they are going to be asked to do more than they can achieve.'

However, he also sounded a warning: 'One important factor is the quality of the Russian soldier. He is a magnificent fighter, brave, hardy and a natural tactician. He can work at night and in extremes of cold probably better than any other soldier in the world.'

It would be this adversary, and his allies, that BAOR would stare down for the next 40 years.

LEFT: **Mary, Princess Royal, visiting members of the newly formed Women's Royal Army Corps at Bad Oeynhausen in 1951 (Stadtarchiv Bad Oeynhausen)**

RIGHT: **Soldiers of the 2nd Battalion, The Durham Light Infantry, on parade in Wuppertal in May 1953 to receive new Colours (SLG John Provan/Allied Museum, Berlin)**

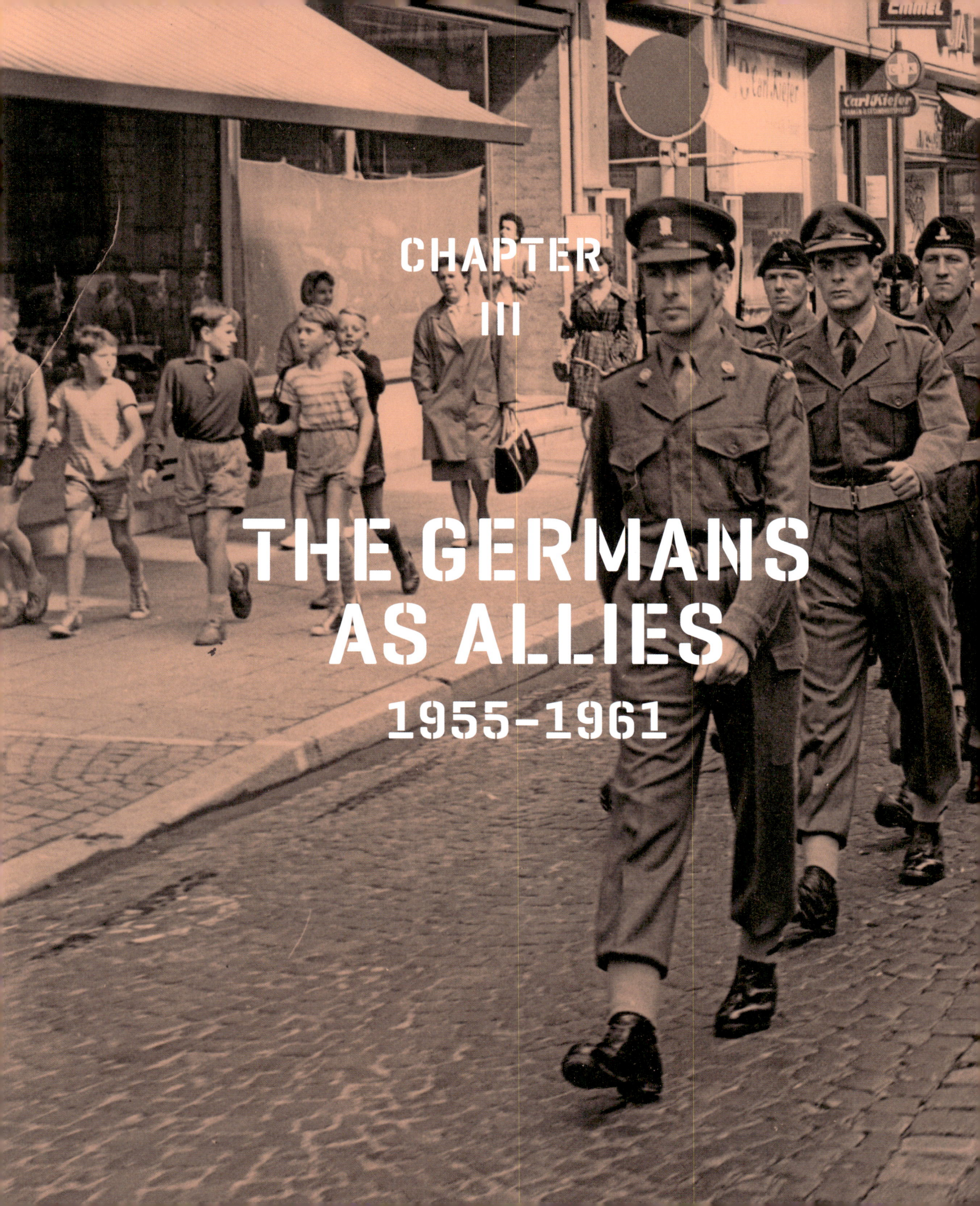

CHAPTER

III

THE GERMANS AS ALLIES

1955–1961

A NEW RELATIONSHIP

The formal end of the occupation of West Germany in 1955 saw the British embark upon a new phase of their deployment. The soldiers and airmen stationed there – and their families – were now ensconced in their garrisons and barracks to act as a deterrent against the Soviets. The Germans were now allies as well as neighbours. But it would be a long time before they were capable of playing a meaningful role in the collective defence of Western Europe.

The Bundeswehr, the armed forces of the new Federal Republic of Germany, was officially established on 12th November 1955. However, due to several obstacles, including many put in place by the Western Allies to guard against a return of German militarism, a process that was intended to take three years took a decade. For the British soldiers, some of whom had fought against the Germans in the Second World War, and others who had grown up in its aftermath consuming a public culture that was obsessed with it, it could have posed some difficult questions. Yet the British reacted with typical pragmatism. General Brian Davis of the Royal Artillery remembered fondly the links between his unit and the German military units and personnel that he worked with at the outset of his career, and how this developed through subsequent years:

'It was really quite close. They were fellow soldiers, actually. I never got involved with anybody who we'd known to have been involved in the death camps and so forth, none of that ... I'd met a number of ex-German soldiers ... as the peace treaty took hand and the German armed forces started to be revived again, a number of them who'd been in the war rejoined the new German army. And they were allowed to wear their decorations and so on, provided there were no swastikas.'

The British had been planning to work with a rearmed Germany for several months before the formal creation of the Bundeswehr. Earlier in 1955, a joint HQ NORTHAG and 1 (BR) Corps exercise called APRIL FOOL had been run. It was a logistical study that looked at how the British could best move to a continental system of logistics so as to better work with their allies. At the time, NORTHAG composed of Belgium, Netherlands, Britain and Canada, but the idea of working with the West Germans in future was explicitly discussed and clearly expected. This paved the way for better integration when West Germany joined NATO later in 1955. It was clear to the British that, should they have to fight, they would do so with at least one multinational corps under the command of NORTHAG, and depending on Soviet actions this could be composed of several different units drawn from their allies. Planning for this multinational eventuality was therefore essential.

While the Western Allies were coalescing around each other, the Soviets were also taking steps to redress the balance of power. West Germany joining NATO acted as a catalyst for the formation of the Warsaw Pact, those countries allied to or under the control of the Soviet Union.

In 1954, BAOR relocated its headquarters from Bad Oeynhausen to just outside Mönchengladbach, near a small village called Rheindahlen. Plans had been in

PREVIOUS: **British soldiers marching through Heidelberg, 30th July 1961 (SLG John Provan/Allied Museum, Berlin)**

'Is BAOR going on for ever?'

Lieutenant Colonel Marcus Lipton, MP, December 1952

LEFT: The front cover of the April 1957 issue of *Soldier Magazine*, focusing on the work of NATO (Crown)

RIGHT: Newly enlisted West German soldiers report for duty at barracks in Andernach in the winter of 1955 (Bundeswehr - Baumann)

place since 1952, and in October 1954 the headquarters was officially opened. The new Joint Headquarters became the command centre for NORTHAG, the Second Allied Tactical Air Force, BAOR and Royal Air Force Germany. It was centred on a block of 2,000 offices, which was soon nicknamed 'The Big House', and covered 470 hectares on land that had been requisitioned especially for the purpose. It was a brand-new military community, designed to be a fully functioning, independent town, and some 12,000 military personnel moved to the area in a few weeks. Relocation of the various HQs from Bad Oeynhausen, Bad Eilsen and Benkhausen was completed in just two months. While it was a social community, it was still very much a military installation and operational base, with

contingency plans in place for if the Cold War turned hot.

The move to Rheindahlen cost DM 130 million (£12.5 million in 1950s money), and was met from the German financial contribution to European defence – another significant windfall from the recent readmittance to their increasing economic prosperity to the European defence community. But this decision was also made for strategic reasons, moving the headquarters to the west of the Rhine, and therefore allowing a greater forward defence in depth should the Soviets attack. However, the move was not without criticism, particularly in the UK. On 9 December 1952, Lieutenant Colonel Marcus Lipton MP asked in the House of Commons, 'Is it not fantastic that

at this time so much money should be spent on headquarters for BAOR? Is BAOR going on for ever?'

Previous discussions had suggested relocating the new HQ to Aachen, even further to the west. However, this plan had been abandoned due to vociferous complaint from the Belgian contingent, in whose sector Aachen lay. They were simply unwilling to accept a HQ in their administrative area that would interfere with their control and also their training. Any move towards Aachen, and a new concentration of British troops, would have involved taking over three Belgian barracks, and relocating their troops east of the Rhine. The Belgians objected due to the repercussions on Belgian public opinion of the displacement of Belgian units, the undesirability of having troops of different nationalities in the same sector, and the undesirability for operational reasons in having Belgian units moved east of the Rhine given the overall planning for how to defend the northern ports.

Initially Rheindahlen (as it became known, rather than Mönchengladbach) was referred to in official British correspondence as the 'Peace Headquarters', even if the British and their multinational allies were standing at, albeit different, levels of readiness for war. This readiness needed to be constantly exhibited through exercises and public statements. But any fighting that would take place would be on a defensive basis. Throughout this period, NATO plans were for deterrence 'rather than preparation for fighting a protracted war in Europe'. They would not fire the first shot, but they would be ready if war came.

East of the Zone, the British were also ensconcing themselves further in Berlin. The foundation of the German Federal Republic had not affected the British troops in Berlin, who remained under the control of the military government there. It was widely acknowledged that the Berlin garrison was completely exposed, and militarily would have been able to offer little resistance should they have been called upon to fight the Soviets, or the new National People's Army (the *Nationale Volksarmee*, or NVA) that had been created in East Germany to match the Bundeswehr. However, their presence in the city was about more than just military utility. They were also important in maintaining morale among the West German population. They were the

proof that the Western Allies were willing to stand up for West Berlin and West Germany.

In West Berlin, the British occupied four barracks: Montgomery, Brooke, Wavell and Smut. In addition, as elsewhere in British Forces Germany, there was also the supporting infrastructure, such as schools, NAAFI, churches and others to provide for the families and dependents stationed there with the serving personnel. There were approximately 3,100 men serving in three infantry battalions, an armoured squadron to provide more firepower that was almost exclusively drawn from a Germany-based regiment and the BAOR, together with an engineer squadron and a number of support units. This was very much the upper limit of troops. Given the complex, and at times fraught, political climate, any increase in troop numbers risked being seen as a provocation to the Soviets. Yet at the same time, any weakening could be interpreted as a lack of resolve. And if the shooting had started, this garrison would have had to be self-reliant. As a note from the Chiefs of Staff Committee stated on 13th August 1953 when conducting war planning for the city's troops: 'The strength of the garrison will be constituted in peacetime. You will plan on receiving, after the outbreak of hostilities, no reinforcements or replenishment of ammunition, petrol or other warlike stores.'

Yet despite the Soviet encirclement, Berlin was still seen as the most exciting part of the deployment to Germany. Perhaps it was because of the danger, and the opportunity to cross into the different occupation zones, but Berlin held a real attraction for those stationed in Germany. David Walmsley, who served with the RAMC from 1955 to 1959, noted that these trips highlighted the differences between East and West:

'It was fairly prosperous, the bit we were in. East Germany wasn't, and we had these little holidays in Berlin where we were allowed to go into the East Berlin Sector as long as I was in uniform. That was completely different, still huge amounts of smashed up buildings and the Wall hadn't come. But the dereliction was tremendous in East Berlin while West Berlin even then had very considerably rebuilt itself.'

But it was the extracurricular activities that soldiers stationed in Berlin seemed to really enjoy, particularly

TOP LEFT: The foundation stone for the main building – the 'Big House' – at Joint Headquarters Rheindahlen was jointly laid on 1st July 1953 by (from left to right) General Sir Richard Gale, GOC Northern Army Group; Air Chief Marshal Sir Robert Foster, Commander-in-Chief 2nd Allied Tactical Air Force; and Rear Admiral Robert Sherbrooke, Flag Officer Germany (Crown)

TOP RIGHT: Building Rheindahlen was an enormous project. Here the architectural model is scrutinised in March 1953 (Crown)

MIDDLE LEFT: The 'town within a town', the purpose built community, as seen from the air during construction before it officially became home to the British Forces community in late 1954 (Crown)

MIDDLE RIGHT: The Big House under construction ahead of its official opening in 1954. Up to 6,000 builders were involved in the construction of JHQ, making it a major source of employment for the people of the region (Crown)

BOTTOM LEFT: The swimming pool, just part of the extensive recreational facilities built alongside the working aspects of JHQ (Crown)

BOTTOM RIGHT: The completed Big House after opening in October 1954.

before the Berlin Wall went up. As Lt Mac McCullagh, who served with the 5th Royal Tank Regiment from 1959 to 1961 as a junior officer, recalled,

'The nightlife was great, not least going to the East Berlin Opera House. The Russians insisted that the only personnel allowed to cross the east–west city border were military personnel, and as such, we had to be in uniform. The Opera House management insisted that the only dress acceptable was Number One Dress, and every night an entourage of British "peacocks" would arrive for the performance. The Tank Regiment had a smart cornflower and dark blue uniform but nothing over the top, but the uniforms of some of the famous cavalry regiments was a sight for sore eyes, especially the sad eyes of the East Berliners. There was always a crowd to watch the British Army show up at the Opera House as that was free entertainment in their dull and grey sector.'

Before the Wall and the hardening of the internal border, some soldiers also had a chance to explore Communist-controlled East Germany. The Very Rev. The Dean of Durham John Robert Arnold remembered his first trip through East Germany on the way to Berlin:

'It was quite a thrill, really, the first time I went to East Germany, in the summer of 1956. I went on the normal train that stopped at Helmstedt ... And it was really wonderful; we went into a hut – it was like being 3,000 miles away, it was just like a hut, say, in the Ukraine, with a smoking stove, with a pipe going up the wall ... there was a portrait of Lenin hanging askew on the wall, in cracked glass. And a Russian officer ... on his desk, he had one of those 'sit up and beg' telephones, where you turn the handle and the bell rings, and an abacus.'

SOLDIERING ON

As relations with the Soviets, and Communist East Germany, crumbled further, the possibility of direct conflict increased. An increasing perceived threat of nuclear war loomed large in British military planning. Nuclear weapons were incorporated into training and operating practices. Gale was adamant this was the case in his assessment of the situation in BAOR in 1955: 'The dominant factor is becoming the nuclear factor.' But it was only in 1960 that the Army in Germany had the equipment and ability to harness this for offensive purposes, when 50th Regiment Royal Artillery, based in Northumberland Barracks in Menden, had been equipped with the Honest John nuclear missile and 8-inch howitzers capable of firing nuclear warheads. The stockpiling of ammunition for this in Sennelager (along with the associated Site Guards drawn from across BAOR for periods of duty) was another factor that had to be planned into the daily life and training

The opportunity to serve in Berlin was welcomed by many. In promotional photographs, soldiers of the 2nd Battalion, Royal Green Jackets, are shown preparing to move from Northern Ireland to Wavell Barracks in Berlin, where they were stationed from 1960 to 1962. The battalion took an unusual mascot with them from Northern Ireland: a seal pup that a Rifleman Halpern had discovered and cared for (Crown)

RIGHT: A *Soldier Magazine* feature on the first firing of the Honest John rocket by British troops – which took place on the Hohne Firing Ranges (Crown)

'The dominant factor is becoming the nuclear factor.'

General Sir Richard Gale, Commander in Chief BAOR, September 1955

regimes of the BAOR. Previously, the expectation was that it was the Soviets, who already had this capability, who would use the weapons in their attack, and the British had been far more defensive in their mindset.

However, it was difficult to plan for something when people were unsure how it would actually impact the battlefield. The tactical use of nuclear weapons in a land campaign was completely without precedent. As a BAOR Umpiring Pamphlet of July 1949 had stated, 'Exercises that are unrealistic are actively harmful, since they tend to teach wrong lessons, breed a false atmosphere and lay open the troops taking part to the shock of surprise when they first meet the enemy in battle.' Training the Army in the use of nuclear weapons was essential, but how could the nuclear element, the scale of potential destruction, be included in exercises? Since 1954, the Army had been using specially made explosive charges to mimic the flash and atom burst of a tactical nuclear weapon to try to introduce more realism in their simulations and training exercises, but they were still quite limited, and could even be safely observed from just 300 yards away. Issues of proximity to the burst and the impact of the fallout all needed to be factored into exercise management, planning and control. There also needed to be consideration as to who had used nuclear weapons and in what quantity; had they been used by NATO forces or the enemy – or both? A briefing note from 1958 on the attainment of nuclear realism quite accurately pointed out that 'One of the most difficult aspects to introduce into nuclear play is a realistic time scale for the introduction of information to players', all of which was harder to quantify without accurate information.

But as General Sir Richard Gale pointed out in his assessment of the strength of BAOR in 1955 – and the strength of the enemy – it simply wasn't clear how

Vol. 16, No. 11 **SOLDIER** JANUARY 1961

THE BRITISH ARMY MAGAZINE

Libya, 4 piastres; Cyprus, 40 mils; Malaya, 30 cents; Hong Kong, 60 cents; East Africa, 75 cents; West Africa, 9d.

HONEST JOHN TAKES OFF

Trailing flame and smoke, *Honest John* leaves the launching vehicle on Salisbury Plain to explode over Ell Barrow ridge, near Stonehenge, five miles away.

★ ★ ★ ★ ★ ★ ★ ★ ★ ★ ★ ★ ★ ★ ★

On the Hohne ranges on Luneburg Heath, Germany, men of 24 Regiment, Royal Artillery, prepare an *Honest John* for firing from its mobile launcher.

A GUNNER in a slit trench on Luneburg Heath pressed a button and with a mighty roar a 27-foot long rocket a few hundred yards away leapt from its mobile launcher in a sheet of searing flame.

Rapidly gathering speed, the rocket shot across the sky at 700 miles an hour and disappeared, exploding in the air immediately above its target several miles away.

The rocket was *Honest John* and it was being fired for the first time by British troops —Gunners of 24 Regiment, Royal Artillery —on Rhine Army's ranges at Hohne.

A few weeks later *Honest John*, the British Army's new divisional support weapon, made its début in Britain, when, its warhead filled with concrete and high explosive, it was fired at a demonstration by the School of Artillery, Larkhill. It, too, exploded and disintegrated in the air, five miles away on a ridge called Ell Barrow, near Stonehenge, only 25 yards wide and 30 yards short of the target.

Honest John is a free-flight ballistic missile and can carry an atomic or high explosive warhead.

PAGE 5

much the Soviets possessed. As such 'this factor is probably the most difficult truly to assess', as 'one cannot be sure of the Russian stockpile, nor of the way in which the enemy will make use of this enormous power'. Even so, necessity compelled attempts at planning, and estimates did exist. In 1960, a report investigating the potential casualties among 1 (BR) Corps in the event of a nuclear attack found that 'the results show that, for example, a 10 weapon attack is likely to produce between 1,900 and 3,700 casualties and a 100 weapon attack between 11,000 and 25,000 casualties'. The risk of nuclear fallout on both enemy and friendly troops was pointed out. It could be used as a ground-denying tactic to slow an advance, but the risk was that, unpredictable as it was, it would then spread over friendly troops. This was particularly relevant to ground-burst weapons. However, once again there was a problem planning due to 'a lack of information concerning the Russian nuclear potential'. Furthermore, how much operational intelligence did the Soviets have? What concentration of weapons would be issued against which targets? All of those factors made planning an incredibly difficult – and in many ways almost futile – exercise.

Yet, as Gale pointed out, 'ground is the thing armies fight for, for it is the will to dominate ground and the people who live on it that is the first cause of aggression'. To counter this potential aggression from the Soviets, and in an effort to better counter some of the British weaknesses by improving their understanding of their potential enemy's capabilities, intelligence gathering on both nuclear and conventional capabilities became an integral part of the British Forces' security and defence. Corporal John Muckler served with the Intelligence Corps in Germany between 1957 and 1958, and remembered his main duties:

'The function of the section was to carry out security surveys of military establishments. It meant that units had to follow certain procedures, protective procedures basically to look after their kit. And at that time the threat was seen as the East German Army and Security Service plus the Russians. Our main focus was the East German Intelligence Service who were busy infiltrating military units. So our other main function was to vet German civilians before they were taken on.'

The main line of defence for the British in Germany were the armoured brigades based throughout the British Zone. The Army was going firm in garrisons such as Bad Lippspringe, Bielefeld, Bünde, Delmenhorst, Celle, Detmold, Dortmund, Herford and Fallingbostel. Training areas had been established from the end of the Second World War, but new ones were added to help them maintain a professional edge. The Bergen-Hohne ranges had been taken over by the British straight away in 1945, and were extensively used, even after control was passed to the Bundeswehr in 1958, where it became a central NATO training facility. Places like Vogelsang had been handed to the Belgians in 1950, but the British would continue to use it. The same year, Reinsehlen Camp was established on the Soltau-Lüneburg Area (SLA), though it would take several more years to agree a legal framework to enable the British to train there all year round.

For many of the British soldiers arriving in Germany from training establishments in the UK, the difference between what they had been trained and taught and what those based in Germany actually did was remarkable. Mac McCullagh recalled being confronted with this as soon as he arrived at Lumsden Barracks in Fallingbostel:

'When I got to Germany, the first thing I noticed on the

TOP: Soldiers of the 1st Battalion The Buffs (Royal East Kent Regiment) leaving Moore Barracks in Dortmund, 1959. The British continued to live mostly separate lives from their West German neighbours (NAM)

BELOW: *Standing Orders for Units Using the Soltau-Lüneburg Training Area* (revised March 1991). The British would establish themselves on the training area in the mid-1950s, and remain there until the mid-1990s (Private Collection)

National Servicemen serving with the 1st Battalion The Buffs (Royal East Kent Regiment) undergoing Bren Gun training in the grounds of Moore Barracks in Dortmund, 1959 (NAM)

first day, there was a parade of tanks going past, Centurions … And the driver was a chap called Corporal Murphy with a fag hanging out of his mouth … We'd just come from a training area where we would be court-martialled if we were seen with a cigarette in the tank – not only in a tank, but within a hundred yards of a tank. You would be out on your ear. And here we were, with an actual front line regiment, where not only did they smoke in the tank but they were also welding their kind of primus stoves to the actual floor of the tank itself inside. And when you got a troop of tanks, the idea was to choose the best cook. And the best cook was then made the gunner, because the gunner had the most room in the turret … The chap I had, Gunson, was a very good cook – and he would cook cross-country. We'd be in the tank, bitterly bloody cold, well below freezing, and suddenly you'd get a nudge and you'd look down and Gunson would say, 'Cup of soup, sir?' You'd be balancing this soup as you travelled cross-country around the Hohne ranges and all around there, and we had a whale of a time, I must say; it was great fun.'

The Army at this time was a mix of National Service conscripts and professional volunteers. Training was vital for everyone on all weapons, from armoured vehicles to the new FN Self-Loading Rifle, which was introduced into the Rhine Army after its official approval by the War Office in 1954. The soldiers had access to back-door training areas close to the barracks for low-level training or to practice for crash outs. Dry training could also be done in barracks.

There were, however, perceptible differences in how National Servicemen and professional regulars conducted themselves. As National Servicemen weren't for the most part planning longer careers in the Army, they could and did play fast and loose with some of the 'rules' imposed on them during training exercises. This was occasionally exploited by their professional superiors, as McCullagh noted:

'So we had these various exercises all over Germany, and it was always a little bit cavalier and a bit wild. For

LEFT: Mac McCullagh's troop of Conqueror tanks from 5 Royal Tank Regiment on a training exercise, taken during McCullagh's period of National Service from 1959 to 1961 (NAM/ McCullagh)

OPPOSITE LEFT: A collision between a British Centurion and a West German civilian car in icy conditions, early 1960s (Crown)

OPPOSITE RIGHT: 200 BAOR vehicles that had been made in Germany and had been damaged in collisions and accidents awaiting repair or being cannibalised for parts at No. 4 Base Workshop, 1956. Between 1950 and 1953 there had been on average 600 traffic accident reports filed per month. Indeed, 10 per cent of all accidents in Germany, Belgium and Holland were caused by British 'non-observance of national traffic regulations concerning vehicle design and equipment.' (Crown)

OPPOSITE BOTTOM: British soldiers receive traffic safety lessons from a German police officer, 1956 (Stadtarchiv Bielefeld)

instance when they'd say that the motorways were impassable rivers, and there were always certain bridges you could cross. So when you'd have an exercise against some cavalry regiment who were frightfully correct and proper, the Colonel would say, 'Right, the National Service officers, we want you to go up the motorway on the other side, and when the traffic's clear go across, take the crash barriers with you.' We got about five miles north of where the action was, wait for the right moment, and all three tanks would go straight across the autobahn to the other side, and they would come in behind the cavalry regiments and beat the hell out of them from the back, and they could never work out how we actually got there.'

While some soldiers could find service in Germany monotonous, there were also active duties that helped break the cycle of training and exercises. For the British armoured units, particularly the Recce Troops, there were duties such as patrolling the Inner German Border. This was an opportunity to catch a glimpse of the potential enemy – though in usual British style this could be done with a certain recklessness, as McCullagh remembers:

'When I was in Recce Troop, we used to do a border patrol from the Baltic place called Flensburg all the way down to Hannover. And we went down with 16 of our Ferrets through all the way along the border. And you'd stop every now and again to examine the border, and there'd be a minefield on the other side of the fence, and ... The East Germans, or the Russians at times, would be kind of hiding out the other side, and they'd look at you, and we'd all lie below the wall and we'd all get our cameras ready, and when we said 'go' we'd all leap up and take a photograph before they had a chance to duck down again ... and this we'd do all the way down the border ... On the border patrols, there was the local excitement, together with the excitement of aggravating the people on the other side ... I suppose we're lucky we didn't start World War III.'

The reasoning for this attitude was fairly clear. Active British training had prepared the soldiers for the possibility of a conflict of devastating consequences – one in which they were on the front line and likely to feel the full weight of the expected Soviet assault. The seriousness of the threat certainly influenced how the British soldier behaved not only on duty, but in his own time as well. In

the words of McCullagh again, 'The life of a tank commander if the Russians attacked was expected to be 36 hours. Optimistic. But at that age you think, "Well it could never happen to me, so let's have fun." And we did have fun, and it was a lot of fun for two years.'

LIVING WITH THE GERMANS

All of the British Army's training and active duty in Germany played out alongside the local German inhabitants, who were becoming increasingly economically prosperous. They were no longer the defeated people of a decade earlier. Yet the British had not really changed their relationship with the locals, and without a renewed level of social interaction, this relationship could be problematic. McCullagh again describes how the British soldiers and German civilians were coming into contact, often in fraught circumstances. Ultimately, this could create a sense of hostility from the Germans:

'We were going through the village of Bieringen and my troop sergeant's driver, Sergeant Ward, was rough that day, he had flu or something ... And my gunner, Gunson, who was about 5 foot high, said, "I'll drive, sir." I said, "Do you know anything about it?" He said, "Yes, I'm a good driver." I said, "Well I'll take your word for it, but take it steady!" So as we went into Bieringen, I went through the corner ... and then the Troop Corporal's tank came round with Gunson at the controls, and I saw him coming down the high street at a hell of a speed. And as I'd turned left I'd seen a car, a Mercedes car, with a trailer full of televisions on their right, unloading into a TV shop. And we turned left all right. The troop sergeant and bloody Gunson came round that corner ... and couldn't make it and went straight over the Mercedes and the trailer full of TV sets. And they were just literally about one foot high, the two of them. Not surprising, 65 tons going over the top. And the Germans came rushing out of the shop. And Gunson had the cheek to walk back, and said, "What's the trouble?" And believe it or not, you filled in a form, you signed it, you gave it to the Germans, and that was the last you ever heard of it.'

It was the Claims Department that picked up the responsibility for this and processed the claims submitted by German civilians looking for compensation.

The West German people were certainly recovering their own identity alongside their economic prosperity. As the war receded in memory, and their own prosperity increased, they were more assertive and less likely to tolerate being treated as a subjugated people. This undoubtedly changed their relationship with the British, who were no longer quite able to enjoy the superior lifestyle they perhaps expected. In the immediate aftermath of the war, employment with the British had meant an income and better rations for German civilians, which made it a very attractive proposition. But this was changing. J.F. Warren, who commanded 30 Heavy Anti-Aircraft

LEFT: An Austin Champ general service military vehicle in Roberts Barracks, Osnabrück, 1962. At least 40 per cent of all Champs – which were known by their civilian designation rather than their military name – were in BAOR between 1955 and 1970, and behind the UK it was the second-highest area of concentration (Crown)

RIGHT: Soldiers of 13th/18th Royal Hussars (QMO) celebrate winning the regiment's Troop Efficiency Shield in 1956 (Crown)

Regiment in Delmenhorst from 1954 to 1957, noted that while for him Germany was comparative luxury, for the older hands it was changing rapidly:

'It was quite new! Everyone said, "Oh, gosh, you should've been here a year ago, it's going to the dogs now! You'd have had three German servants until last year! You've only got two now." That sort of thing. We had a boilerman and a nanny, or a putzfrau or some name like that, that would look after children. Still, pretty good by my standards! But it was gradually going down and before we left I think it had gone, you know, likely to get one servant. And, quite right. Germans were taking over everything in those days. Now Delmenhorst barracks are German barracks again.'

Gillian Northey had moved to the Zone with her husband when he had been posted to Hameln in 1958. As they had married when her husband was under 25, they had not been entitled to a quarter in Chatham, and been forced into a private rental that had been rather unpleasant. But a year later, when they reached Hameln they were allocated a quarter, which amazed them both: 'To us it was like a palace.' Northey remembers the friction that existed with their German neighbours, a definite hangover from the war and the occupation, but rather than accept it, the Northeys saw this as a challenge to be overcome:

'The quarters were on a hill, with Lieutenants at the bottom, going up according to rank. So our immediate neighbours on the opposite side of the road were German. We sensed their unfriendliness, and they were very frosty, which was understandable as we were occupying their country, for which they were paying through taxes, so we were determined to try and break down the barrier. We bought a German car, my husband spoke only German when away from office and home, we sometimes attended the local Lutheran church, joining in everything going on in town, shopped locally and eventually invited neighbours to our home at Christmas time.'

Eventually, Northey was invited to coffee and cake by the local German wives, and ultimately established a friendship that lasted for decades.

Royal Irish Fusiliers in Celle Altstadt, 1961 (*Cellesche Zeitung*)

For many, the apparent coldness of the Germans was a barrier to attempting to integrate. Others found it hard to leave camp and interact with Germans in the local towns. Those who did, however, enjoyed their lives in Germany far more for the opportunities it offered.

Warren was luckier than most in that he was able to escape the confines of camp and interact with local Germans at a social level, though this was far from official:

'We met quite a lot of German people in Bremen – friend, did all sorts of things with them. They were very nice. My wife spoke German quite well, and so she used

TOP: The regimental skiing team of the 13th/18th Royal Hussars (QMO) in the Harz Mountains, 1957 (Clive Haynes)

BOTTOM: Despite the new alliance that formally ended the occupation, it took a long time for the occupier mentality to end in the British psyche, and the British retained numerous privileges. They were still very much used to holding a superior position as the victors in the war. Concerns about inconvenience to the West Germans were limited. This view of Brixton Barracks (later Richmond Barracks), then a RAOC depot, in Bielefeld in 1952 shows how the main street was simply blocked off to non-military traffic in the 1950s (Stadtarchiv Bielefeld)

to shop in the markets. The difficulty was the language ... I'm afraid, having a wife who spoke German, I just didn't find the time – I should have – to learn German myself. And the Germans that I met all spoke perfect English, which was very nice too.'

For those without these advantages though, life on some of the quieter British garrisons could be monotonous. Leaving camp became a matter of personal choice and confidence.

The authorities did try to provide as much entertainment as possible. By 1958, for example, there were nearly 50 Globe cinemas operated by the Army Kinema Corporation across the garrisons. But those lacking the confidence, ability or opportunity to venture into the local towns – even just to visit the shops – were confined to the facilities that were provided for them. While the NAAFI provided a taste of home and rapidly expanded its range to include fashion and consumer items, it could still be limited as the only source of shopping, and life on the ration system, good as it was, became less beneficial, particularly when the UK began its own economic recovery. For some the camp walls almost served to keep them in, rather than keep the Germans out. Even though the larger garrisons such as Rheindahlen were sometimes described as being closer to holiday camps than military facilities due to the provision of shops and extracurricular activities, not all British personnel were lucky enough to be stationed there. For Warren, the impact living on a small station had on life in Germany was quite clear:

'Delmenhorst was not a huge town, but it had a ... linoleum factory. That's one thing I shall always remember, the smell of the linoleum factory, coming away across the country to the barracks. That and the sound of the bells: they had a big church with two very heavy bells, which used to toll and clang, wonderful sound. Other than that Delmenhorst was nothing, really ... As a station it was pretty dim.'

Indeed, one of its principal advantages was its proximity to other areas of interest, which made it a 'good place to get away from'. The quality of the adventure training opportunities that were offered to soldiers in Germany at least, including both summer and winters sports, were unlike anything else in the world at that stage. In particular the skiing resorts at Winterberg or in the Harz Mountains were seized upon by many.

Not everyone enjoyed the lifestyle in Germany, or responded well to the military circumstances. Even between 1955 and 1961, a definite hierarchy was emerging between the various postings. Those in larger towns such as Celle or Paderborn were seen as very attractive. But some of the smaller stations and postings, or the more isolated – such as Fallingbostel – were seen as a bit more bleak. Regardless, each station developed its own activity plan to help build a sense of community among its inhabitants. Sports, choirs and drama societies all sprang up, and sought to help offer recreation activity for those who were off duty or for the attached families. For many, these were vital in helping provide a sense of community to compensate for what had been left behind in the UK.

For those willing to venture off camp, however, Germany offered great potential. But it was the military personnel who were most able to enjoy these, rather than the families. As McCullagh noted, it was a brand-new country waiting to be explored. For the young and the single, this provided almost unparalleled opportunity:

'On Recce Troop you've got wheels not tracks, which means you can go anywhere you want, you're not worried about tearing up the tarmac. And so we'd say, "Let's do a training exercise all the way down to southern Germany" ... We'd draw rations for two weeks in a three-tonner, and all 16 Ferret armoured cars would line up and away we'd go ... off down to the Möhne dam ... to see what damage was done there. We then had a canoe exercise all down the Rhine. It was fantastic fun. For a young man you couldn't beat the Army.'

Still, exploration of the wider German countryside risked bringing the British soldiers and their families into contact with the German people in unexpected ways, as Warren remembered:

'Well, there was a nudist camp just up the coast – never got as far as that ... Now, if you're a keen bird watcher, there were avocets just down along the coast. The Brigadier, when we were there, was very keen on that. I don't know if he got as far as the nudist camp.'

The British Families Education Service school in Lübbecke in 1957. The British had simply commandeered an existing vocational school when establishing education provision for the children of service personnel, but like much of the real estate that had been acquired in the aftermath of war it was not handed back swiftly [Stadtarchiv Lübbecke]

At a professional level, there still appeared to be a divide between the British and their neighbours. The relationship between the two, however, was not as clear-cut as perhaps may have been assumed. Indeed, while the British were quite cavalier in their attitudes when it came to using the training areas and their treatment of German property, they were assiduous in their provision of financial compensation for any damage caused. They were no longer an occupying power, free to behave as such. Some of the local German farmers recognised the opportunity the British could offer them, as reported by McCullagh:

'When we were training on a bigger exercise like BROWN JUG, which is a NATO exercise, the Germans would be out pleading with us, the farmers, pleading with us to leave the road and go over their field, because they would claim so much per acre of damage. And they'd almost bribe you to do it. Not that we did, but they were there actually, saying, "Please can you please come over the field, we'll give you a big meal or we'll entertain you or something, but go over my field," so they could make a claim.'

For farmers making a claim the British and their exercises could herald the start of a second harvest.

Despite living alongside each other, there still remained fundamental differences in culture between the British

and the West Germans. Without the regular social interaction of later years, the Army and the Germans lived next to each other, but lived largely separate existences. This physical divide resulted in a mental and cultural divide, which could often manifest itself through something simple, such as a failure to appreciate, if not understand, one another's sense of humour:

'And they could never understand us because it was always a standard thing that we all had dogs ... and the idea was every time you went through a German village you'd put a Tank Regiment beret on the dog, with headsets on the dog, and then you'd all close the hatches down, you go through the village, and out the other side. And the Germans would shake their heads and say, "The crazy British, they have the dogs commanding the tanks!" They could never work out that humour; that would never happen in the German Army.'

CHAPTER

IV

WALLS AND WIRE

1961-1973

THE WALL GOES UP

Overnight on 12th/13th August 1961, East German border guards laid nearly 100 miles of barbed wire around West Berlin. The Allied sectors had always been isolated islands in a Communist sea, but the wire barricade now cut the city off from the outside world. The 1948 blockade had been an escalation in the relations between the Soviets and the West, but people in Berlin had been able to move between the different sectors fairly easily. The new wire, however, ended that. Established crossing points between the Western and Soviet sectors were closed. Neighbourhoods were divided down the middle. Families were separated.

Officially the wire was laid to protect the East from the 'Western Fascists' seeking to undermine the Communist state, but it was clear that it was designed to keep East Berliners *in*, more than West Berliners *out*. Thousands of people, among them many young professionals and skilled workers, had fled from East to West Berlin – 2,400 on 12th August 1961 alone – and the East German government, and their Soviet supporters, wanted to put a stop to it. The Berlin Wall came to symbolise the Iron Curtain between Western Europe and the Eastern Bloc.

Soon after the wire was laid a brick and concrete wall was built, which was steadily fortified. Measuring nearly 100 miles around the western sectors, and 27 miles through the middle of the city along the border between East and West Berlin, it evolved into a fearsome obstacle. Two 12-feet-high walls were separated by a heavily guarded patch of ground called the 'death strip'. It was covered by watchtowers, crossed by barbed wire and even had soft sand so that the guards could spot the footprints of anyone trying to escape. It was under constant surveillance, and the East German border guards could shoot on sight anyone they believed to be attempting to escape and defect to the West.

Refugees from Berlin's East Zone wait to be processed at the Marienfelde Refugee Camp in West Berlin in July 1961 (CIA)

PREVIOUS: **The Berlin Wall in the 1970s (Pete Modley)**

After the Wall was built, there were initially only three checkpoints that enabled travel from West Berlin to East Berlin and the outside world: Checkpoint Alpha, at Helmstedt, enabled crossing of the Inner German Border from West Germany and access to West Berlin via Checkpoint Bravo at Dreilinden. In the centre of Berlin, the more famous Checkpoint Charlie gave access from West to East Berlin. Later border crossings were also established.

But the wire and walls were only the latest development in a crisis going back to 1958. Soviet calls for the Four Powers to leave Berlin and demilitarise the city had been ignored. In April 1959, wary of the increased threat, the British, Americans and French had created the LIVE OAK contingency planning committee to deal with Soviet threat to Western access to Berlin. It was to remain in operation until 1990.

The Wall, while an obvious indication of the growing hostility between Western Powers and the Eastern Bloc, added a new sense of drama to what was widely seen as the most exciting posting for British forces in Germany. It introduced new duties, such as patrolling the Wall, but it also introduced new rituals to daily life. Prior to the

Wall going up and the restrictions being put in place, British personnel and their families had enjoyed considerable freedom in moving between the sectors of Berlin. Even after the Wall, and the regulation of crossing points, a new form of dance was initiated. Allied military personnel and civilian officials of the Allied occupation authorities could enter and exit East Berlin freely, but serving personnel could only enter in uniform, and be in the Soviet sector for a set period of time. As the Allies did not recognise the East German state or their authority to regulate Allied military traffic to and from West Berlin, identification was only ever to be shown to the border guards, never handed over.

Unlike the British Zone in West Germany, where the British had stepped back from their occupation and government role and seen the West German government in Bonn rise and take political control, in Berlin they were still very much occupiers. While civil government did exist in West Berlin, and work in partnership with the Allies, the British Military Governor remained the ultimate political and military authority in the British sector.

This, and the latent threat of the Communist encirclement,

LEFT: **East German infantry line up to seal off Berlin's key crossing point: the Brandenburg Gate, late August 1961 [CIA]**

ABOVE: **East German soldiers dig holes for a new barbed wire fence near Potsdamer Platz, late August 1961 [CIA]**

gave service in Berlin a particular character as compared to the British Zone. Life in Berlin also retained several aspects that often made it feel like an extension of the colonial service the Army had spent most of the 19th century doing. The Service personnel and their families had a heightened status, real spending power with the exchange rate and good-quality housing maintained by the city of Berlin. Some even had domestic staff, again paid for by the city to create employment among local civilians. RAF Gatow was seen as a good station. The four barracks were well-built, well-equipped and comfortable. With the Berlin HQ being at the Olympic Stadium, facilities were unmatched anywhere else in Germany. The Maifeld polo ground, built for the 1936 Olympics, was considered the finest in the world – and doubled as an impressive parade ground.

However, even these sites were not immune to the Wall's intrusion on Berlin life; as Montgomery Barracks was located at Sakrower Strasse on the border between the British and Russian sectors of Berlin, when the Wall was built it ran along the perimeter of the camp, with East German observation posts keeping the barracks and its inhabitants under constant observation and surveillance. At RAF Gatow, the situations were reversed. The Wall ran alongside the western side of the airfield, and on the other side was a tank unit of the East German Army. It was always a fence rather than a concrete wall, but the neighbours were clearly visible from the RAF control tower.

When it came to the inhabitants of the British sector of West Berlin, the relationship between the British and the German civilians was also slightly different than elsewhere in West Germany. Isolated and threatened as they were, West Berliners recognised the role the British played in Berlin, and saw them as protectors against the far-worse alternative of being forcibly united with the Communist East Berlin and the wider East Germany. The Wall's construction confirmed this, and helped raise the popularity of the British and other Allied forces in Berlin further. Even if their military value was limited, the impact on morale of their presence in the city was significant. The British had embarked on a public programme of ceremonies and parades that served as a charm offensive, fully embracing the British military calendar and transporting it to Berlin. There were Guards of Honour and the Queen's Birthday Parade,

which saw the garrison Troop the Colour, as well as the annual Allied Forces Day Parade in July of each year. These were major events that drew crowds of Berliners to the Maifeld and the grounds of the British headquarters, and showed the British off to West Berlin. In 1966, it was the turn of the Royal Anglians and David Harding to Troop the Colour and, as he recalls, thousands of Germans came out to watch the parade at the back of the Olympic Stadium.

Another highlight of the social calendar – for the British military community and Berlin civilians – was the Berlin Tattoo, a huge music festival in a packed-out Olympic Stadium that took place over several days. Massed bands drawn from the British Zone and those of the Western Allies, as well as precision marching and display teams, all combined in a festival of military pageantry. The British had been holding military tattoos in their Zone and Berlin since 1947. Despite initial criticism in Parliament about the effort in cost and manpower to not only put on the event, but also to transport soldiers to Berlin for the purpose of performing, the tattoos were seen as delivering real value in terms of training for the soldiers taking part, as well as morale for them and for German civilians. They were not demonstrations of military power or a triumphal parade by a conqueror to

East German police officers monitor train tracks near the border between East and West Berlin a day after it was closed by the Soviets, 14th August 1961. The nearly empty train shows the impact of the closing [CIA]

the conquered – though those of course had taken place in the aftermath of the war; instead they were a showcase to display skill and professionalism, a spectacle rather than an act of intimidation. They were about entertaining the locals. The 1947 Berlin Tattoo even donated the profits to the welfare of German children. After the Berlin Wall went up, the events became even more important in maintaining social and friendly links with the German people.

Yet even after the Wall and the wire, and the hardening of the city sector borders, there were some rituals that needed to be continued that maintained links with the Soviets. With the division of Berlin in 1945, important sites fell within the British area of control. When the Soviets had been sole occupiers of Berlin immediately after the war in 1945, they had chosen a central site in the Tiergarten public park to build their War Memorial. Symbolically located between the Brandenburg Gate, the old Reich Chancellery and the Reichstag, it lay on the last battleground in the city. However, when the city had been divided this memorial fell inside the British Zone, the only place where Russians were permanently in the western sector, and its inauguration parade was in November 1945. With cooling relations in the Cold War, access was still maintained for the ceremonial guards, and for commemorative events. Once the Wall went up, this access was continued, preserving the agreements made when the city was initially divided 15 years before. However, if anything the escorting of these Soviet ceremonial guards to their positions was about protecting them from those elements of the civilians of West Berlin who were still angry at what the Soviets had done to the city. The British had even erected a barbed-wire barricade around the Soviet War Memorial to shield it from vandals and protect the Soviet soldiers on duty.

Other areas of cooperation included maintaining the quadripartite system of guarding Spandau Prison, where those convicted at the Nuremberg trials were housed. It was one of only two Four-Power organisations to survive the breakdown of the Allied Control Council in 1948. For a month at a time, Berlin's four occupying powers held control of the prison, and provided all the guards and security. Thus, British soldiers in Berlin could be right up close to not only the Soviets when they handed over control, but also the remnants of the Nazi regime.

A view from the British observation post in the old Reichstag, looking beyond the Wall into East Berlin, early 1970s (Pete Modley)

Aside from ceremonial duties, there was also operational training to be done. Despite being cut off in Berlin, military training continued in the designated training areas. Ruhleben in Charlottenburg would be used to practise urban tactics, and the Grunewald for more open exercises – as open as could be in an urban environment. Despite the fairly hopeless strategic position should the Soviets attack, the training was still realistic in order to maintain standards, and enjoyable for most of the soldiers who took part. The creation of the Wall also created new duties – it needed to be patrolled and observed.

Outside of military duties, there remained the opportunity to enjoy the social life of a young, cosmopolitan city. For the young and single in particular, Berlin was fantastic for the low cost due to the preferential exchange rate given to British personnel, and the vibrant nightlife, especially around Charlottenburg – or 'Grotty Charlotty', as it was soon nicknamed.

John F. Kennedy visited Berlin two years after the Wall was built, and on 26th June 1963 he delivered one of the most famous speeches of the Cold War. In front of 450,000 people in West Berlin, he proclaimed: 'Today, in the world of freedom, the proudest boast is "Ich bin ein Berliner!" … All free men, wherever they may live, are

citizens of Berlin, and therefore, as a free man, I take pride in the words "Ich bin ein Berliner!"'

Despite the small and unfortunate linguistic error that resulted in the leader of the free world labelling himself a donut in front of his German audience, it focused the attention of the globe on what was happening in Berlin. The Wall made Berlin the centre of the world, the place where the ideological battles between East and West, communism and capitalism would be fought. For the vast majority of British personnel living there as spectators and participants in global events, this made it one of the most interesting and desirable postings available in Germany.

BACK IN THE ZONE

Call ups for National Service had ended on 31st December 1960, and in 1963 the last National Serviceman to be demobilised, Second Lieutenant Richard Vaughan of the Royal Army Pay Corps, left the Army. Vaughan had actually served in West Germany, but after he completed his mandatory service – which had been extended slightly after the Berlin Wall had been built – the Army returned to the all-volunteer, professional force that it had been for so long.

The large number of men absorbed into National Service had become a burden to the Army, tying up regular soldiers in training new recruits. National Service also drained workers from the economy, which resulted in opposition from the public, the government, industry and many high-ranking officers. The Sandys review led

OPPOSITE: President Kennedy visiting the Berlin Wall, 26th June 1963 (John F. Kennedy Presidential Library and Museum, Boston)

ABOVE: British soldiers of 2nd Armoured Division (Lübbecke) shown in Gut Benkhausen, around 1963 (Stadtarchiv Lübbecke)

to the 1957 White Paper on Defence, which signalled the intention to return the British Armed Forces to a smaller but more effective force, capable of being deployed quickly. Nearly a third of the reduced Army would still be committed to West Germany and Berlin, however. As for the RAF in Germany, the White Paper cut the 2TAF in half, reducing it to 18 Squadrons and recasting it as a nuclear strike and reconnaissance force through removing its ground attack and fighter capabilities. Those personnel on leave in the UK at the time were simply told not to return to Germany. By the end of 1958, the airfields of Wahn, Celle, Bückeburg, Oldenburg, Wunstorf and Ahlhorn had all been handed back to the new West German Luftwaffe. On 1st January 1959, 2TAF had been renamed RAF Germany, and further reductions took place. By 1962, RAF Germany had 12 Squadrons under its command – which would remain its steady state for much of the Cold War.

Voluntary recruitment for the Army had understandably tailed off during the National Service years, but without a steady supply of conscripts the Army had to begin recruiting again in earnest. It began to offer competitive employment, as well as an opportunity to travel – something which appealed to prospective recruits like Ken Railton:

'I grew up in Newcastle upon Tyne and joined the Royal Artillery as a boy soldier in 1964. I was offered an apprenticeship as a draughtsman at one of the local shipbuilding companies, which would have been a job for life, but I didn't take it. An apprentice had to work for five years and for small money, whereas the Army gave you a good wage and also offered apprenticeships. My elder brother was in the Army and enjoyed it. My father had died and there was no money, and so to try to support the family I joined the Army at 15. The adverts read: 'Join the Army and See the World' and the idea of adventure also incited me to join up, but I didn't know where I was going to end up.

After two and a half years' training in the Junior Leaders' Regiment, I moved to Celle in Germany, home of 94 Regt RA, where I worked as a surveyor in a one-off posting for nine years. For half of the time I was there, I worked in Paderborn as a sports instructor detached from the unit ... My first impression of the country was that it was very clean and tidy compared to the grubby streets of north-east England. Everything was very picturesque – the trees, the roads, the houses; it was a big difference.'

LEFT: Despite having been established in their Zone for decades, there were still housing shortages in some garrison areas. Here, British soldiers and their families move into mobile homes that were to serve as their quarters in Menden, February 1962. Two hundred fully furnished caravan homes were sent to Rhine Army from Britain as a temporary measure to ease lack of accommodation. Some 8,675 were being built or planned in December 1961 for the Rhine Army (Picture Alliance: DPA)

RIGHT: Other families were far luckier. This is British Army service housing on Reineburg Strasse in Lübbecke, 1967 (Stadtarchiv Lübbecke)

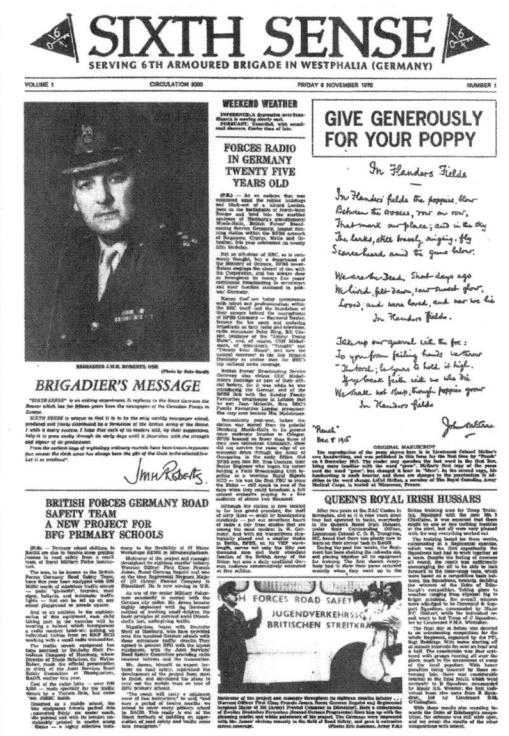

For many, the Army remained an alternative to unemployment, and for many the unexpected bonus of arriving in Germany and being introduced to a new way of life proved to be a major positive. Nigel Lawn, who served in the Royal Signals, recalls his motivations for joining up, and his first impressions of the country:

'I was born in Birmingham. There was no work where I was in England, so I joined the Army, signing on for 13 years. I did basic training in Catterick and from there I went to Bulford. I served in Germany in Verden with 1st Divisional Headquarters and Signal Regiment. When I came to Germany in 1970 it was something different to England, and besides everyone liking the beer, sausages and scenery, it was a different mentality. I noticed that Germans were more punctual.'

Of course, it wasn't only the British based in the British Zone. The Canadians maintained the 4 Canadian Infantry Brigade Group (known from 1968 as the 4th Canadian Mechanised Brigade Group), which was headquartered in Soest, but also had locations at Hemer, Werl and Iserlohn – some 6,700 troops by the mid-1960s. This all added to the cultural mix. The Canadians had their own newspaper, *The Beaver*, which was printed in and

distributed from Soest. When the British 6th Armoured Brigade moved in, they introduced a new weekly newspaper to replace it. *Sixth Sense* was the first post-war newspaper produced and distributed by a formation of the British Army of the Rhine. The first edition, in a run of 8,000, was released on 6th November 1970.

Transport to Germany was also changing. Movement via troop trains was being phased out, and the RAF was taking a greater responsibility in terms of air transporting. Ken Railton was not alone in it being his first time on an aeroplane, flying into Hannover and then moving on from there. Between October 1961 and October 1962, British United Airways made an average of 314 chartered flights between the UK and Germany per month. British European Airways operated a regular service from Hannover to Berlin. The RAF was going through a period of change too, in terms of equipment and their stations. RAF Geilenkirchen was handed over to the new West German Luftwaffe in March 1968, its last British inhabitants, No. 92 Squadron, moving to RAF Gütersloh with their English Electric Lightnings.

The Army that new recruits were arriving into was more settled, and had laid down roots in Germany.

LEFT: Serving in Germany offered great opportunities to an entire generation of soldiers. Here, Captain Christopher White-Thomson of the 1st Battalion, The Royal Fusiliers gives some of his men a few points on German geography as part of an orientation briefing, based on his own previous experience of serving there, before the battalion's departure for Osnabrück in June 1963 (Crown)

RIGHT: The first edition of *Sixth Sense* appeared in November 1970, and continued weekly until the end of 2017 (Crown)

Fifteen years after the war, the BAOR had established a comfortable routine, a steady way of life and work. While were variations depending on the regiment or corps concerned, Railton describes the typical daily routine:

'The daily existence in the normal unit was parade in the morning and then, for us, vehicle park maintenance and the normal checks. Sport was always once a week – football, rugby or whatever. Most of the guys stayed in the barracks in the evenings and had a duty-free beer. There was beer downtown, but it was expensive. Like most soldiers I would lie on my bed and read a book in my free time, or you'd go with your pals down to the NAAFI and have a beer. On the weekends I was always away doing my hobby. Your normal soldier on the weekend would sleep till 11am and then go downtown and have a few beers.'

For the officers commanding these men, the routine was important. It wasn't uncommon for the soldiers to get themselves into trouble if they weren't otherwise entertained. Major General Walter Courage, who joined the 5th Royal Inniskilling Dragoon Guards at Athlone Barracks in Sennelager as a young subaltern in 1960, remembers that one of the most important things was keeping soldiers occupied. This was either through vehicle maintenance, enemy vehicle recognition tests, skill at arms training, sport on a Wednesday afternoon, adventurous training or the large exercises. For some, particularly the reconnaissance squadrons of the armoured regiments, there was patrolling the Inner German Border to be taken up in earnest – which like the Berlin Wall had been increasingly fortified on the East German side; more than 850 miles of heavily defended positions ran from the Baltic in the north to Czechoslovakia. There were also more extensive international competitions, such as the inter-Allied gunnery tournament or the Nijmegen Marches.

Even so, despite the increased levels of threat, and the training for crashing out of barracks to pre-sited positions as part of the General Deployment Plan, for many the Soviets still remained an abstract threat, beyond comprehension. Even after the Warsaw Pact invasion of Czechoslovakia in 1968, for many the actual political situation, with its peaks, troughs and flashpoints, was

Troopers Jim Oliver and Roy Cruise of the 10th Royal Hussars on a border patrol with an officer of the British Frontier Service at Travemünde in Lübeck Bay in 1967. They were on a four-day patrol, before returning to the regiment in York Barracks, Münster (Crown)

not something that registered. For many soldiers below company commanders, the looming threat to the east remained mostly out of sight and out of mind. Ken Railton summarised many people's feelings:

'At age 17, you didn't take too much interest in politics; being in Germany was an adventure and I felt kind of neutral. I guess the Army was there to protect, as opposed to being the guy in charge and taking over. It was working together with the local people to maintain the NATO image of keeping the Russians out. At the time the big threat was the Russians coming and invading Western Europe, and that was what we all had in our minds. The Soviet Union was the big threat as far as we were informed in the 1970s. That was our mission: to stop this supposed invasion. We were going to be the heroes and save the world.'

While Warsaw Pact propaganda was pushed into the West, occasional glimpses of the Soviets could be found in the Zone in the form of the SOXMIS vehicles – driven by the Soviet Military Mission. Some soldiers spent whole postings to West Germany without ever seeing one, but for others sightings were quite regular. Jim Griffiths, who had completed his National Service in 1956 before signing on as a professional soldier with the Light Infantry, was luckier than most: 'I regularly saw SOXMIS vehicles, because they were stationed in Bünde and I was in nearby Herford and you could see them going out. Sometimes they went out in big furniture wagons. In those days you had to report them as soon as possible.'

The British authorities were eager that the Soviets

working in the mission be tracked and made to observe the permanent and temporary restricted areas of the Zone. Each British soldier was issued with a SOXMIS card, with details on how to recognise their vehicles, how to detain them with the correct legal procedure that the liaison missions operated under, and the telephone number in Herford to whom their position could be reported. Some of those who did report even received a small thank you card from the Royal Military Police (RMP). However, many British soldiers doubted how enthusiastically those Soviet soldiers stationed with SOXMIS actually were in pursuing espionage. They lived within a compound in a British married officers' patch in Bünde, and if they weren't sighted out on the road then they were often found enjoying the comparative luxuries of the NAAFI in Herford, with their entitlement to duty-free cigarettes and spirits.

The Soviets remained the major threat, but the main 'foreign' influence that the British Service personnel came into contact with were the local Germans. There were still traces of the legacy of non-fraternisation in the early 1960s, as Courage found in the beginning of his time with his regiment. After returning to the mess following a night out in a local German bar with a fellow young officer, it became apparent from his more senior colleagues that it was not 'the done thing' to drink and socialise with Germans off camp. However, these attitudes were becoming more rare. Soldiers began to go in to town more proactively as West German pubs and clubs became worth going to for more than just an opportunity to meet West German women.

A major driver of this was the introduction of rock music to the social scene. From the Beatles playing shows in Hamburg to the famous Jaguar Club in Herford attracting British bands like the Who and Manfred Mann, the British Zone became a cultural hotspot. They were interesting to West Germans and British soldiers alike, something not lost on the German inhabitants of the garrison towns. Siegfried Eckstein, who had moved to Herford in 1946 as a child, remembers the changes of

Coldstream Guards and officers of the Bundesgrenschutz (Federal Border Guards) on a border patrol, 1969. The opportunity to catch a glimpse of the Cold War enemy – even through binoculars – was rarely passed up (Kaspar Coward)

the 1960s and early 1970s: 'When I was around 18, rock music started in Germany – Bill Haley and the others, and so we met young soldiers of our age at the pubs, dancing halls and swimming pools and it was a fantastic time ... British soldiers were there but not in uniform.'

Eckstein had seen first-hand how the rules on where soldiers could and couldn't go in civilian areas had been relaxed:

'In the 1950s and early 1960s, when the British soldiers went into German pubs, they thought German beer was like English beer, but it wasn't. The soldiers drank from big glasses and it could be that they got a bit drunk. It wasn't a real problem but the Army said, "We'll stop soldiers going to German pubs." So there was a sign in the window: Out of bounds. And we Germans thought, what is that? That went on for many years, but we thought that was not the right way. The ban finally went and all the soldiers became part of the pubs and restaurants and dance halls. In the dance halls the soldiers tried to find a German girlfriend and it was the same for the German boys, and sometimes it could be a bit of a problem. But in the end, everything was good.'

The interactions between the British and West Germans helped close the cultural gap, and the exchange was sometimes reaching back to the UK. For example the folk song, 'The Happy Wanderer', a performance of which was made by an Anglo-German children's choir from the Rinteln area and recorded by the British Forces Broadcasting Service (BFBS), became a major hit in the UK. Bands started forming that included both British and German musicians. Sport also became a major way for British soldiers to meet with local Germans, and they began playing on the same local German teams when duties and postings allowed. Encounters were no longer limited to either fights or confrontations with farmers about the damage inflicted by the British while out on exercise. The times really were changing.

SERVING THE SERVICES

Throughout the British deployment to Germany, the one constant link with the comforts of home was the NAAFI. Wherever the British Army was based, NAAFI was there.

A NAAFI Dividend Stamp – a familiar aspect of life in the Zone for thousands of customers (Private Collection)

These included both the small stations, such as the sole shop providing for the Kiel Yacht Club and the 12 British, 16 American, three French and 25 Danish families there, as well as the small NAAFI shop and airmen's club for the 26 RAF families at Putlos in the north, and the much larger garrisons in the south. Across the Zone, NAAFI ran the shops and entertainment centres that helped give a taste of home to the British Service personnel and their families.

The 1960s did not begin particularly well for NAAFI, however. The decision to end National Service had a substantial impact on the NAAFI, stripping it of many of its customers. Furthermore, as the British retreat east of Suez began in earnest, NAAFI was losing more and more customers and markets. This meant the focus fell on West Germany, as one of the largest concentrations of British forces. Even so, it still closed 26 establishments in the Zone.

From 1957, the NAAFI distributing warehouse had been established at Krefeld. It claimed to have handled 1,000 tons of throughput per week. Over 500 people worked there, including Germans. The commercial transport fleet consisted of 450 vehicles, covering anywhere up to 16 million kilometres each year. But it wasn't just a warehouse. It was a complete facility, rivalling some of the smaller military stations. There was a transport garage and workshop, a staff hostel, a club and a bakery. It was also the first place where the NAAFI used computers to help with stocktaking, having installed two in 1956. These were replaced again in 1966. This made the NAAFI far more agile in identifying what products were selling well and where, and getting new stock to

The NAAFI at JHQ Rheindahlen, March 1971 (SLG John Provan/Allied Museum, Berlin)

places that were selling fast, while removing poor-performing lines. It could also help with the fluctuating exchange rate and the depreciating value of sterling that NAAFI needed to remain wise to, and that influenced the price of goods in the Zone.

In 1961, Service personnel and their families could order from a 128-page catalogue with a bewildering array of products: television sets, LP records, washing machines, typewriters, cameras, children's garden swings and sports equipment. The NAAFI had it all, and more. They claimed to supply 15,000 different saleable items. Personnel could even buy NAAFI-branded ground coffee and tea. NAAFI were able to import so much instant coffee into Germany without paying duty that it had to be rationed, for fear that the temptation would be too strong for Army spouses not to sell it on to the local Germans, who were paying far more for a more limited supply.

The year 1961 also saw the introduction of the Hire Purchase scheme, which resulted in the purchase of more than 1,000 cars from the NAAFI by Service personnel. This scheme offered favourable terms to obtain loans for British and continental cars. They were certainly good value, with a 20 per cent deposit and repayment over three years at a rate of 6 per cent interest on the original loan. However, if customers could not meet these repayments, NAAFI could and did contact commanding officers, and the instalments were deducted direct from the pay packets of the recalcitrant. This docking of pay obviously angered the troops who fell victim to it, who had not realised that NAAFI could influence Army discipline in such a way. Other independent dealerships also began marketing exclusively to British Service personnel in both Germany and the UK – though all purchases in Germany were made through the NAAFI as the official procurement

LEFT: A mixture of REME and RAOC soldiers at Hobart Barracks on Detmold Air Day, 1971 (Kaspar Coward)

OPPOSITE TOP: Soldiers under undertaking instruction at Bad Oeynhausen Nautical Academy, around 1968 (Crown)

OPPOSITE BOTTOM: Kiel Training Centre, 1968

agency. The widespread introduction of cars into the British Army of the Rhine, a luxury that had previously only been enjoyed by some officers, closed the distance between the UK and the German bases. Trips back to Calais became more common. When France abruptly left NATO in 1966, Zeebrugge over took as the main continental port for travel to and from the UK.

Some unexpected items were big sellers for the NAAFI; £25,000 worth of musical instruments were sold per year in the 1960s, for example. There is even a story that, in order to satisfy British tastes, NAAFI taught a German farmer how to grow marrows just so they could be sold to the British forces. During the 1968 foot-and-mouth crisis, when West Germany banned meat imports from Britain, NAAFI even employed a sausage factory inspector to teach German and Danish producers to make British sausages – transplanting a taste of home rather than replacing it entirely with locally sourced, German-made wurst.

As a result of these sorts of policies, NAAFI's turnover in West Germany and Berlin increased from £17 million a year to £26 million a year during the 1960s. Seventy family shops served 25,000 service families. In 1972, NAAFI unveiled a 14,000-square-foot supermarket at JHQ in Rheindahlen, filled with £250,000 worth of stock and 300 unique NAAFI own-branded lines. It was the biggest NAAFI store in the world. Takings were estimated to be £3 million annually. It was more than capable of competing with the American PX, to which the British stationed in the multinational HQ used to enjoy access, and became so popular that day trips would be organised for service wives from as far afield as Hohne just to shop there.

Ultimately, for many, the convenience and familiarity of the NAAFI meant that there was no need to leave the British garrisons, or to go into the local German towns. In many ways, this could lead to the British isolating themselves further behind their own walls and wire. Nigel Lawn was not alone when he recalled his early years in Germany: 'My contact with German civilians was very little indeed, as I stayed basically inside the camp all the time. We had little contact with the people in Verden. All shopping was done in the NAAFI and we had no reason to go into town, except maybe at night to go to the discos and local pubs.'

Other organisations made the gap between the UK and Germany smaller. BFBS had begun broadcasting the BBC show *Two-Way Family Favourites* in 1955, the theme tune

'With a Song in My Heart' heralding its arrival for 90 minutes each Sunday. BFBS had moved from their original home in the Hamburg Musik-Halle to Cologne, and they could be heard across the airwaves in each garrison – and were often enjoyed by the West Germans too.

As British forces in Germany moved through the 1960s and into the 1970s, the challenges of establishing themselves in their garrisons and re-orientating themselves to the new, atomic threat had mostly been met. Provision was made for the forces and their families, and a routine was established. But the coming decade would reveal new challenges, requiring the Armed Forces to adapt once again.

CHAPTER

V

AT HOME
IN GERMANY

1973-1982

TRIPWIRE IN BERLIN

During the years of the British Army in Germany, the threat of the Soviet Union had always loomed large. While somewhat intangible, it was always there, governing the daily routine of their soldiers and their families. However, the period of détente between NATO and the Warsaw Pact reduced the danger of war breaking out. The Strategic Arms Limitation Talks and the Helsinki Accords meant that from 1969 the tensions between East and West were reduced, at least until 1979 and the Soviet invasion of Afghanistan.

This thawing Cold War meant that those living on the front line were slightly more free to enjoy living in Germany. This was particularly true in Berlin. While the Wall remained up and physically and mentally dominated life in West Berlin, the decrease in tension of the 1960s meant that, while remaining vigilant, life could be very good. Indeed, in some ways, the Wall itself and the aura associated with it could serve to make it even more attractive for those stationed there. It defined Berlin and the Cold War. As Colonel Simon Fordham, who served with the Royal Irish Regiment and Royal Irish Rangers, recalled:

'The battalion was being posted to Berlin, and I was very much looking forward to this ... My first real view after going through the transport was a red-and-white barrier. And so the whole impression of the Wall, and guards, and everything, came all sort of flooding there ... And it was remarkable ... It all confused me as to where the Wall was, where you were allowed to go or not ... And it was a cat and mouse game between them and the Russian Recce platoon, taking photographs of each other, trying not to cause international incidents and all this sort of thing.'

From the soldier's perspective, service in Berlin was a great opportunity to mix and mingle with a young,

A British Military Policeman controlling Allied traffic passing through Checkpoint Charlie in Berlin, 1973 (Crown)

PREVIOUS: Schloss Bredebeck in Bergen-Hohne. Bredebeck was the Officers' Mess of the resident cavalry regiment in Hohne, located on the Bergen-Hohne training area. It was used for sporting events, hunts, and other social and ceremonial occasions (Private Collection)

vibrant city. This new generation was less likely to hold the same attitudes to the Western occupying powers that their parents did, and even less so after the Wall went up and global politics had placed West Berliners and the Western militaries on the same side in the Cold War. For Brigadier Norman Allen, who served with the Royal Military Police in Berlin for six years during the 1970s, this made it a fantastic posting: 'The locals … loved us. We were called the amis, the entertainers … we had lovely housing … We had very excellent vehicles, wonderful communications … Anything we wanted, we got!' For Fordham, 'Berlin was great, because on a social side … Berliners live this 24-hour-day existence … and it was such a unique place.' Walter Courage, who commanded the armoured squadron based in Smuts Barracks in the mid-1970s, recalled the unparalleled sporting opportunities that being based in the old Olympic complex offered: 'It was a great sporting place, fantastic cricket ground on the Maifeld, by the Olympic Stadium.' Overall, he remembered Berlin thus:

'It was a very relaxed atmosphere, funnily enough. It was great fun, because the Berliners welcomed us enormously. We had incredible facilities there, the Berlin budget was something else, so we had a wonderful officers' club, we had FRIS [Family Ration Issue Service] … one had the ability to visit East Berlin through Checkpoint Charlie, though one had to wear uniform. We had the Havel training area … the facilities in the barracks were fantastic. But there was a job to do, so from that point of view, and actually at the time, whether I realised it or not I don't know, but there was no way we could have defended that if they'd come in with all their might.'

Many of the British took the opportunity to observe the large parades held by the East Germans and the Soviets in East Berlin, particularly on Republic Day on 7th October, which commemorated the foundation of East Germany. The 1979 parade of the East German People's Army was the largest yet seen: 37 main battle tanks – including 25 brand-new, Soviet-built T-72 tanks that had recently been delivered to East Germany – 84 armoured vehicles, 18 rocket-carrying vehicles, 95 rocket launchers and 87 artillery pieces; 42 armed helicopters even flew over East Berlin for the first time. While it was a great spectacle, and an opportunity to

An Army Air Corps Gazelle flying past the Brandenburg Gate while carrying out airborne observation of East Berlin, 1970s [Army Air Corps Museum]

gather intelligence on Warsaw Pact forces, these parades could certainly be slightly intimidating, and served to underline the vulnerability of the Western Allies – something not lost on Allen:

'The big parades in East Berlin – and they were big parades, too – you'd suddenly realise that there were whole regiments of tanks, and a regiment is three or four battalions of tanks lined up there to parade. And we

A ZSU 23/4, a Soviet anti-aircraft system, on the streets of East Berlin, prior to the October parade in 1981 (Crown)

had only a handful of tanks in the British sector. *Probably we could've mustered … I don't know what the total would've been with the French and the Americans, but never more than 50 or 60 tanks. It would've been a very brief battle I'm afraid, but we were a tripwire, and the tripwire held.'*

It wasn't only the serving military who enjoyed life in Berlin. It was a great posting for Army families too. Jenny Savory, who lived in Berlin from 1976 to 1979 when her husband was posted there, recalls how, 'Everyone had parties … You could do anything. You could sail on the Havel. I learned to sail a dinghy on the Havel … the German horses were fabulous … Life was good.' There were also the nightclubs in Berlin. The FRIS deliveries were a real highlight. After the Soviet blockade and the airlift, the garrison maintained a year's supply of food at all times, but as the various items reached close to their perishing points it was released to the garrison and replaced with fresh deliveries. This provided those living in Berlin with good-quality food for very reasonable prices.

The British also played a major role in the social side of garrison life, both for their own benefit and for those of the local Germans. Courage recalls, 'We had a lot of events with the Germans too, the Tiergarten Open Day … there was the Military Tattoo, which went on for a week and a bit, and there was the Queen's Birthday Parade.'

The social events at the home of the general officer commanding the Berlin garrison, the Villa Lemm on the banks of the Havel, were also legendary. For the wives, there were regular coach trips into East Berlin for shopping, where the spending power of the British was maximised by a very favourable exchange rate from Deutschmarks to East Marks. There were also big social events that took place in the East, which the Wall had not curtailed. Just like the generation that had served before in Berlin, the British continued to visit East Berlin, and to enjoy the cultural richness cultivated there. Savory remembers:

'All the officers and their wives were encouraged to go through [the Wall]. And we used to go through in a

VILLA LEMM

coach, and we'd go to the opera ... All the girls wore their best ball gowns, and all the husbands wore all their mess kit, and all we had to do was hold our closed passports up against the window as we drove through. And they weren't allowed to stop us, they weren't allowed to look at anything, and that was it. It was brilliant. And after we'd been to the opera, we used to go out for dinner ... it was the most fabulous German restaurant, and they used to have chateaubriand and gulls eggs, and they had a three-piece band, and as we walked in they played "God Save the Queen".'

There were also opportunities to interact with Soviet soldiers in some of the shared, or overlapping, duties and rituals that the opposing sides in Berlin maintained. British soldiers could, and did, play a full part in these. They could range from guarding the remnants of the Nazi regime to managing the movement of British personnel in and out of the Communist encirclement. Yet these rituals were what made service in Berlin unique. Fordham did both:

'I was captain guard for guarding Rudolf Hess, twice. And this one time when he got ill, I was captain of the guard that took him to the BMH hospital. And what was amazing there was that all of the arrangements to look after him, all the operating procedures, were all written right at the end of the war. And no one allowed any of them to change. So in the hospital there had to be an armed soldier every six feet, all the way up to his room – he had a special room, and all the rest of it. If one doctor saw him, it had to be an American, French, Russian or British doctor. Or four of them at the same time ...

When I was captain of the guard of the freight train ... instead of about an hour of the passenger train going

through, the freight train would take about ... three days. And it was obviously shunted off and moved at awkward times. And it meant that when we got to the checkpoint, with the Russians, we were there for about three hours. And so, I'd go in and we'd chat together about life in Russia, life in Europe, what we were getting up to and all the rest of it. And it was just remarkable, because after that stage, clearly the Soviet forces were what we had studied and expected to be attacked by, and here I was, meeting these people face to face, which was fascinating. And of course they were just like me, like soldiers anywhere and everywhere.'

For Fordham, encounters with the Soviets, and his journeys into East Berlin, left him with the sense that 'you really were in this sort of time warp', such were the contrasts between the Communist side and the modernity of the West. Even various British traditions lived on in Berlin long after they had elsewhere in the Zone; BAFVs, for example, were only withdrawn from Berlin in 1979. Julia Payne, who served at Teufelsberg on attachment from the Women's Royal Army Corps in 1976, and then spent another two years in Berlin between 1979 and 1981, noted that occasionally Soviet intelligence, the GRU, would try and turn some of the garrison, particularly at the checkpoints on the corridor when soldiers moved individually. She was approached by a Russian claiming that he wanted to improve his

LEFT: Signboard from outside the Villa Lemm in Berlin (NAM)

RIGHT: Troops from the British Berlin garrison drawn up on the Maifeld as part of the Queen's Birthday parade in 1976 (Crown)

English and wanting to arrange further meetings, but also that it was all part of the game.

Outside of the formal protocols and rituals of working with the Soviets, service in Berlin was still serious soldiering. Soldiers patrolling the Wall and checkpoints routinely carried live ammunition, in case the Russians tried to break through. There were also big ROCKING HORSE exercises, where the entire garrison would crash out and practise defending West Berlin – which while fun for the soldiers could be intimidating for the local civilians. The encirclement of Berlin and the politics of the Wall meant the British had to maintain a diplomatic presence – something not lost on Allen and the other members of the RMP, who manned the checkpoints and were therefore often in close proximity to the Soviets. Allen commanded a Company responsible for access along the Autobahn from Helmstedt into the city, as well as various liaison roles. He recalled,

'Someone said Berlin's the only place in the world where a military policeman could start or prevent the Third World War. Well that was an overstatement, but we were the lubricant in a very difficult machine at times. Because we were there and always there, and were prepared to eyeball people at low-key. I was dealing with an incident one dark night on the Autobahn, and Volkspolizei appeared, hands on their pistol holsters, and I greeted them, "Guten nacht!" and reached my hand out, and they had to take their hands out and shake my hand; they were really reluctant to do it, but you know, I was cooling the situation. And … one was aware that things could blow up. But they never did … It was a tricky diplomatic situation. And our chaps, and our girls too, dealt with it wonderfully. And we did have lots of low-level incidents, but keeping the lid on was important. Vital.'

But while many of the British living in Berlin tried not to dwell on their slim chances of survival should the Cold War turn hot, the brutality of the ideological divide was never far away. Tours into East Berlin revealed the militaristic state, with armed policemen constantly visible. Yet despite the dangers, people from East Berlin and East Germany regularly tried to escape to the West. Some were lucky. The 1970s saw two escape and defecting attempts land at RAF Gatow, in 1978 and 1979. But the majority of people tried to smuggle themselves over, through or even under the Wall where it divided the city. Allen remembered this vividly:

'We had escapes, we had people coming over the Wall … We had a nasty event on the Spree in the middle of Berlin. The Spree marked the boundary in the middle there. And one escapee was shot in the water and died; another one was struggling and my second in command rescued him. Got a bollocking for it from the ambassador for risking his life, and a pat on the back from the General, who said, "Quite right, but don't do it again, will you?" '

This undoubtedly caused anxiety for those serving in the city, something Lieutenant General Sir John Kiszely recalled from his service as aide-de-camp to the General Officer Commanding, Berlin, Major General Scott Barrett, while still a young captain in 1973:

'There was certainly a sense of tenseness about it … You were at something of the sharp end … I don't think that we really thought that there was a very high chance of deterrence failing at the time I was in Berlin, but that didn't stop the feeling of tenseness that there was a wall around you and people were being shot trying to escape from it.'

One of the most obvious focuses of this was the crossing at Checkpoint Charlie, which the British used to get into East Berlin: 'It was always pretty spooky, because this was a frontier like no other frontier really, where drama was happening – not on a daily basis but quite regularly – and at a very tense crossing, a tense atmosphere … There were certainly lots of border guards around with weapons that you knew were loaded and ready to fire.'

Yet because Berlin was surrounded, that tense feeling pervaded the whole British sector. Gillian Northey lived in Berlin between 1976 and 1979, when her husband was posted there as the Area Works Officer, and she recalls the Intimidation of it all.

'It was intimidating living with the ever-present threat of invasion by the Russians, within earshot of their exercises. We were, after all, living the Cold War. We had to be careful in our behaviour. Each officer's quarter had its RED telephone and the house phones were bugged.

Items from a Berlin escape pack issued to British soldiers serving in West Berlin, which included a compass, a silk map of Berlin and Germany, money, a saw and a notice in four languages asking for safe passage (Barry Davies)

The fence around our house was electrified. We were constantly photographed and our movements monitored by the Russians and our escape plans were in place. My son was taken up one day in the reconnaissance plane along the 'corridor', and he was told not to put his hands up at the window as the Russians would think he had a camera and was taking pictures and therefore [would be] liable to be shot down.'

There were still important operational and professional lessons to take from being in such close proximity to Britain's allies – as well as a major enemy. Berlin was very rewarding at the professional, as well as the social, level. Allen described it as 'probably the most challenging and enjoyable time of my career'. Fordham learned a huge amount from being stationed in such an isolated place:

'Berlin was sectioned off, obviously, with the Americans, ourselves and the French. And I learnt quite quickly that [in] quite a lot of these large-scale situations and operations, it actually is very important that an officer plays his part in getting on with other contingents, with other armies. And understanding that they're not going to be the same as you, but actually if you're going to end up fighting side by side, it's best that you [get] to know them before you actually have to do it for real.'

Major General Charles Dair Farrar-Hockley, who was Brigade Major in the Berlin Infantry Brigade from 1979 to 1981, noted that working with the Americans and French, as well as the local West Berlin political structures, had advantages but could also put limitations in place:

'[We] were encouraged, or allowed, to go out to the different boroughs in the city of Berlin, and they would give us buildings that were due for demolition for people to train on, new buildings under construction – U-Bahns, for example, which hadn't got to a point where they could be damaged, and really our opportunity culminated in a brigade-level exercise with tanks rumbling in from the north of the city, with the full permission of the Senate of West Berlin, who had

warned the public and said, "Provided you don't have a battle during the morning rush hour or evening rush hour, you can do it when you like." Over three days we ran this exercise, and it was a tremendous boost to military confidence, as well as (curious enough in those days) to the people of the city, who realised we were serious about defending them should something happen.'

For the families as well, it was a real highlight. Gillian Northey lived in Berlin between 1976 and 1979, when her husband was posted there as the Area Works Officer. For her, 'it was all excitement. The social life in places like Berlin was marvellous ... It was all an adventure; it was a very good life.' The facilities, the excitement of the Wall, the opportunities to go into the East, as well as the incentive for people from the UK to come out and visit – all made it a great posting. Savory agreed: 'It was very special, a very special time. I don't know if everybody loved it as much as I did, but I found it the most super place.'

A NEW THREAT

The implications of détente were also being felt elsewhere in the Zone. For many people, the risk of the Soviets smashing their way across the Inner German Border and taking on 1 (BR) Corps and the rest of NORTHAG had always been a remote possibility, but not much more than that. Training had obviously been geared towards that possibility, but as the years went by without a devastating Soviet assault, and as the wider global geopolitical situation changed, for the majority of the British forces serving in the Zone the chances of a Soviet attack receded. As in Berlin, the majority of people did not give the exact implications of any possible attack much thought. In many cases, this was a case of ignorance being bliss. The more senior officers, especially those involved in intelligence work, maintained a vigilant watch across the Inner German Border, and were alive to any possibility of the Warsaw Pact forces moving to a war footing.

As Lieutenant Commander David Morgan, who served with the RAF on two tours in West Germany between 1973 and 1976 and again from 1979 to 1981 before transferring to the Royal Navy, noted,

'War had been a constant concern in Germany. During my first tour there I had been heavily involved in intelligence work and had become convinced that an attack by the Warsaw Pact upon NATO forces was only a matter of time. Many of us kept spare cans of petrol in our cellars in order that our families might have a chance of making the Channel ports before Germany was overrun. Several times a year there were a few tense hours when the sirens would sound, summoning us all onto base, and no one was sure whether it was an exercise or for real. I had instructed my family to head west if they didn't hear that it was a drill within a couple of hours.'

Morgan shared the general sense of pessimism about what would happen if the Soviets attacked: 'We had no illusions about how long we could keep flying in such a hostile environment and reckoned on 30 per cent attrition every day. In other words, after three days we would probably cease to be an effective force. It would have been a bloody battle with little hope of survival.'

The Soviet threat remained the central threat that the UK orientated itself towards in Germany. Détente had an impact on military spending; it made it easier, for example, for the 1974–75 Mason Review to implement a reduction in defence spending from 5 per cent of GDP to around 4.5 per cent over ten years, moving the UK's defence expenditure closer to the NATO average. But four major commitments were still deemed essential: the UK's contribution to NATO front-line forces in Germany; anti-submarine forces in the eastern Atlantic; home defence; and the UK's nuclear deterrent. However, specialist reinforcement forces were identified for cuts, and overall there was to be a reduction of 11 per cent in manpower over a ten-year period. The UK was prioritising Germany and the Cold War over theatres like the Mediterranean, from where all forces were withdrawn with the exception of Cyprus, and severely limiting its out-of-area ability.

After the early 1980s recession, there was again a

Four members of 12 Air Defence Regiment, Royal Artillery, in their NBC or 'Noddy' suits, changing a tyre of a Landrover while on exercise at Haltern near Munster, 1978. The regiment were based in Dortmund at the time (Crown)

desire to reduce military spending. This new climate led to the 1981 Defence White Paper, formally known as *The UK Defence Programme: The Way Forward*. While the NATO commitment and Germany remained a priority, it was not immune to reduced spending. The review was driven by a need to save money, and decisions were made more on a financial, rather than a strategic, basis. The Regular Army, for example, was to be reduced to 135,000 men, a loss of 7,000, which was to be partly offset by the gradual expansion of the Territorial Army by a figure of 16,000. Two thousand would be lost from Germany through the withdrawal of a divisional headquarters, leaving the BAOR standing at a strength of 55,000, with divisions centred in Verden, Soest and Herford. In 1985, there were 158,000 British Service personnel and their dependents living and working in Germany.

It was, however, not all bad news for those based in the Zone. In Nott's statement, it was announced that four armoured regiments would be equipped with the new Challenger tank, while there would also be an increase in the order of the MILAN anti-tank missile. For the RAF,

while it was being cut by 2,500 personnel, the upgraded AV-8B Harrier was being procured. Two F-4 Phantom squadrons were also to be retained rather than being phased out with the introduction of the Tornado.

But while these defensive reorganisations were taking place, a new threat to the British Service personnel and their families in West Germany was becoming more and more apparent. NATO may have been the main focus for the military at this time, but increasingly the actions of the IRA were intruding into life, both in the UK and in Germany, with several attacks. JHQ at Rheindahlen was first targeted by the IRA in 1973; a car bomb was planted in the car park of the Globe cinema and timed to go off as the film ended. However, the film had finished earlier than expected, and the car park was largely empty when the bomb exploded. No one was injured, but a couple of cars were damaged. On 16th February 1980, Colonel Mark Coe was shot dead outside of his home in Bielefeld.

David Ackroyd was a teacher at Queen's School in Rheindahlen between 1979 and 1982. He recalls some of the threats that affected him as a civilian and his pupils, as well as the military community:

'You checked your cars underneath for bits of wire. You never left your windows open. If you even left a little crack open, the Royal Military Police would put a note in saying, 'This is a bomb, please report for education', or something. You were very aware ... The IRA were definitely a threat. They were on the garrison ... How much it really was I'm not entirely sure, but yes it was a definite threat.'

Ackroyd, like all of the British community, was forced to adopt constant vigilance, which became 'a way of life' for anyone associated with the military. Personal folding mirrors were handed out to every service person. While ostensibly the Cold War was the dominant threat, the IRA's actions meant that they had the greater impact on the British:

'This was more IRA than it was Russia ... I think it was the more real threat yes. We did have bombs go off – the Russians didn't do it! ... For personal security you considered the IRA a greater threat than the Russians ... To the extent that even at one point our BFG car number plates reverted to Mönchengladbach, German. We were

aware, out in the country, that you were in a British military forces car, even though it was your personal one. And even coming back here, visiting Portsmouth and relatives there, I was requested to put it in the Dockyard, under Dockyard security, rather than leave it on the streets in Portsmouth.'

Julia Payne, who lived in Rheindahlen from 1982 to 1984 and again from 1988 to 1990 as an Army wife, also recalled this constant vigilance, which only increased: 'We were far more worried in Germany about the IRA threat. That was much more imminent and likely ... Nuclear war is highly unlikely but very serious; an IRA bomb is less serous but much more likely.'

The West Germans shared this new danger. Frank Föste, who lived in Bielefeld, remembers the impact the IRA campaign had on him due to the close proximity in which he lived and worked with the British:

'During that time there was a lot of trouble with Northern Ireland and some wives of soldiers worked in my firm, and we had to check the vehicles upon their leaving, put a mirror under the car – just like it was in camp. They never told me, but the RMP would walk around my building at night. Once, I was in the sergeants' mess on camp, and someone asked me to

OPPOSITE: The 5th Royal Inniskilling Dragoon Guards taking part in training exercises at Vogelsang, West Germany, 1973 (Crown)

ABOVE: Under-car mirror and torch kits like this were issued to all personnel with BFG registered vehicles to counteract the terrorist threat (Private Collection)

move my car, because they thought there was a bomb in the vehicle standing next to mine. I said, "First you find the bomb, and then I'll move my car!" Once I was drinking a beer in a pub full of soldiers and there was a loud bang outside, and everyone threw themselves onto the floor except me. It was just a car backfiring.'

As Operation BANNER intensified from 1969 onwards, the British Army was increasingly drawn into Northern Ireland. The need for more troops meant that units from the German garrison towns were deployed to the province on short emergency tours of four months, or even longer postings. John Kiszely, who had deployed to Northern Ireland from Germany in 1970, and went again in 1974 with 1st Battalion Scots Guards from Waterloo Barracks in Münster, remembered: 'It came to be a regular feature of life in Germany. You knew in a two-year tour that you might be deploying to Northern Ireland.'

Many of these saw armoured regiment soldiers dismount and conduct operations as infantry. This interrupted the training cycle in Germany, as it required the units to convert from armoured warfare to counter-insurgency operations. Kiszely noted that, while this provided an opportunity for active service and appealed to some like himself,

'Some people, I think, might have thought it was a distraction from proper soldiering, which was countering the Soviet threat in West Germany. There was always this slightly uneasy balance as to priorities, and if the pendulum swung too far you could be focusing far too much for too long on Northern Ireland to the detriment of your preparation and your professionalism in Germany and vice versa.'

While some aspects of life in Germany for the Cold War warriors were certainly changing, others had set themselves into a familiar – and, for the most part, an enjoyable – routine.

A WAY OF LIFE

Outside of the deployments to Northern Ireland, existence in the Zone continued much as it had for decades. The British were an accepted part of life in

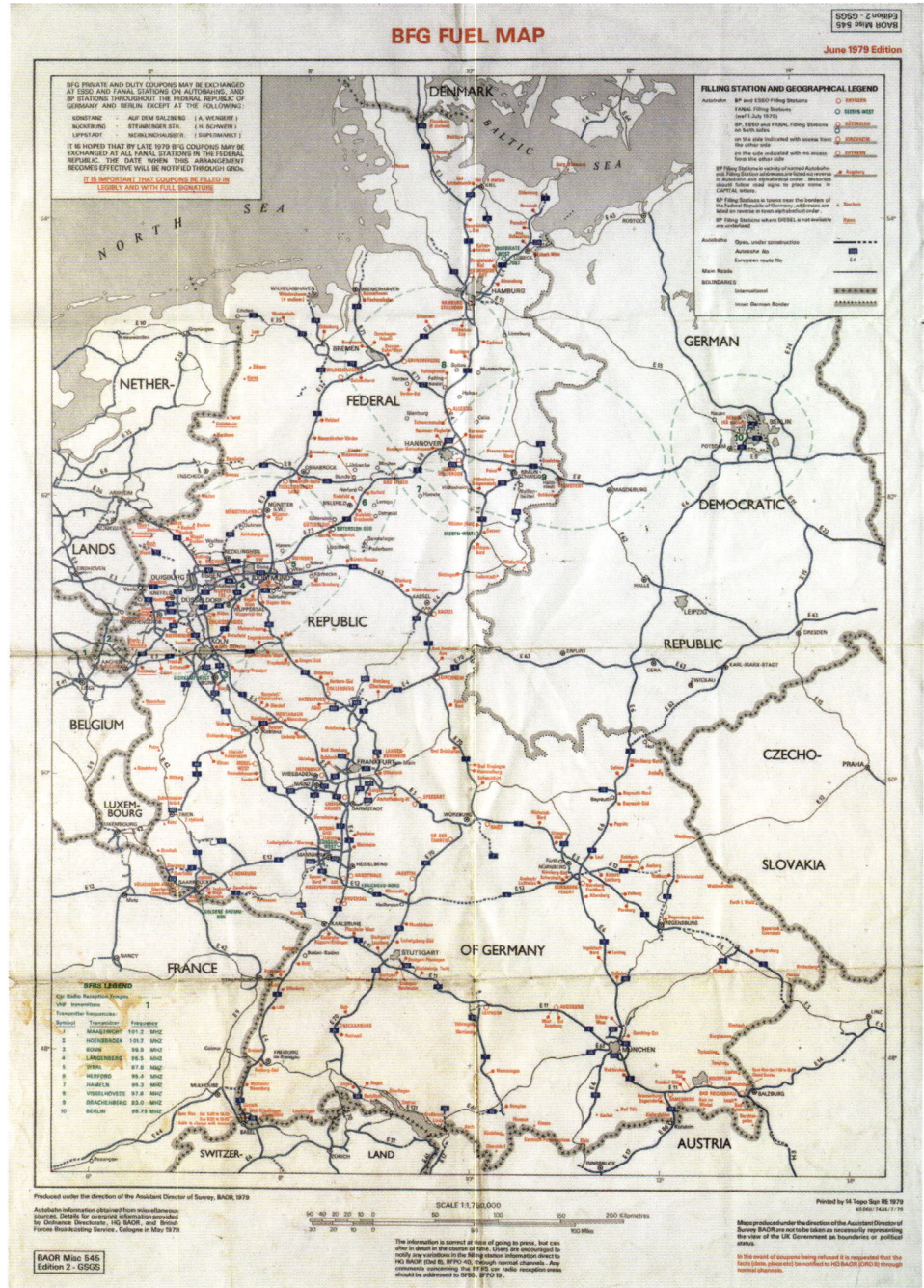

A 1979 BAOR Fuel Map. Maps such as this were issued to BFG car owners and became an essential part of touring Germany, alongside a BAOR road map. The Fuel Map showed the specific location of Petrol Stations in Germany that would accept the BFG Fuel coupons [NAM]

West Germany by the locals, though there were flashpoints. Often much of the trouble that arose in the local towns came about when two regiments were located in close proximity, and rivalries boiled over. Osnabrück Garrison – or Osnatraz, as some nicknamed it – had a large concentration of soldiers in various barracks, and attracted a bit of a negative reputation.

But with inflation and a weak economy in the UK, service in Germany was once again an attractive option. And the country continued to have an impact on the new soldiers who were joining the Army. Pim Hogben served with the 16th/5th Lancers, and first arrived in Wolfenbüttel in 1976:

'I'll never forget my first trip to Germany because we'd just finished in Cyprus, and the clothes we had were all summer clothes and arrived in Germany in January. And by God did we know it was cold, so my very first memory of Germany was how cold it was. It became apparent, in a very short time, how clean, efficient and well-built Germany was. Everywhere you went was super clean.'

Brian 'Harry' Clacy did three postings in BAOR between 1975 and 1993, first with 10 Regiment Royal Corps Transport. The cleanliness of the country also struck him on arrival:

'Everything seemed so clean and tidy and efficient in Germany. That was my initial impression. It wasn't like 1970s England, where it was a slightly dirty place because of the binmen and electricity strikes and what have you. And if you speak to most soldiers, that is their initial impression of Germany – the cleanliness. It was super – we had Local Overseas Allowance [LOA], which basically doubled your wages, and there were tax-free purchases. It was lucrative; everybody wanted to serve in Germany, but foremost because it was such a beautiful country. I made a lot of friends in Germany. I served in Verden, Wolfenbüttel, Bielefeld and Detmold, and I fell in love with the German people, and so did my wife and in-laws.'

Ken Blake also served with 10 Regiment Royal Corps Transport. The cleanliness was something that he noticed immediately after stepping off the plane in 1978:

'My first trip to Germany was on a flight from RAF Brize Norton, and it brought us into RAF Gütersloh. We got off the VC10 and on to a bus and were brought to Bielefeld. It was a very clean country. I could not believe how clean it was. It was beautiful. Everywhere you went it was colourful. I come from the London area; it was a dirty sort of city, but Germany was so clean it just took my breath away.'

The favourable contrast with the UK was something that struck Hogben, too:

'My favourite posting of all, irrespective of anywhere in

TOP: Margaret Thatcher, then Leader of the Opposition, visits King's School, Gütersloh, in January 1976 (Crown)

ABOVE: The 443 exercises in Germany, and the opportunity to watch the Army in action, often proved popular with the local German population, even if the noise of tanks rumbling past was too much for some (IWM)

the world, was Wolfenbüttel, which was a beautiful town. It was six years of total bliss, a whole town to just one single regiment. It was fantastic ... I left home at 15 and it didn't really become apparent how really good life in Germany was, like cleanliness, the efficiency of the German system, until my return posting back to Tidworth, where you really noticed the difference between the two countries – and the negative part being the UK side. I went to Wolfenbüttel in Germany in 1976. It was the best posting I ever had and it lasted for six years.'

This new generation of soldiers had a different mentality to their predecessors about what the Army was in Germany to do. For Hogben: 'My feelings on why the Army was in Germany were that it was more of a protector and also an ally. But I've always thought they were equal to us anyway. I always thought that the Army was posted in Germany – especially my unit, who was the close reconnaissance unit – to defend, protect and obviously to train.'

Similarly, for Clacy, the NATO commitment and keeping the Russians out, maintaining the forward defence for

the UK, was the primary reason for service in Germany:

'We were all told in training that we were in Germany to keep the Russians at bay, and the East Germans on the other side of the Berlin Wall. I suppose it was in the back of your mind all the time – we were constantly under threat, and I think the German people, too, felt under threat from the Soviet Union at that time.'

This new generation also had different thoughts about the Germans. The occupation mentality was gone, and as more and more soldiers ventured off camp and into the local community, they had more and more contact with local Germans. This meant that, whatever thoughts they'd had prior to the arrival, these did not last long. Hogben summed it up best:

'My thoughts about Germans before joining the Army were literally brought about by reading comics, the nasty Huns and things like that, but it soon became apparent that Germans are really not that way. In fact, I would say that the Germans are just like English people but with a different language ... Thoughts about the

LEFT: An aerial view of RAF Hospital Wegberg in 1984. It served the community at JHQ Rheindahlen, and its maternity wing was the birthplace of thousands of children born to parents in both services and the civilian support staff who were working there and in garrisons and stations nearby [Crown]

TOP: An RAF Harrier flying over the Mohne Dam [Crown]

ABOVE: A Wessex of 18 Squadron RAF flies past Castle Neuschwanstein in Bavaria. Bavaria was used extensively by the British for exercises and recreation. 18 Squadron operated the Wessex out of Gütersloh between August 1970 and November 1980 in support of BAOR [Crown]

Major General Martin Farndale unveils the Crossed Keys sculpture that the 2nd Armoured Division gifted to Lübbecke in November 1982 as a gesture of thanks before their relocation to York (Lübbecke Stadtarchiv)

Germans and what they did in the Second World War were discussed to a certain degree. However, there was no ill feeling towards the German people. It was just a fact of life about what had happened in the past.'

Blake was very conscious about the difference between his generation and those who had come before:

'My father fought during the Second World War, and my thoughts about the German people were different to what his thoughts were. I'm from a different generation ... We were in Germany to defend Europe and the free world, not just to defend Germany. I never felt that I was an occupier or a dominator; I was in Germany purely as a friend and felt part of the German people. If the Russian army came over that border, there weren't a lot of us to defend it. But we were going to do the best we could to help the German army to repel or to at least hold them back until we could get more reinforcements into Europe ... We were briefed on the history of Germany when we got there and were taken to places such as Bergen-Belsen concentration camp to show us what could happen when you have a political party that takes

over full control of everybody. It was an education for us all, because it could happen anywhere, not just in Germany with the Nazi regime ... My opinion of the Second World War was, it was over and that was it. We were part of a different European freedom and were okay about it.'

There were still some barriers between the British and the Germans, and some reluctance. David Ackroyd recalls of the locals in Mönchengladbach:

'Did we mix much with the Germans? Not a lot ... Within one mile of the garrison you were hardly spoken to by the Germans. Within ten miles of the garrison, there were a few people you could talk to and might become friends with. But it was very rare to go to a party where Germans were in the party unless it was an official party, and they were German officials.'

However, soldiers were changing. They were actively reaching out to the Germans. An increased number of sports clubs brought them together, and more and more soldiers were venturing in to the local towns.

97

The Rhine Army Summer Show in Bad Lippspringe grew in popularity from its relatively humble beginnings in 1949, and became a major part of the BFG calendar. This aerial picture shows RASS in 1994 (Detlef Wittig)

Hogben was a good example of this:

'The contact that I had with Germans was very little at the start, but my confidence grew and I started learning German, and managed to engage with a young lady for 18 months. I have to be very thankful to her as she taught me most of my German, and from that day on I never looked back, and eventually I became 100 per cent fluent.'

The language barrier proved a problem for many, though. German was still not taught to soldiers as standard, nor was it required of junior officers, and so the majority that wanted to learn had to pick it up in whichever way they could. Whether that was limited to 'ein Bier, bitte' or something more extensive remained a personal choice. Blake commented on some of the challenges that came from attempting to use the local language:

'Trying to speak German with a little bit of English involved was quite funny. The German people would always turn around and speak English to you. They could see that you were trying to speak German and were stuck. We got away with an awful lot with their help. I had full contact with German people every single day – on the road driving, going down to the shops, going to the bars and having a drink, ordering our food in restaurants.'

This increased openness and willingness to engage was not lost on the local Germans. Carlo Dewe grew up in Herford, and was one of many Germans who took advantage of it, and reciprocated by engaging with the British:

'We saw the military lorries and soldiers in uniform very often, but later, in the rock 'n' roll era of the 1970s, they appeared more and more in civilian clothes and began to mix more. They came to clubs, cafés and events, and we then saw them as friends. The older generation of Germans – my parents and grandparents – were very hostile towards the soldiers and wondered why they were here ... Later on, because of NATO countries working together, the British Army was no longer seen as an occupying force, but rather as a friendly force here to protect us from the Russians ... My first contact with the British was when I was 15 in the 1970s, when a friend and I tried to start a school band. We had no equipment, but we had this dream to be like the Beatles or the Rolling Stones, and some of the soldiers based in Herford had very good equipment – amps and microphones – and so we met in the barracks. At that time there were few restrictions; you could enter the barracks without any problem. They lent us their equipment; we jammed together and became friends, though they were ten years older than us. I had a good

friend who was a British Army soldier responsible for organising gigs in barracks. In the 1980s, when I had my own established band, we would often play in the barracks at all kinds of events. Sometimes it was very strict, when we were told to stay in a corner until it was time to play. Then there were other times when we could mingle among the soldiers and guests. I will always remember the rather awful British food at that time. But we ate it and we were happy.'

For some, the forming of relationships with the locals actually took them out of Army life altogether. Ken Railton left the Army in 1975 to continue his relationship with his German girlfriend – who later became his wife – rather than be posted to Hong Kong, even though his German was 'limited to two words: bier and bratwurst. I ended up working with the Army supplying drinks and later on coin-operated machines.'

One of the official things that was bringing the British and the Germans closer together were the large open events, notably the Rhine Army Summer Show (RASS). The first iteration of this had taken place at Bad Lippspringe in 1949 as an equestrian show, but its evolution came to reflect the changing nature of the relationship between West Germans and the British forces. In 1960, the first Anglo-German Horse Show took place. It then grew and grew, and while the equestrian element remained a core part of the festivities, it also included trade stands, a car show, military displays and beer tents. In 1979, BFBS took part for the first time, and being live on air helped give it more of a festival feel. In 1981, it even included a German funfair for the first time. John Kellas, a NAAFI

department manager in Münster-Gremmendorf from 1973, noted the impact this had on the whole community:

'One of the major bridge-building events was the Rhine Army Summer Show, where tens of thousands of Germans would turn up. It started as a small horse-jumping show and over the years turned into a full-blown, fantastic day out with funfair and stalls. It was a fabulous time when the mixing of Germans and Brits took place. Germans were allowed to drink beer in the NAAFI tents and loved it.'

Frank Föste agreed: 'Of course I went to RASS, but that was a completely different thing, it was great. Germans could learn about the British way of life, especially in the first years of the show when it wasn't so much a business. The Families' Day, which was held in Catterick Barracks, Bielefeld was really good.'

Much of the credit for the closer relationships between the British and their German neighbours belongs to the staff of the Joint Services Liaison Organisation (JSLO). The JSLO had been created in 1955 after the Federal Republic of Germany was created and became a sovereign nation, and their role had been to act as a point of contact between local German authorities and the British. They were based in the Villa Spiritus in Bonn, and the staff reported to both C-in-C BAOR and RAFG, meaning that there were both Army and RAF personnel in its ranks. There was Legal Department, a Customs and Immigration Department, a Police Advisory Branch, Joint Linguistic Services, a Press Office, a Training Section and a mobile team of Liaison Officers on the ground.

Training was a constant aspect of life in the British Zone. Here, soldiers can be seen taking part in an exercise in Osnabrück in January 1978, dug in by the side of a road somewhere in West Germany, 1979, and on the move during an exercise in January 1980 (Crown)

The Service Liaison Officers (SLOs) were housed in each of the garrisons, and had responsibility for exercise clearances on private land, serving of non-criminal court and legal documents to soldiers and dependants, liaison at a local and higher level on civic and political matters, orchestrating and running civic events, monitoring the local press, and attending events on behalf of the local commander. For many Germans, they became the face of the local British garrisons.

The 1970s and early 1980s saw the culmination of a huge shift in British attitudes towards their German neighbours. But there was still the core business of soldiering to be done, and that remained a major focus of their lives.

1972, soldiers had also been making the long flight from Gütersloh or Brize to Calgary and then on to the British Army Training Unit Suffield (BATUS) for armoured training on the Canadian prairie.

All of this was designed to build up to the major autumn field training exercises, where enormous mock battles were fought over the West German countryside – though with increasingly greater consideration for the German farmers and local civilians trying to go about their daily lives. In September 1980, Britain organised the largest training exercise since the Second World War with Exercise CRUSADER. It would ultimately cost £82 million. A major part of this involved moving 30,000 troops from the United Kingdom to West Germany as rapid reinforcements, including 20,000 Territorial Army

TRAINING

Training remained a major part of life for British Forces in Germany, including training designed to prepare them for war. The training cycle had formed itself into an accustomed routine. There would be near continuous low-level training. The ACTIVE EDGE callouts would also test a unit's ability to mobilise and deploy quickly, and the random and spontaneous calls became something that soldiers would dread. In between, adventure training would be offered to soldiers, and Exercise SNOW QUEEN, which saw thousands of soldiers ascend into the Alps for skiing, became a major highlight. Since July

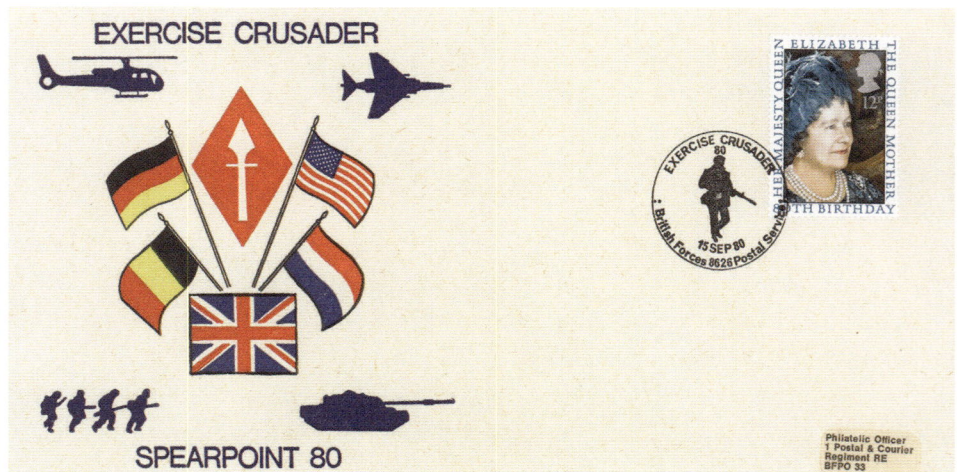

soldiers. RAF Wildenrath was attacked by saboteurs representing Soviet Spetsnaz, and driven off by the RAF Regiment, and electronic warfare was heavily rehearsed. Blake took part, and remembers that even with additional care being given to minimise damage and disruption, moving so many large vehicles, armour and troops across parts of Western Germany could lead to damage and accidents:

'EX CRUSADER 80 was quite a formidable exercise, with lots going on. I had a road traffic accident on the exercise – two German people in a car hit my lorry in a head-on collision. They were overtaking a line of vehicles in the rain as we were coming round a bend in a convoy. He was 21 and she 17, and both died. I knew I hadn't done anything wrong, but it was an RTA that actually stopped most of the exercise at that moment in time, because everybody thought that, being a driver, I hadn't had enough sleep. We'd only just had a six-hour kip and breakfast, and I'd only gone 50 miles down the road when the accident happened. So I was fully aware, fully awake and fully functioning at the time. It wasn't the only RTA during Exercise CRUSADER 80 – there were another two. The occupants of a car were killed when its driver pulled out in front of a convoy and was hit by an APC.'

The exercises were also multinational, and CRUSADER 80 showed participants the incredible scale of any potential conflict. A 400-man force of the United States 82nd Airborne even parachuted into the middle of the exercise area.

Training throughout this period was increasingly realistic. As détente ended with the Soviet invasion of Afghanistan in December 1979, war again became a distinct possibility. But the need for realism in training also brought dangers. There were accidents that resulted in injuries and deaths to some of the British soldiers taking part. On the night of 11th September 1974, for example, six Territorial soldiers from 15th (Scottish Volunteer) Battalion, the Parachute Regiment, died after a mis-drop resulted in them landing in the Kiel Canal and drowning near the town of Sehestedt in Schleswig-Holstein while taking part in Exercise BOLD GUARD. It was the highest loss of TA soldiers during a major NATO exercise. A memorial carrying the names of those who died still sits by the canal.

Captain Vic Cowrie visiting Sehestedt memorial on the 15-year anniversary of the accident in 1989 (Crown)

But at the same time, the culture of training for the real thing was what made the British forces in Germany so professional. It was something many responded to, and felt gave great value to their experiences of living and working in Germany. Squadron Leader Jerry Pook flew in Germany on Harriers as a ground attack pilot, and he recalled with fondness that there were few restrictions limiting what he as a pilot could do, therefore presenting him with the opportunity to improve his skills. He could fly low wherever he liked, developing and increasing his aptitude for this demanding skill that was a necessity of his role as a ground attack pilot. Also, because Germany was so heavily fortified,

'Everywhere you went there were real targets on the ground, which you could make simulated attacks on, or take pictures of. And of course there were big exercises; we'd take part in all the Army exercises when they'd have huge numbers of vehicles out, and we'd be on one side or the other. In addition to that, what made it even better was that our rules stated that in flight, in peacetime, any other jet we saw … you could jump on them and attack them, so it really kept you on your toes. Every airplane you saw was a potential enemy, so we had the most wonderful air combats.'

However, sometimes the military skills learned through all

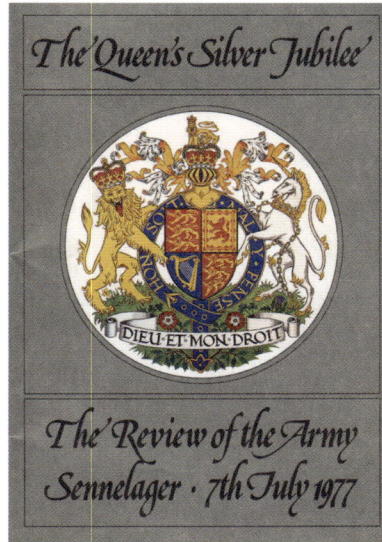

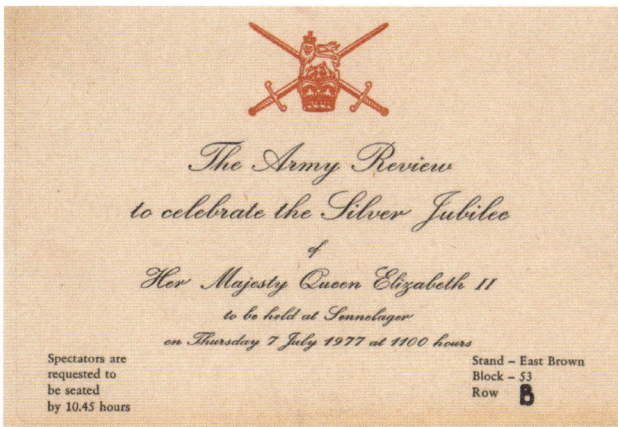

TOP LEFT: Her Majesty Queen Elizabeth II reviews soldiers drawn up for the Silver Jubilee Parade at Sennelager (Crown)

TOP MIDDLE: The programme from the Jubilee Parade (NAM)

TOP RIGHT: Commemorative merchandise was produced and sold by the NAAFI. As well as featuring an image of the Queen, this mug showcased the close alliance and cooperation between the British and West Germans in NATO.

BOTTOM RIGHT: The Stalwarts of 4th Armoured Division Transport Regiment, Royal Corps of Transport, after the parade had finished. They were based in Glamorgan Barracks in Duisburg. After the parade finished, their vehicles were held behind due to restrictions on moving military vehicles at weekends, and they formed up for this photo (Terry Byrne)

OPPOSITE: A British soldier on patrol during Exercise FULL HOUSE in West Germany, March 1978

this training could be put to wider use. One of the major events that took place in BAOR in this period – both for soldiers and their families – was the huge military parade that took place as part of Her Majesty Queen Elizabeth II's Silver Jubilee at Sennelager on 7th July 1977. The review was organised and performed by 4th Armoured Division 1 (British) Corps, which represented not only BAOR but also the entire British Army. It was the central military occasion of the Silver Jubilee, and broadcast on both British and West German television. It was the biggest gathering of British military troops and equipment in one place since the Second World War, involving 3,000 men and 550 armoured vehicles, among them the launchers for the Lance missile, which had begun to replace the Honest John as the Army's tactical nuclear missile in 1975. Music was provided by 24 different bands from the Royal Armoured Corps, infantry and Royal Artillery, the massed bands being led by Dettingen, the Drum Horse

of the Queen's Own Hussars. There was also a fly past of helicopters supplied by 4th Regiment Army Air Corps.

The famous windmill by the airstrip on the training area provided the backdrop behind the Royal Box as the parade vehicles went past, where the Queen, Prince Philip and the Federal President of West Germany, Walter Scheel, and his wife shared the saluting base. The last parade of this scale had taken place among the rubble of Berlin in 1945 in the immediate aftermath of the war; the preceding decades had brought the two countries closer together, and this parade took place under very different circumstances, in a very different climate. There were 3,000 German guests in attendance, along with thousands from British families. There was even a commemorative mug, sold through the NAAFI. It was a celebration of a British community that was much more comfortable in Germany than in had been in previous decades.

CHAPTER VI

FROM TWO TO ONE

1982-1990

THE RITUAL DANCE OF DETERRENCE

As the British forces in Germany moved into the 1980s it faced multiple challenges, but the Soviets and the Warsaw Pact remained the most pressing. The conflict in the South Atlantic, while intense, was short, and did not draw huge resources from West Germany. Yet it had a sizeable impact; the Soviet forces were surprised and impressed by what the British had achieved – which certainly influenced international relations. For the forces themselves, who had experienced the real thing, it had proven very different to the expectations of how war against the Soviets would have been. Lieutenant General John Kiszely, who had sailed south with 2nd Battalion Scots Guards in 1982 and returned to Soltau the same year as Brigade Major in 7th Armoured Brigade, felt this keenly:

'I think it was slightly frustrating after the Falklands, [going from] doing it for real to going back to something where you're playing at soldiers, to put it unkindly, i.e. training for war. And one did get frustrated with what appeared to be the pettiness of training in Germany, compared with the Falklands, where certain things mattered a great deal and other things didn't matter much – and that wasn't necessarily the order of things in Germany. But you just got on with it.'

In the aftermath of conventional conflict after preparing for so long, it meant that 'some of the things about Germany appeared to be a façade of how good you appeared to be rather than how good you actually were'. However, as Kiszely noted, 'Nevertheless, the British Army of the Rhine, the British Army in Germany, was – and took pride in being – very professional at what it was doing. Took exercises, for example, very seriously. Took the level of training very seriously. Took readiness for whatever might come seriously.'

There was a definite distinct culture to service in Germany, with many unique aspects that weren't replicated elsewhere in British military life and service. Germany was the centre of armoured warfare and the main focus for British Army spending, but the reserve, out-of-area forces that were held in the UK in readiness spent little time there – normally only playing enemy forces during large exercises. Germany remained, in many ways, an alien environment to them, with a very different way of life. This was commented on by General Sir Rupert Smith, an officer who completed the majority of his regimental duty with the Parachute Regiment: 'There was a divide ... You just didn't go to Germany if you didn't recognise a tank ... There were whole streams of people who were in one or the other streams.' It was particularly apparent when he attended the Staff College in 1975:

'The "Continental Army", as we called them in Camberley, were marked by having a generous LOA; they drove big cars,

PREVIOUS: British soldiers from 1st (UK) Armoured Division on Exercise White Rhino in West Germany, 1989

Volvos, they drank gin at lunch, and talked about the Corps and divisional attacks. We, in what we called the "Colonial Army", brewed beer in our baths and had a Renault IV or Citroen 2CV for a car. On the other hand, we tended to own our own houses, and we talked of very different operations. And it was this cultural, as well as military experience, divide that was so evident when it came to putting that sort of hundred officers together at Camberley.'

Even those soldiers with long experience of Germany noted this peculiar way of living. Kiszely, for example, described it as being, 'quite like maybe, I suppose, cantonments in India. There was an element of cantonment about the barracks life in Germany at that time.' This coloured and affected how the British would live their lives and the levels of contact they had with the local Germans. While increasingly barriers were being broken down, the security situation with the IRA meant that the British were also becoming more withdrawn. The cultural and social aspects of this particular brand of soldiering therefore became more entrenched.

From 1984 Field Marshal Sir Nigel Bagnall – when as a General in command of NORTHAG – sought to redefine NATO's strategy of forward defence, and also sought to implement reforms that would close this cultural divide within the Army. At the tactical level, Bagnall aimed to prioritise the deep battle with more mobile defensive operations, a unified corps approach rather than allowing the divisions to fight their own battles. At a cultural level, there were efforts to close the gap that existed between the 'Continental' and 'Colonial' armies. In 1984, directions were that this gap needed to be closed and a plan was formed and issued that the top stream of the COs of the 'Colonial Army' were to go to BAOR, and vice versa. This saw staff officers from elsewhere in the Army – like Smith – deliberately brought to Germany. In September 1985, he went to Germany as Chief of Staff of 3 Armoured Division at Soest, the first time he had been stationed in Germany in an Army career that had begun in 1962. The different cultural outlook among the soldiers was immediately apparent: 'What was evident in Germany ... there was this ritual dance of deterrence and garrison life, and it wasn't dissimilar in its way to the Raj. At this time of year you went up into the hills, and in this time of year in BAOR it was the skiing competition, or a couple of these exercises.'

One major feature of this life, a direct continuity from previous decades, was the constant training that took place, which took the form of exercises. These took place at all levels, from individual, to small unit, to company or squadron, to battalion and regiment training, before moving on to brigade battlegroup and then culminating in the major field training exercises. The need for professionalism and high standards was rigorously enforced. It was about readiness in case the Cold War turned hot. Kiszely remarked that, 'it was up to senior commanders to promote that feeling, that you better be ready because

A Chieftain in the OPFOR role on Exercise KEYSTONE in 1987. Even in the middle of the exercise there was still an opportunity to take a break, as the crew of this Ferret were doing (Carl Schulze)

this could happen, and that [was] also something that applied to all ranks'. Battalion commanders had to embody effectiveness – they had to perform. When it came to ACTIVE EDGE, for example, 'this was a make-or-break, career-defining exercise for commanders'. The battalion, its vehicles and their kit, had to be at their General Deployment Positions within the set time, and ready to fight, for when the brigade commander would inspect. Should their battalion fail the Brigadier's inspection, 'the commanding officer would be facing the woodwork outside the brigade commander's door the next morning at eight o'clock. So this was treated extremely seriously, and quite right too.'

Was it all for show? Was there ever a chance of the Cold War turning into a full-blown shooting match? It was something that those living in the Cold War's shadow had mixed feelings about. Obviously commanders had to make sure the soldiers under them thought it would happen regardless of their own personal opinions. Rupert Smith, for example, believed that, 'for my part, it was an "if", not a "when". And the things that would make an "if" start to become a "when" weren't evident to me. But I'd probably held that view as early as the 1970s, at some point, and probably felt reinforced in this view as things remained stable.' The 'party line', however, was that there was 'an imminence to this thing ... otherwise the ritual dances of deterrence would lose meaning very quickly'. Not all soldiers were convinced. Brigadier Mark Armstrong, who as a young officer first served with the Royal Electrical and Mechanical Engineers [REME] in Germany in 1982, remembers that deterrence worked, and so allowed his colleagues and friends to enjoy life there:

'When I joined up there were 55,000 soldiers in Germany who were bored [and] used to drink a lot, and we used to party quite heavily. And it was a good existence, because, actually, they were never going to attack us and we were never going to attack them, so it was a nice little sort of stand-off we had there.'

Yet officers still had to inspire the recognition of the threat in their troops to ensure readiness, professionalism and effectiveness could be maintained. Training still had to be realistic, and it had to acknowledge what would need to be done should the 3rd Shock Army crash across the Inner German Border.

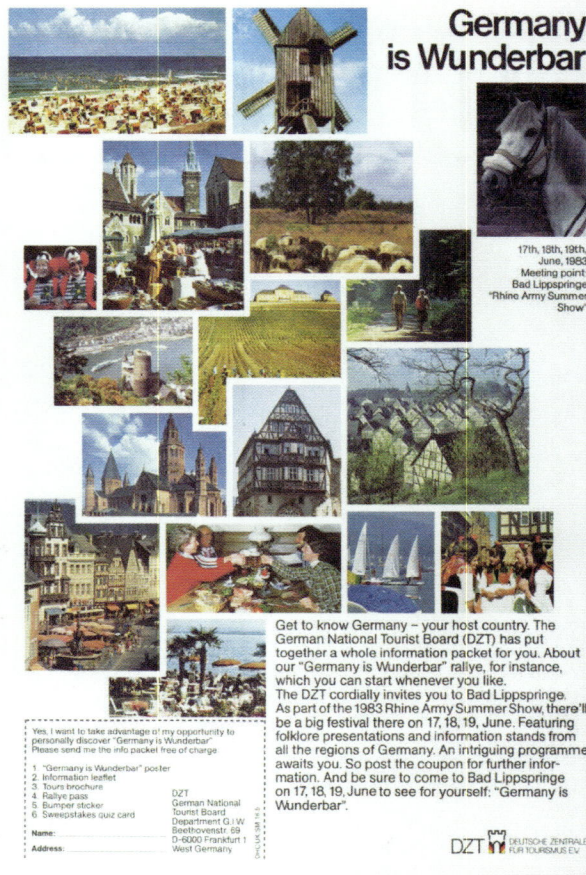

Germany is Wunderbar

LEFT: The West German Government recognised the economic value of having the British stationed there, and sought to capitalise on it further by promoting in-country tourism. This poster, 'Germany is Wunderbar' appeared in Soldier Magazine in May 1983 (DZT)

OPPOSITE: HM The Queen visiting the Royal Artillery in Dortmund, reviewing troops at Napier Barracks in 1984 (Chris Atkins)

The field training exercises – many highly choreographed – were deliberately competitive to push higher standards. But while many soldiers still did not necessarily think they would ever have to put the skills into practice, they did recognise the implications of what they were learning to do, and the intelligence they were picking up regarding the forces and capabilities of the Warsaw Pact through publications like Threat magazine. For Jim Toms, who arrived in Verden in 1984 for his first posting as a young Signaller with the Royal Signals, the constant drilling of the scale of the threat had a major impact on his life in the Zone:

'You were constantly briefed on the threat, there was a lot of information put out there about GSFG group, the Group of Soviet Forces Germany ... I suppose I was a bit more exposed to it, because I worked on the intelligence side. At 1 Div I worked on G2 Int, and a bit of exposure to artillery intelligence as well, and then in 14 Sigs I was electronic warfare. So I was very aware of it. You were aware of the threat, you knew what they could do to you. The assessment was we had about 30 minutes and we'd

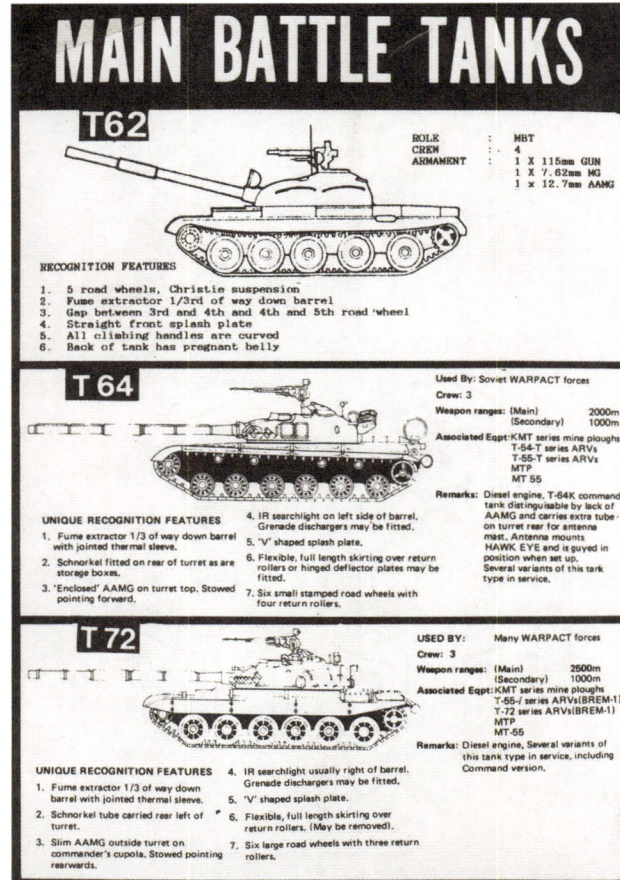

LEFT: *Threat* magazine, 1984 [NAM]

RIGHT: A 1984 copy of *Threat*, with one of the pages detailing some of the equipment used by the forces of the Warsaw Pact [NAM]

be dead … So you were hot as you could be on your NBC drills, you put your NBC kit before you even got out of barracks. And it was very ill-advised that you took it off before the end of the exercise. You lived in the damned stuff, it was awful. Especially in summer. Weren't so bad in winter. Summer was absolutely dog-awful.

I think in the Signals you were very aware of who was over the other side, what their capability was. I was pretty good at recognition for example … There was a *Threat* magazine that they published … with the latest updates on what rocket systems had been spotted, and things like that … I don't think many people dwelled on it too much, but there was an appreciation that we were there to protect, we were a shield or a speed bump … There was definitely an appreciation of what they could do to us. If it had happened, we were quite determined to do whatever we could … You just put it to the back of your mind and cracked on.'

This was not a singular, gung-ho attitude regarding the consequences of what might happen should a shooting war begin. Kiszely shared many of the same sentiments:

'I think there was also a feeling, knowing the strength of the Soviet Army, that one's chances of coming out of it unscathed were rather low. At that stage the nuclear deterrence theory was of a tripwire; at some stage the battle would go nuclear, but there wasn't a great deal of thought about how you in your NBC suit and gas mask and respirator would be surviving the event of nuclear weapons being thrown about the battlefield, and I think a feeling that, if this does happen, our job is to die gloriously. And that in itself produced quite a happy-go-lucky, fatalistic mindset that encouraged eccentricities, encouraged maybe behaviour that would be thought rather odd nowadays, and I suppose encouraged officers of style, who had the leadership qualities to hold their command, of whatever size, together by their leadership and personality, because if you dwelt too much on the realities of what might face you, you might not have the cohesion to stand and fight. And I think *there was a huge determination certainly in our battalion, and I'm sure there was in others as well, that you were damn well going to stand and fight, and if that was the end of you and the battalion then so be it.'*

Ultimately, 'the likelihood of the Soviets invading was low, but if they did the probability that you would die was high'.

Training was a constant aspect of service life in order to build self-confidence in people's abilities and equipment. And training was not just about preparing for *a* war, but *the* war. Kiszely noted that 'there was certainly an ethos that training for war was something you very much needed to do and excel in, and that was the main activity that occupied your waking hours'. There was, however, a challenge that came with organising exercises that retained a professional edge without becoming mundane and repetitive. As Smith pointed out: 'You've got these long-service BAOR warriors, of all ranks … You rarely came out of that bubble. They were tied to this annual cycle of exercises, which inevitably were very similar, and difficult to make hugely novel. If you made it too novel you could send all the wrong signals to Brother Boris the other side of the Iron Curtain.'

Exercise ABLE ARCHER in 1983 had been a good example of this risk – the command post exercise had been so realistic that the Soviet Union thought that NATO were using it to hide their preparations for an attack on them, and took steps accordingly. The world was brought as close to a nuclear war as at any point since the Cuban Missile Crisis in 1962.

In Germany, the '443' system of land clearance gave the British Army wide freedom to exercise across the same terrain, both physical and human, that they expected to potentially fight over. It was a scenario that simply could not be replicated elsewhere – even at BATUS. Rupert Smith remembers that, when commanding 6 Brigade, he had the freedom to experiment with the concept: 'I was able to do, when I was doing experiments with helicopters, really quite adventurous exercises … You had enormous opportunities to be quite imaginative as to manoeuvre and to handle mass.'

The British also became bolder in their field exercise planning. On the back of CRUSADER, Exercise

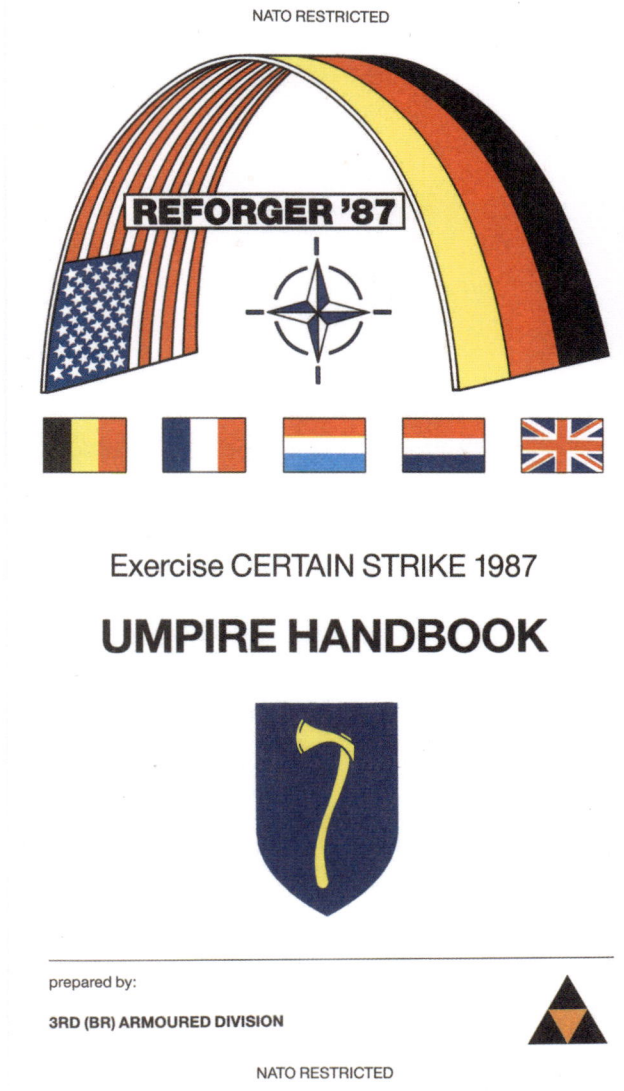

Exercise CERTAIN STRIKE 1987

UMPIRE HANDBOOK

prepared by:

3RD (BR) ARMOURED DIVISION

NATO RESTRICTED

An Umpire's Handbook from Exercise REFORGER in 1987. The name came from the 'return of forces to Germany' concept developed by the United States, that would see them rapidly reinforce their troops in Germany by moving units across the Atlantic from the States. Other NATO nationals also participated. It was an annual exercise that involved predominately US troops moving across the Atlantic from the States to Europe. The 1987 version was called CERTAIN STRIKE (NAM)

LIONHEART took place between 3rd September and 5th October 1984. It was the biggest exercise held since the Second World War, and the largest NATO had ever orchestrated. After four years of planning, and costing around £31 million, 131,000 NATO troops descended on the 1 (BR) Corps area to battle their way across it. The exercise was broken down into two parts. Like CRUSADER before it, the first stage, Exercise FULL FLOW, was about testing the ability of the military to transport 57,000 troops and equipment from all over the UK to the battle zone in north-west Germany. There were 32,000 personnel transported on 290 flights, and 150 sailings across the North Sea and the English Channel carried 23,600 personnel with 14,000 vehicles. To handle this mammoth task, civilian car ferries and aircraft were called into service.

The second stage of the exercise, SPEARPOINT, involved 120,000 British troops acting as the Blue forces in a major field training exercise. The opposing Orange forces were composed of 6,300 German troops from 1 Panzergrenadier Brigade, 3,500 Dutch troops from their 41st Armoured Brigade and 3,400 Americans from 1st Armoured Brigade. The recently reconstituted 5th Airborne Brigade from the UK also formed a second opposition group, joined by elements of the Life Guards and 10th Gurkha Rifles. While it was undoubtedly choreographed, realism was put at the heart of the exercise. There were 750 Main Battle Tanks involved, and most crossings over the Rhine were conducted with combat bridging, making the assumption that all civilian bridges had been destroyed. The ability of the Army and RAF to cooperate was also tested, with the creation and maintenance of temporary airfields by the Royal Engineers for the Harrier GR3s of the air force. Above the ground, the air forces of five nations engaged in Exercise COLD FIRE to test the struggle for air supremacy.

Scale and mass were a major component of the exercise from an effectiveness perspective, but they also had an important impact on morale. The sheer scale impressed those who took part, which made enduring the tribulations of living in the field, and even spending days in NBC suits, worthwhile. Jim Toms had only arrived in Germany a few weeks before the exercise began, and

virtually the first thing he was confronted with were the preparations taking place:

'The day I flew into ... Gütersloh on the air trooping transport ... I can remember seeing freight trains loaded with armour moving, and it was just, 'This is the real deal.' You really got the sense of scale of what was going on in Germany, how big NATO was, the power of the organisation ... It was absolutely gobsmackingly impressive to see.'

Being a part of it 'was huge ... It was brilliant.' But exercising at such sale and intensity was not without risk; three soldiers died during the exercise and seven were seriously injured.

LIONHEART was an exercise that defined an entire era. It was also an opportunity for testing new tactics, and exploring the capabilities of new equipment. It was the first major exercise where the British used the Challenger 1 Main Battle Tank, which compared favourably to the Abrams and the Leopard II Main Battle Tanks in service with the US and Dutch and German forces respectively. The Warrior armoured vehicle, still in the early stages of development, was also tested, as were the Saxon armoured personnel carrier and the tracked Rapier air defence. Tracked Rapier had only been accepted by the Army in 1981, and in 1983, 11 (Sphinx) Air Defence Battery, of 22 Air Defence Regiment, who were based in Napier Barracks in Dortmund, were the first to be

LEFT: **Troops of 22nd Armoured Brigade dig in during Exercise LIONHEART (Crown)**

RIGHT: **A Chieftain Armoured Vehicle Layer Bridge in action draws the crowds during the exercise (Crown)**

A Lynx of the Army Air Corps on a fly past of the Hermannsdenkmal in Detmold in the 1980s. 'Herman the German' was a familiar to landmark to those who were stationed in the area (Army Air Corps Museum)

equipped with it. LIONHEART was also a major PR exercise; in addition to several members of Parliament, there were 165 observers from the Commonwealth. This was Britain showcasing its military might for all to see, and to convince them of its power – including those across the Inner German Border. It was deterrence in action.

By the end of the decade, a part of this process of overt military display involved having representatives of the Warsaw Pact militaries invited as observers. Smith recalls the impact this had on his perception of the potential enemy: 'It wasn't long, by which time I'm brigade commander, that we're being visited, we visit their exercises, and you begin to see the Russians, and the Warsaw Pact armies, or particular officers of it, fairly regularly on exercises, and that humanised them, if that's the word.'

Yet things didn't always go smoothly. When Smith was commanding 6 Brigade in the late 1980s, he went from an airmobile brigade back into an armoured brigade. He was running an exercise as part of a divisional FTX, and was visited by a Russian delegation of observers:

'There was a formula for this. You had a big tent, you get more coffee, it's about 10 o'clock in the morning, and you told them what you'd been doing the day before, how it had gone, where you were going to go in the next 24 hours, and they could then choose where

they'd like to go look. And then the next day you'd repeat the process, and they could ask you questions about what they'd seen and so forth.'

Part of the exercise involved crossing the Weser:

'By dawn, the bridge had broken, bits had floated off with tanks on it, and were somewhere downstream. I had a brigade split by a river with no bridge to connect them up, and so on and so forth. So I told them what had been happening, and said it was a complete cock-up, that the next 24 hours you can watch me try and sort it out again and get everyone on the same bank. And we couldn't do things because of the air threat, and so forth, and we had to wait until dark. Anyway, I told them. At the end of it, they're all having another coffee, and this Russian, I think he was what we would have called a brigadier, and an East German officer came down and said to me, "Can we have a word?" And I was sort of dragged off to the side of this tent, and this Russian said, "You really musn't do this, you'll never get promoted, you should never give briefings like this!" And I was given this career-enhancing lecture about not telling the truth, and so on and so forth. By 1991, I'm a Major General, and standing in the Staff College having been invited back to give a briefing on what we'd done in the Gulf, and in the audience were a whole load of Russians with their big hats and so forth. And when I'd finished, this same chap

ON MONDAY 23 MARCH 1987
AT 10.25 P.M.
THE IRA TRIED TO CALL TIME
BUT
B MESS KEPT ON DRINKING

came bounding out of the crowd and said, "Ah, you took my advice!" '

But for the majority of the British serving in Germany, the main 'enemy' of all the training remained an abstract concept. The IRA, in contrast, were intruding more and more into domestic and professional life, with deadly results. On 23rd March 1987, they targeted Rheindahlen with a 300-lb car bomb, which exploded outside the visitor's officers' mess on Queens Avenue, injuring 31 people, including 27 West German military officers and their wives. Nine soldiers from the Royal Corps of Transport were injured when Glamorgan Barracks in Duisburg was bombed with two separate devices on 14th July 1988. A bomb attack on Roy Barracks in Rattingen on 6th August 1988 injured three sappers and a civilian. The same month, WO1 Richard Heakin was shot and killed at a set of traffic lights outside Ostend on his way to catch a ferry back to the UK to go on leave, his car being identifiable by its distinctive BAOR number plates. On 2nd July 1989, Corporal Steven Smith of the Royal Tank Regiment was killed by a bomb in Hannover. On 7th September 1989, Heidi Hazell, the wife of a British soldier, was murdered in her car as she waited outside their home in Unna, near Dortmund. On

26th October 1989, two IRA gunmen opened fire on a British vehicle as it left a petrol station at Wildenrath. RAF Corporal Maheshkumar Islania and his six-month-old baby daughter, Nivruti Mahesh, were both killed. Her mother, Smita Islania, survived but suffered deep shock. On 1st June 1990, Major Mike Dillon-Lee of 32nd Heavy Regiment Royal Artillery was murdered outside his home in Dortmund by IRA gunmen.

There were other threats and near misses with bombs that were found and defused. Keith Bailey, a former Blues and Royals soldier and Royal Military Policeman, recalls the ever-present threat:

'Back in the early 1980s, when terrorism was at its height, and when I was based in Ripon Barracks in Bielefeld, an officer drove into camp and parked on the main square after his car had been checked. As he got out of his vehicle, he heard a clunk. A live, magnetic device about the size of a Malteser box had dropped onto a wheel. There was a timer on it and he was very lucky it didn't go off. These things became a regular occurrence, which is why we checked under our vehicles with special little mirrors issued to us. That soldier was lucky. A friend of mine in Northern Ireland who drove

past a 500lb bomb that I had passed earlier wasn't. It was a sad time and it sticks with you for life. For a while after leaving the Army, many of us still checked underneath our cars even though we were civilians and no longer part of the military.'

To help make vehicles less distinctive, the iconic black-and-white number plates used by the military were removed under a process called Operation HAGEN. It was two years in the planning and came into effect on 1st April 1990. If Service personnel drove a left-hand-drive car, then under the BFG system they had been issued with a German number plate according to the station or landkreis where they lived. If they moved station, then they needed to get a new set of German plates to go with the new area. Right-hand-drive cars, however, were issued with a new UK number plate, complete with an invented dealership for authenticity. If the German police tried to trace these cars to issue speeding fines, for example, they wouldn't get an answer on the system, but they could apply in writing via the Police Advisory Branch [PAB]. All fines would be handled by PAB via the unit or direct to individual, following German rules. Many soldiers who thought they could escape punishment were often caught out.

Regardless, hand-held mirrors were issued as standard kit to soldiers and their families, and were swept under cars before any journey, regardless of who was driving. A lifestyle of vigilance that had begun in the previous decade was ramped up even higher.

UP CLOSE AND PERSONAL

For the majority of those training in preparation for war with the Warsaw Pact forces, there was very little understanding of the prospective enemy. There was minimal contact. However, for those in Berlin, the opportunities to come into contact with the enemy were far greater.

For some, direct liaison work with the Soviets was a core part of their role. The British Commanders'-in-Chief Mission, better known as BRIXMIS, to the Soviet Forces in German (or the GSFG) was formed on 16th September 1946 under the Robertson-Malinin Agreement, with the express intention of acting as

LEFT: A poster that was on display in Berlin for British forces stationed offering advice on personal security, and urging vigilance against the terrorist threat [NAM]

BELOW: A BRIXMIS Tactical Recognition Flash [NAM]

a go-between for the occupying powers, a chance to maintain professional contact. They had freedom of travel, aside from permanent and temporarily restricted areas, across the Soviet Zone. However, as the Cold War took hold, and particularly after the Wall went up, the 11 officers and 20 other ranks working in each successive mission were ideally placed to gather military intelligence through reconnaissance, surveillance or even the acquisition of Soviet material. They were drawn from across the Army, RAF and Royal Navy, but the majority were from the Army. There was a solid core of Intelligence Corps soldiers and NCOs. They weren't spies in the conventional sense, though. The 'tours' of the Soviet Zone, three-day expeditions, were conducted in uniform and in clearly identifiable vehicles, but the RAF also contributed through flying Chipmunk aircraft out of Gatow. The tour teams were made up of a driver, who never left the vehicle, an NCO with a tape recorder who recited everything he saw, and an officer who took pictures with a camera. Although the Mission was based in London Block next to the Olympic Stadium in Berlin, there was also a Mission House in Potsdam in East

One of the BRIXMIS Chipmunk aircraft conducting an airborne observation of the Soviet sector of Berlin (Crown)

Germany. Undoubtedly bugged, it was used for formal events, and the social side of liaison work.

But the tours were the main function of BRIXMIS. In their touring vehicles – Opel saloons and then later Range Rovers and Mercedes-Benz G-Class – the soldiers would go anywhere they could. On three-day tours of the Soviet Zone they would break into Permanent or Temporary Restricted Areas, or even Soviet or East German military facilities. They would track convoys of armoured vehicles, on the roads, on the railways and across country, constantly taking photos and recording their observations so as to gauge the strength and readiness of Soviet forces in Germany and the East German Army. The RAF pilots attached to the mission would also go up in their Chipmunks and carry out surveillance from within the designated airspace that the Allies were still able to enjoy.

One of the most notable intelligence coups of BRIXMIS took place when a three-man team broke into a Soviet tank gunnery range in East Germany on May Day 1981,

when Soviet forces were typically stood down. Two of the team climbed inside one of the new T-64 Tanks that had just been introduced, and narrated all that they could see for the tape recorder while taking photos. One of those who took part, Sergeant Anthony Haw of 14 Intelligence Company and the Green Howards, was awarded a British Empire Medal for this action. The recommendation for the medal, as appeared in the *London Gazette* on 12th June 1982, elaborated further:

'Sergeant Haw joined the Mission in November 1980. Since that date he has been on almost continuous intelligence gathering tours in East Germany as a Tour Non-Commissioned Officer. Often working in arduous and sometimes hazardous conditions, and always under circumstances imposing constant strain, he has shown himself to be an exceptional NCO, possessed of skill, coolness, courage and determination.

His performance reached a peak on 1st May 1980, and it is his actions on that date that deserve special recognition. He was tasked as Tour Non-Commissioned

SPERRGEBIET

Unbefugten ist das Betreten, Befahren und die bildliche Darstellung verboten. Zuwiderhandlungen werden bestraft.

10 БРИТАНСКАЯ ВОЕННАЯ МИССИЯ ПРИ ГСВГ

Officer to accompany Captain McLeod to certain areas where useful physical intelligence might be obtained due to the relative Stand-Down of Soviet Forces on May Day. One of the tasks of the tour was to endeavour to effect entry into Soviet Armoured vehicles, if the opportunity presented itself. Such an opportunity did present itself which was exploited fully due to the experience and skill of Captain McLeod ably assisted by Sergeant Haw. The two were able, after a long, careful and potentially hazardous reconnaissance, to enter a building containing Soviet T-64 Tanks.

The results of this exploit were quite superb, and were due in no small measure to Sergeant Haw's professional

skill, coolness and courage, and total disregard for his own safety. Throughout the period in the building he and Captain McLeod were at great personal risk, and under constant strain, deep in a hostile environment with no way out if detected – always a possibility in such an area irrespective of May Day.

This dedication to duty, regardless of his own safety, his coolness, skill and vital assistance to his Tour Officer were of the very highest order and deserving of special recognition, which I strongly recommend.'

BRIXMIS didn't always get away cleanly. They were fired upon and if they were caught they would be taken into custody. Major Arthur Nicholson, a member of the US Military Liaison Mission, the American BRIXMIS equivalent, was shot and killed by the Soviets in 1985. With their official liaison status, the tourers had some protection but the Soviets and East German police were always trying to catch them. Major General Brian Davis, who was a Brigadier and the Chief of the Mission in 1982, related the standard process that would follow if any of the BRIXMIS mission were caught:

'If you were caught and hemmed in, they'd then send for the nearest garrison commander, because they'd be just soldiers doing their training with perhaps a Major in charge who probably didn't know any English anyway. So they'd circle the car, and some could be quite unpleasant about it. And then a Major or Colonel from the nearest barracks, who had a bit of English but not a lot, would come and we would be escorted to the

TOP LEFT: Serving with BRIXMIS gave personnel the change to collect some unique and interesting souvenirs. This flag of the German Democratic Republic was liberated from outside the Soviet Military Cemetery at Treptow Park in East Berlin by General Peter Williams during a Flag Tour, immediately prior to the annual National Day parade of the GDR on 7th October, while he was serving with BRIXMIS in early October 1974 as a young officer

MIDDLE LEFT: Mission Restriction Signs such as this were used in East Germany to denote areas where even the BRIXMIS tour teams couldn't go. Stealing them was considered a rite of passage for BRIXMIS tour members [NAM]

TOP RIGHT: The medals awarded to Anthony Haw for his military service, including the British Empire Medal he was awarded for his actions while serving with BRIXMIS in 1980 [NAM]

BOTTOM LEFT: BRIXMIS cars were all marked with a distinctive number plate, that was used to both designate their unique status, but also mark them out for any Soviet or East German forces [Keith Richards]

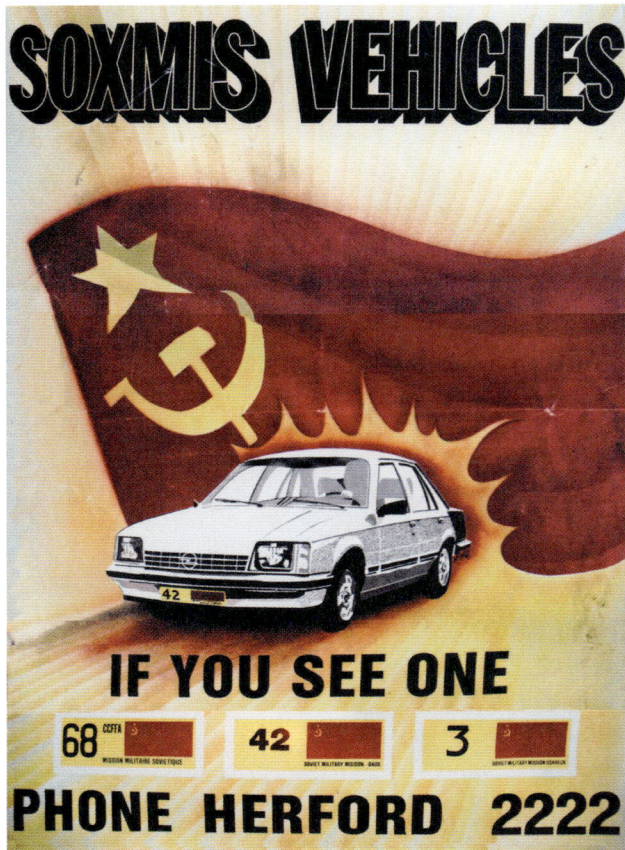

SOXMIS VEHICLES

IF YOU SEE ONE

68 | 42 | 3

PHONE HERFORD 2222

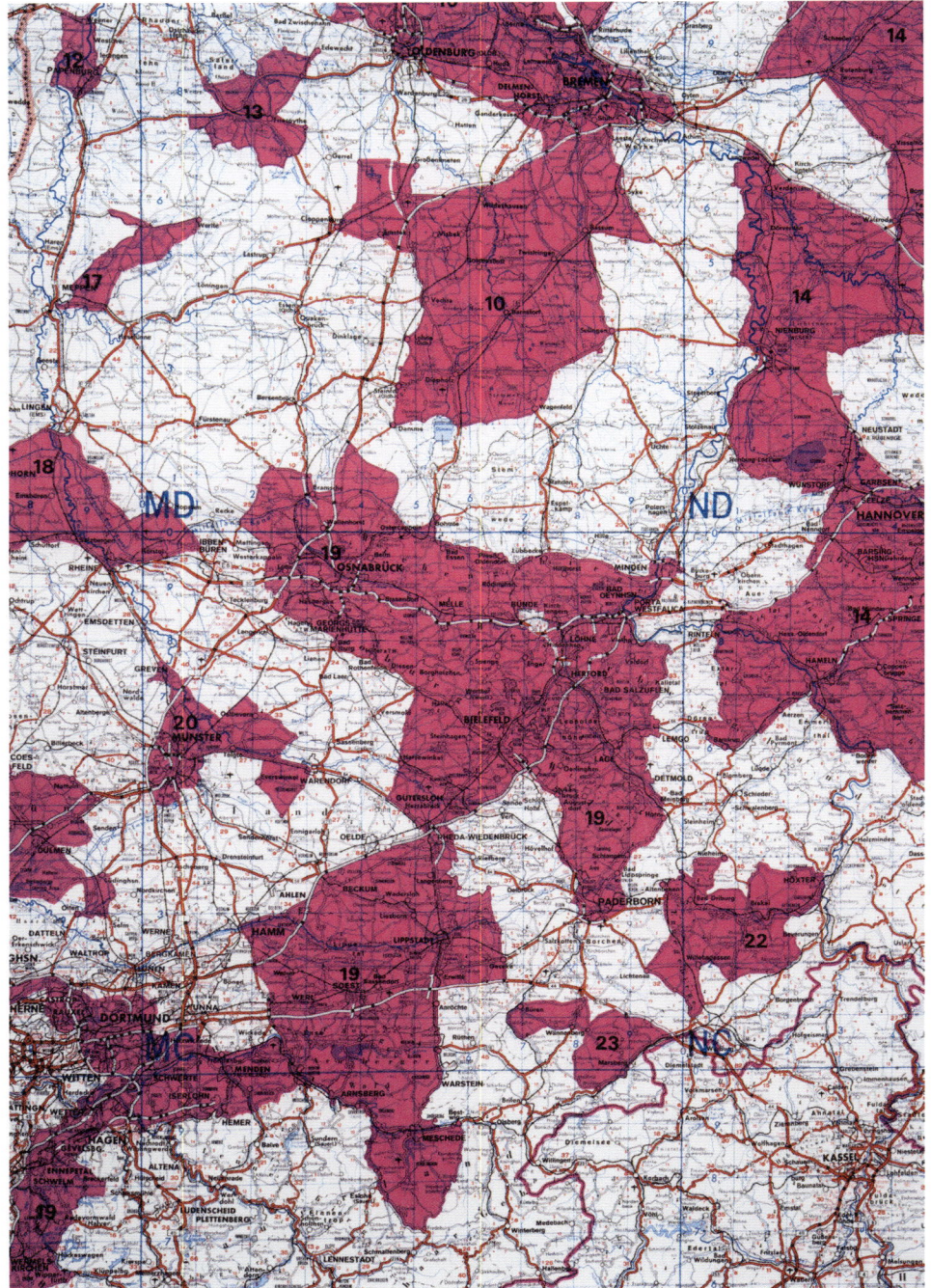

barracks, where they would say, "This chap was doing this, and taking a picture of that," and our reply was always, "None of your business. Mind your business. We're liaisons to the Russian forces. What we do is up to us, nothing to do with you." And they would then produce – it could take 24 hours, you'd sleep in the car with guards, or be locked up in an interview room – they would eventually produce an Akt ... which means a list of crimes which you then had to sign – which you didn't sign at all, which they got very depressed about. And eventually lots of phone calls would be made and you would be released. But instead of letting you carry on running around the countryside, you'd be escorted to Potsdam, and delivered back to your lot. Bloody amusing.'

The stress and tension of the tours was not for everyone. Davis noted that: 'You had to keep happy with it; it could get you down. I had several tour officers who couldn't manage it, being chased and trapped and all the rest of it. And they had to go, medically they had to go, which was a pity.' This aggressive, proactive

intelligence gathering was somewhat at odds with the attitude of the French liaison mission, and also their Soviet counterparts:

'SOXMIS ... operating in the British Army area, 1st British Corps in West Germany, they rarely drove round, hardly ever saw them. My mate saw them in the West, and I saw them while I was in the regiment ... They would spend all their days driving around in full uniform, not our sort of war-y-looking stuff. And just sort of drive

LEFT: A poster from the early 1980s informing British soldiers what to do if they saw a SOXMIS vehicle [Frank Föste]

RIGHT: Detail of a map showing permanently restricted areas for members of SOXMIS. The exceptions between the areas were the Autobahn routes, down which the SOXMIS vehicles would often patrol [Private Collection]

around the barracks and drive away again, and they were never seen on the training ground ever. They must have had some sort of camera work, but I didn't see it. But they didn't do what we did and have three nights in the woods and climb over walls and all that stuff, they didn't do any of that. They just saw themselves as a liaison mission at the highest level. Saluting and shaking hands and honouring each other's days and, leftover from the war, whereas ours was very much, as you can see, intelligence gathering.'

There was, however, an important social aspect to the Mission, which Davis was fully immersed in as the Chief. He became well-acquainted with the Soviet high command in Germany, despite their full knowledge of what he and his command were doing:

'They had three big events: the formation of the Soviet Union … Red Army Day was another day, I think that was in May sometime; and the third one was defeating the Germans, in May 1945. And that was another piss-up. And I went officially to those, all dressed up as a guest of the Commander-in-Chief. I was on his staff, technically, as his British liaison officer. And they were incredible. They would go on, and on, and on. And you're toasting something, there's booze, and as you finish it they fill more booze, and you get little plates of food, but you reach for stuff all the time, and it's all stuff to absorb alcohol, bloody great tables of it. And you get called upon to toast. So you toast the Queen, you toast the British Army, you toast the Russian Army, you toast the Russian Navy just in case there's a bloody sailor there. … Toast the end of the war, of course, toast the heroic Soviet Union who defeated Berlin in wonderful so on and so forth. And after ten or eleven hours of this, you're feeling pretty dodgy, because it's all vodka. And you're running out of toasts. I was called upon by old Zaitsev, very late in the day, in the proceedings. Got up. And I toasted my grandmother, and I had an interpreter because I was determined not to do a lot of Russian because you could get caught out if they knew you knew the language … My interpreter … translated "General Davis will now give a toast to his grandmother, who survived the German Blitz on London" – which she did. Big cheer! And they all stood solemnly from the Commander-in-Chief down and toasted, "Mrs Weber, from London town!" '

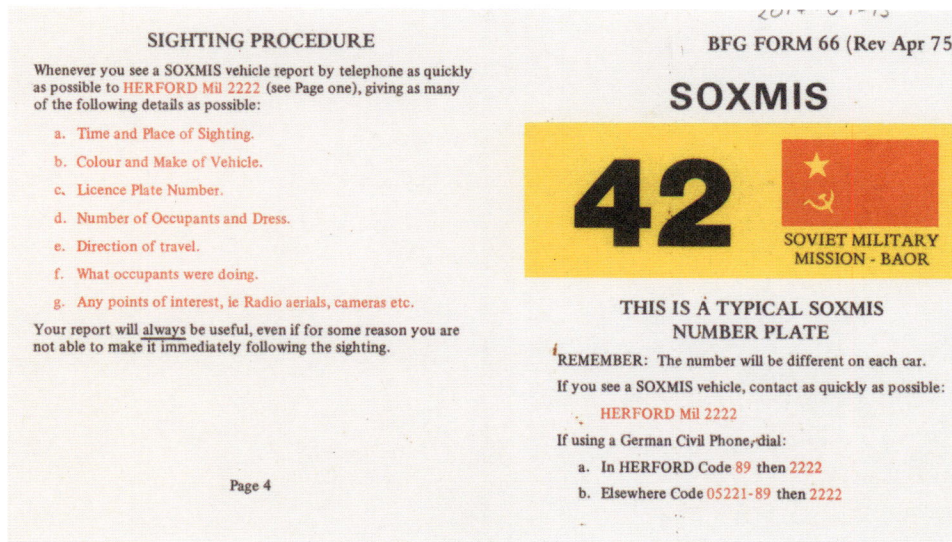

SIGHTING PROCEDURE

Whenever you see a SOXMIS vehicle report by telephone as quickly as possible to HERFORD Mil 2222 (see Page one), giving as many of the following details as possible:

a. Time and Place of Sighting.
b. Colour and Make of Vehicle.
c. Licence Plate Number.
d. Number of Occupants and Dress.
e. Direction of travel.
f. What occupants were doing.
g. Any points of interest, ie Radio aerials, cameras etc.

Your report will always be useful, even if for some reason you are not able to make it immediately following the sighting.

Page 4

BFG FORM 66 (Rev Apr 75)

SOXMIS

42

SOVIET MILITARY MISSION - BAOR

THIS IS A TYPICAL SOXMIS NUMBER PLATE

REMEMBER: The number will be different on each car.

If you see a SOXMIS vehicle, contact as quickly as possible:

HERFORD Mil 2222

If using a German Civil Phone, dial:

a. In HERFORD Code 89 then 2222
b. Elsewhere Code 05221-89 then 2222

SOXMIS Recognition Cards like these – or BFG Form 66 – were standard issue in the British Zone. This one was carried by Michael Wickens during his service with the Royal Engineers (NAM)

Culturally, as well as professionally, there were great advantages to taking a posting with the Mission. Those working for BRIXMIS and their families also had the added advantage of being able to go on cultural tours in wider East Germany, and visit cities like Dresden that were deep behind the Iron Curtain. These events were undoubtedly followed closely by the Soviets and the East German Stasi, but they were extremely enjoyable – one, because it enabled those members of the Mission to see more of East Germany beyond what could be glimpsed from the corridor into Berlin, and two, because the spending power of the West was enormous in the economically backward East.

BRIXMIS was formally disbanded on 31st December 1990, after the collapse of the Berlin Wall, bringing to an end a unique role within the British forces in Germany. For Davis, it had been, 'One of the jobs I enjoyed most really. You really felt you were doing something useful. I thought it was terrific, I thoroughly enjoyed it. As did pretty well everybody else.' Other soldiers had looked on enviously. For Jim Toms,

'We were in awe of the guys in BRIXMIS. That was like, "God, I'd love to do that job!" You know, that would be the ultimate job, I think, for a lot of people. Certainly the guys I spoke to were very impressed with those sorts of people, to be up close and personal with the enemy. And that's how it was seen. They were definitely seen as the enemy.'

But Germany was changing, and with it the world.

AFTER THE WALL

On 9th November 1989, the Berlin Wall fell, bringing with it the collapse of the forcible division of Berlin. With the Group of Soviet Forces in Germany unwilling to intervene to support the East German state, panic and uncertainty gripped the border guards when confronted with an enormous crowd of protestors. On the back of a wave of popular protest, the checkpoints were thrown open, allowing people to move back and forth. Over the next year, the Wall was progressively dismantled.

As the crowds took to the Wall, news of what was happening spread round Germany. It was greeted with shock in the various British garrisons. Geoff Payne, who had first been posted to Germany with 50 Missile Battery Royal Artillery in Menden in 1975, but was in Rheindahlen with the Intelligence Corps in 1989, remembers the shock with

which it was greeted, and the celebrations in the various messes of JHQ. Some people even drove up to Berlin to be part of this seismic event in history. Other personnel picked it up later, as was the case with Jim Toms:

'We were actually out on the ground. We were doing a deployment exercise, and we were in some wood, and somebody must have been listening to BFBS on the radio … You were obviously aware of what was going on in the news … but then that night, when the Wall came down, somebody said, "They've opened the Wall." And it was like, "You what? What do you mean they've opened the Wall? Nah, you've got to be having a laugh." It wasn't until we got back to camp and packed everything up and could see the news … there wasn't this immediate impact on us.'

The British in Berlin weren't only spectators to the events. They responded to a request from the Berlin

Major General Robert Corbett, the 21st and last British 'Stadtkommandant' in Berlin, along with his RMP Close Protection bodyguard, Corporal Richard Ornsby, speaks to the media at the opening of the Wall on 9th November 1989 (IWM)

LEFT: A West German man uses a hammer and chisel to chip off a piece of the Berlin Wall as a souvenir, November 1989 (US Department of Defense)

RIGHT: West German citizens gather at a newly created opening in the Berlin Wall at Potsdamer Platz, November 1989 (US Department of Defense)

Senate to help provide emergency supplies for the influx of East Berliners rushing into the West. As duty battalion, the 1st Battalion The Royal Welch Fusiliers provided beds and bedding for 600 people at the city's exhibition centre, issued 1,000 blankets and even set up mobile canteens at crossing points. At Gatow, two hangars were given over to the Senate for use.

The opening of the borders between East and West Germany and the move towards reunification brought a whole new type of German flooding into the British Zone. In Celle, close to the old Inner German Border, Toms recalls that suddenly: 'There were lots of scabby old Trabants – they might have been brand new but they always looked old – in the town. And squaddies being squaddies, they were tipping them up; it sounds horrible but it was just this weird thing about the enemy's coming here, because the East Germans were as much the enemy as the Soviet Union.'

Troops stationed in Berlin were able to watch the Wall being demolished around them – and many picked up their own souvenirs of this piece of history. While there were celebrations following the collapse of the Wall, it put BAOR and the British forces in Germany into a watchful stance. How would the East Germans react? How would the Soviets? The collapse of the Wall, while a cause for jubilation, was not the immediate end of the Cold War.

It also heralded the end of an era, which would be most keenly felt in Berlin. There was no longer a need to patrol the Wall, or observe the other side. At RAF Gatow, the role of the 'Unscheds' – unscheduled flights – and the

Pembroke reconnaissance aircraft used as part of Operation HALLMARK were, if not defunct, suddenly uncertain. The Cold War, and the sense of isolation the Wall created for those at Gatow – right up against the wire as they were – had resulted in a unique atmosphere, which Kirkpatrick commented on:

'Gatow was a very small station. Very, very friendly. Totally different air force ... The station staff were all very friendly. We were all on first name terms ... We were just hanging out together. Most stations' squadrons hang together, eat together, drink together in the mess, but pretty much there were enough people in that squadron to keep people together. Gatow, you'd go to lunch and sit with the police, the girl from the tower, everybody. We just ganged together. It was really weird. Really funny, really nice.'

But what now, what would come next? The British forces in Germany, and their families, would need to react and adapt to the new world they were entering. Jim Toms captured this feeling:

'It was odd. I remember seeing the first Mi8 Hip helicopter flying over Celle. And that was a real, "What the hell?" I've been taught to look for this stuff, and watch out for it, and report it, and then all of a sudden there's one flying over the town where I'm based. It was just weird, and we're not at war; it was a very strange sense, really. But there was also a thought of, "What now? What are we here for? What's going to happen to us here in Germany now that all this is coming to an end? What is the purpose of British Forces Germany?"'

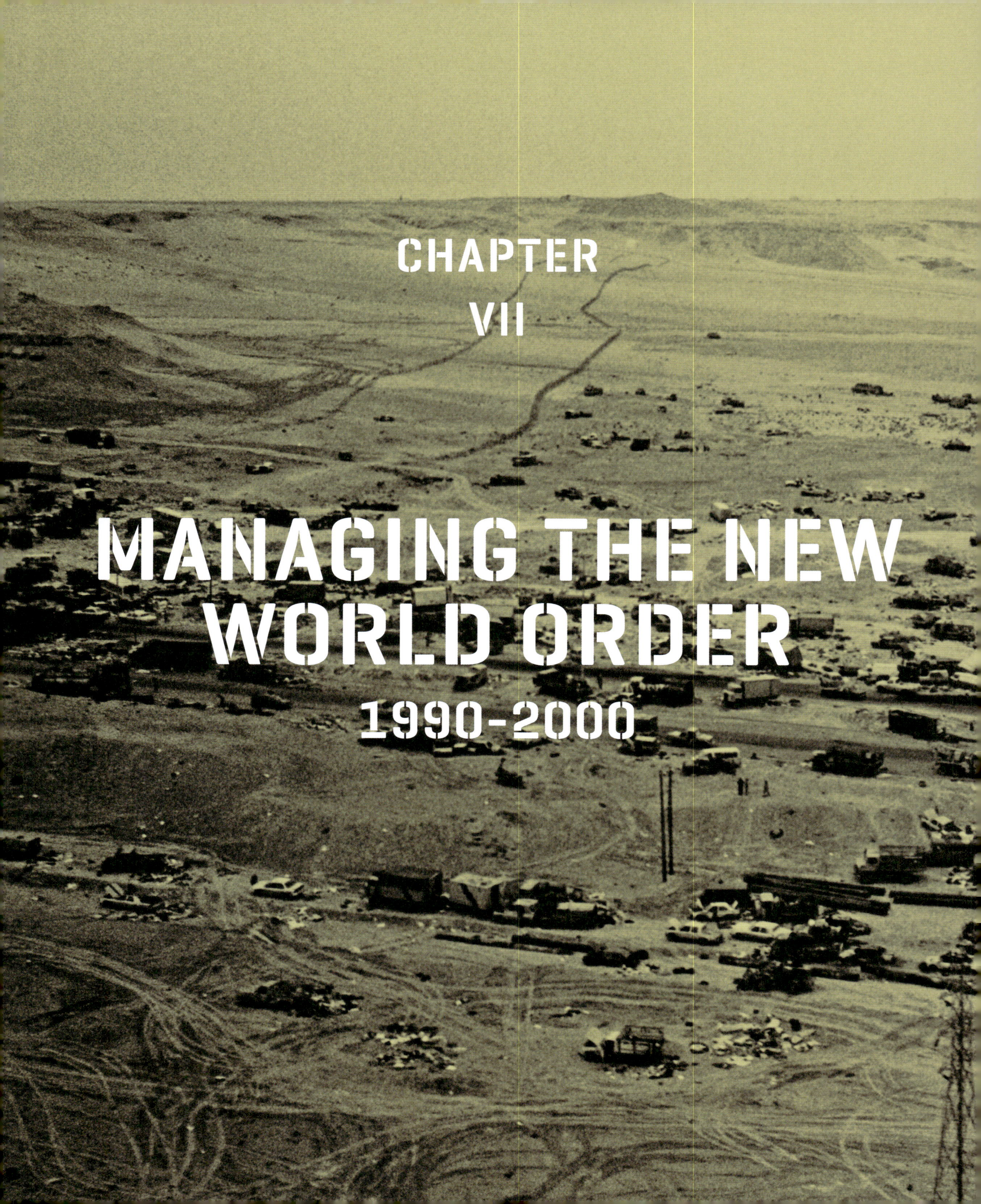

CHAPTER VII

MANAGING THE NEW WORLD ORDER

1990–2000

WAR, BUT IN A DIFFERENT PLACE

The fall of the Berlin Wall in 1989 heralded a rapid change in the established world order. In quick succession, the Soviet Union fell apart and the Warsaw Pact collapsed, led by Poland and Hungary breaking away. The British forces in Germany, which had stood on the frontline of the Cold War in Europe – and elsewhere – had accomplished their task.

But as the Cold War ended, questions were asked about what the British Army of the Rhine was going to do, and what the future held. The crisis that developed in the Middle East after Iraq's invasion of Kuwait on 2nd August 1990 allowed the British Army to focus on what it does best: soldiering.

The international community had condemned the Iraqi invasion. Saudi Arabia had appealed directly to the United States and NATO for protection, and the US committed troops as part of Operation DESERT SHIELD. This was then followed by the UK. With the backing of the UN, an international coalition formed. Soon after the invasion, RAF jets from Germany had been deployed to Saudi Arabia. Initially, the British contribution was confined to air and naval assets, but eventually the UK would contribute the second-largest contingent, some 53,000 personnel in total. The deployment was given the name Operation GRANBY. In August 1990, rumours began that 7th Armoured Brigade would leave its bases in Soltau, Bergen-Hohne and Fallingbostel and deploy to the Saudi desert, which was publicly confirmed on 15th September. The Desert Rats were returning to the desert. They would be followed later by the 4th Armoured Brigade from Münster, and the divisional troops of 1st Armoured Division from Verden.

Major General Rupert Smith had only arrived in Verden as GOC of 1st Armoured Division in October 1990, but he was in the Saudi desert by 12 December. He believed that the Gulf filled the void of the end of the Cold War, requiring 'a complete refocusing' across the Army, and especially BAOR. For most soldiers, the Gulf was a shock.

The Prime Minister, John Major, addresses troops of 7th Armoured Brigade in the Gulf after hostilities had ended [NAM]

PREVIOUS: Scenes of destruction on the Basrah road during the Gulf War [Crown]

The British logistics base for operations in the Gulf at Al Jubail (NAM)

For decades the Army had been preparing for a war in northern Germany. Even with war in the South Atlantic, and the ongoing and serious commitment in Northern Ireland, North Germany remained the primary, and regularly confirmed, focus for operations. Jim Toms, who was in Celle with 14 Signals Regiment, described it from his perspective:

'All we knew is that all of a sudden we're not fighting in Germany, we're going to the desert ... It was a shock ... Your entire focus as a soldier in Germany – as a soldier full stop – was to fight a war in Europe, should it come to it ... War came in a different place to where you expected it to. But hey, that's life.'

Additionally, deploying to the Gulf was a cultural shock. It would see an entire division – a quarter of BAOR's strength – deploy out of Germany at the same time, with all their vehicles. Even so, there was a sense of excitement in getting to take part among the BAOR warriors. In some cases, units were brought up to strength with volunteers from elsewhere in BAOR – which caused problems for some with their spouses when they claimed they had no choice in the matter. But there were no shortages. Brigadier Mark Armstrong of the REME recalls, 'People were pretty excited about it ... over the past 25 years there had only been Northern Ireland, which was steady state, and then that little bit of the Falklands, so I think that there was a sense that this was something that people wanted to be involved in.' Armstrong himself had just found out he had been selected to represent Great Britain in luge and had a chance to go to the 1992 Winter Olympics:

'Having been selected to represent Great Britain, I phone up my CO, and he said, "I've selected you to command an independent comapany out on Op GRANBY, would you like to go there? You've got five seconds to make up your mind, but you can stay doing the sport if you want." But I knew what I got paid to do. And that was the end of my competitive sporting career.'

For Toms, 'I was desperate, desperate to go. I was 23, 24, and you want to do your job; you want to do it for real.'

It wasn't only the soldiers who needed to adapt, but their families as well. Those left behind in the West German garrisons were used to their partners and parents deploying for weeks at a time on exercises, or perhaps for short tours to Northern Ireland. But the scale of this was something different. New welfare systems were put in place to help them keep in contact with those overseas. Single-sheet airmail letters – 'blueys' – helped the soldiers stay in contact. Maps would be issued to the families showing their progress through the Gulf as the campaign developed. *Soldier* magazine helped keep the families informed, as did various garrison magazines, and were used to help soldiers and their families exchange messages as the campaign went on.

Despite the soldiers' enthusiasm to take part, the ability of the British to adapt to fighting in the desert was going to be sorely tested. Armoured vehicles and airframes had to be repainted and modified to cope with the desert sand. There was a shortage of desert camouflage, particularly in NBC suits, so soldiers arrived with their jungle or woodland Disruptive Pattern Material uniforms. It would also test the British in terms of the available kit. Rupert Smith noted how one division had been hollowed out just to send 7th Armoured Brigade. When the troops were enforced further and brought up to a division, other divisions in BAOR then provided more of their own kit for those going overseas. As Smith pointed out, they, 'took everything we wanted from the rest of BAOR, so they just came to a standstill'.

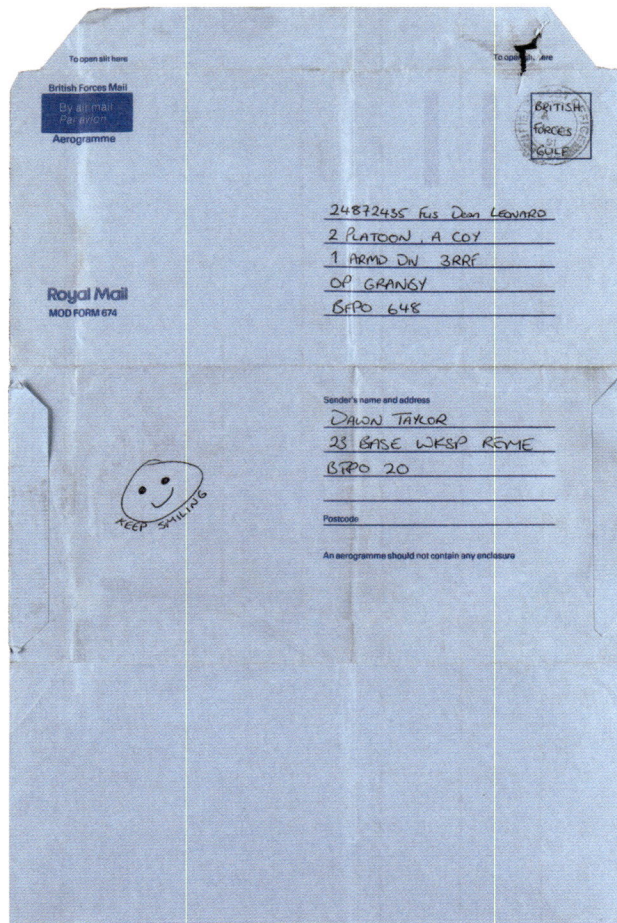

Major General Mungo Melvin, who was the senior planner in the 1st Armoured Division headquarters at the time and deployed to the Gulf, agreed: 'The challenge of the first Gulf War was huge for the Army. It took the whole resources of 1st British Corps to mobilise that division.' Part of this challenge also involved some of the strategic thought behind BAOR. In expectation of fighting the Warsaw Pact, every vehicle in BAOR had been maintained in fighting order, ready to go at an hour's notice. But there was no depth. In a campaign where it was expected that there would be a resort to nuclear weapons once conventional forces were quickly exhausted, sustainability had not been so high on the agenda. But for the Gulf it was essential, and the movement by air and sea to Al Jubayl highlighted some weaknesses in BAOR that had never been tested – as Smith summarised: 'Some of this showed how much of a wing and a prayer we'd been operating on during the 1980s, at least in terms of resources. Some of it was a direct consequence of the distance and the nature of the deployment.'

A Bluey sent to Fusilier Dean Leonard during Operation GRANBY. Leonard served with 2 Platoon, A Company, 3rd Battalion Royal Regiment of Fusiliers and deployed from Barossa Barracks in Hemer. The Bluey was sent from Dortmund (NAM)

In November 1990, the nature of the deployment also began to change, shifting from a defensive posture on DESERT SHIELD, to offensive on DESERT STORM. This tactical shift was something the British had to adapt to, given that all preparations and field training exercises in Germany had concerned how to fight a defensive battle before launching a counter-attack. For the pilots of the Royal Air Force, there was also a need to adapt their tactics to the operational reality of the Gulf. Wing Commander George William Pixton, who commanded the Jaguar Force flying out of Al Muharraq, Bahrain, consulted with his US colleagues about how best to proceed in their ground attacks. Pixton had learned his craft in West Germany, flying out of Laarbruch and Brüggen, where a rigorous training regime had taught pilots how to fly at low level, including how to identify 'about 25 different categories of target' while flying at 450 miles an hour. But when discussing tactics with his US colleagues, the message was quite clear: low level against the Iraqis would not work as it would leave the jets vulnerable to huge amounts of small-arms fire, something the Americans had learned the hard way in Vietnam. So the decision was made to conduct medium-level operations instead. Pixton was awarded the Distinguished Flying Cross for his individual flying and his leadership of the Jaguar detachment in the Gulf.

Some things were similar, though. For example, the threat of NBC attack resulted in regular and constant drills. BAOR warriors had drilled in NBC in Germany, but in Iraq it took on an added significance. As Armstrong noted:

'There was the threat of the Scud missiles ... That put a bit more realism onto the fact that this wasn't a game, that this was something quite serious. Whereas in training, I think it's fair to say, in Germany in training over previous years people, yes people did NBC training, nobody really likes it, nobody likes wearing a respirator for a long period of time, nobody likes going through the process that you do when you put suits on and off and all the rest of it. Suddenly this was real and people were paying a lot more attention to it and wanted to know, and I guess it focused the mind.'

There was a real sense of apprehension across the forces deployed to the desert. While there was certainly confidence the mission could be achieved, the scale of the challenge was not underestimated. For Toms, it was clear that,

while they wouldn't be fighting the Russians, it would not be easy, and he and his friends thought: 'These guys are going to be good. There's a lot of them, and they're going to be good. We'd better be better. But we were up against the hardware we trained to fight against; we pulled in some other kit. We thought this could be nasty ... We had no idea how it was going to pan out.'

The British spent months in the desert training, working up to peak effectiveness, waiting for the offensive to begin. It was finally launched on 17th January 1991 with a devastating air war targeting Iraqi infrastructure and troops. The ground campaign began on 24th February, and 100 hours later it was over. The devastating attack by the Americans, supported all the way by the British, had utterly crushed the Iraqis. Forty-seven British personnel had been killed in action and non-combat actions.

The British experience in Germany had undoubtedly played a major part in delivering success in the desert. Mungo Melvin was adamant on this: 'Service in Germany maintained the Army's professional edge. It was important for its war-fighting power.' That the war had come on a different continent almost didn't matter. It had been vindication of everything the British had spent decades training to do, combined with the increased tactical agility Bagnall had introduced. The culture of professionalism, the training, the sheer practicalities of

Re-arming a Challenger tank in the desert, 1991. The Army's Challengers destroyed some 300 Iraqi vehicles during the conflict. On 26th February 1991, a Challenger recorded the longest confirmed kill ever recorded, destroying an Iraqi tank at a distance of 2.9 miles (NAM)

Campaign map depicting Operation GRANBY and DESERT SABRE, which was carried out by 1st (UK) Armoured Division between October 1990 and March 1991 during the Gulf War. The British secured the right flank of the sweeping left hook that encircled the Iraqis (Crown)

working with large amounts of armour had all been tested in Saudi Arabia and proven successful. As Rupert Smith noted, 'Just the whole business of putting an armoured brigade onto trains and tank transporters is a little exercise in itself, and doesn't happen easily; people need to practise and know what they're on.' Ultimately, in his mind, 'We certainly couldn't have done 1990–91 in Iraq if we hadn't had some of that experience, both in the actually practicalities of putting those armoured vehicles onto tank transporters and things, but also the staff work to manage it.'

But as the British Army were fighting in the Gulf, dramatic changes were taking place in Europe, and at an enormous pace. And enormous changes would be taking place in the Army too, all of which would have a major impact on service life in Germany over the rest of the decade.

CHANGE IS THE ONLY OPTION

The threat of the Warsaw Pact, which had been so routine, was now gone. It had been the defining role and point of the British Army of the Rhine and the British forces in Germany for half a century. On 31st March 1991, it disappeared forever. Similarly, the Inner German Border had disappeared, and on 3rd October 1990, East Germany ceased to exist as part of the process of reunification. An entire way of life for the British, of regular duties, procedures and ways of thinking, was suddenly being transformed. The question was now being asked as to what the British Army was actually going to do.

Even before the British forces had proven their capabilities and value in the Gulf, discussions were being had at the political level about how to respond to

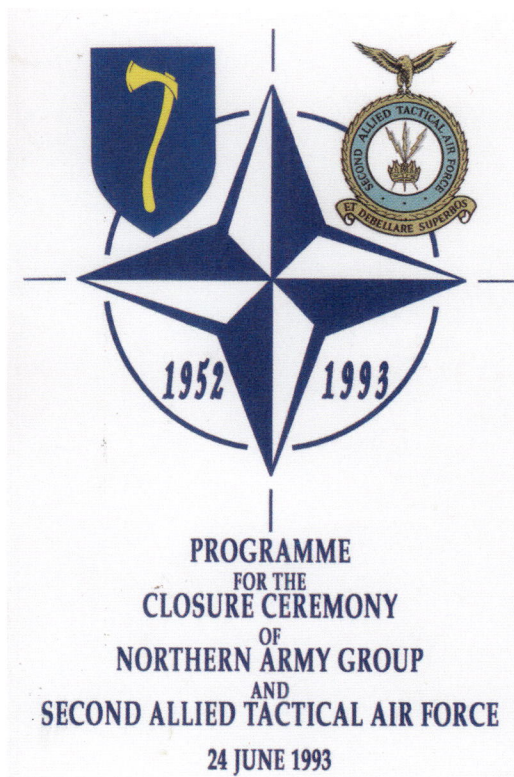

PROGRAMME
FOR THE
CLOSURE CEREMONY
OF
NORTHERN ARMY GROUP
AND
SECOND ALLIED TACTICAL AIR FORCE

24 JUNE 1993

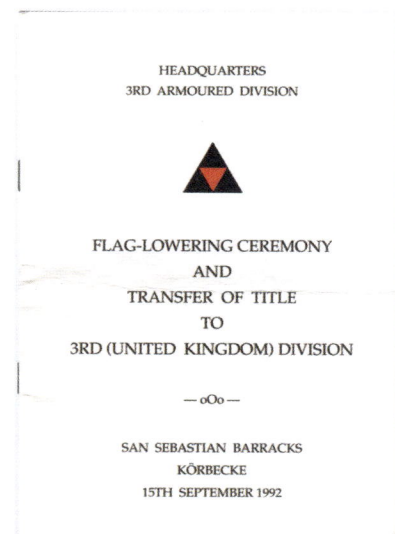

HEADQUARTERS
3RD ARMOURED DIVISION

FLAG-LOWERING CEREMONY
AND
TRANSFER OF TITLE
TO
3RD (UNITED KINGDOM) DIVISION

—oOo—

SAN SEBASTIAN BARRACKS
KÖRBECKE
15TH SEPTEMBER 1992

the new geopolitical reality. In 1990, discussions were held in Whitehall about how to embrace the so-called 'peace dividend' delivered by NATO's victory in the Cold War. A defence review was conducted to ostensibly better appreciate the new strategic landscape – but also to identify where savings could be made on defence spending. The review would become known as *Options for Change*, and its central aim was outlined by the then-Defence Secretary, Tom King, in July 1990:

'*Our proposals will bring savings and a reduction in the share of GDP taken by defence. We need force levels which we can afford and which can realistically be manned, given demographic pressures in the 1990s. The aim is smaller forces, better equipped, properly trained and housed, and well motivated. They will need to be flexible and mobile and able to contribute both in NATO and, if necessary, elsewhere.*'

The aim of *Options for Change* was to create a smaller but more flexible military that could be deployed in different circumstances as part of an international coalition alongside either NATO partners or as directed by an international body such as the UN. It would not be the only defence review of the 1990s, but it would certainly be the most far-reaching, and have the greatest impact on the Service personnel living and working in Germany. As King said on 23rd July 1991, 'Since the greatest threat previously came in the central region in Europe, it was on Germany that the major part of our Army was focused and it is from this area that the largest part of our reductions now comes.'

The physical transformation of the British forces in Germany

was huge. The largest cuts that came as a result of the review fell on BAOR, which was reduced from 55,000 to 23,000; 3rd Armoured Division in Soest became a mechanised division and moved to the UK, 1st Armoured Division's HQ moved out of Verden and into Herford, replacing the dissolved 4th Armoured Division and being renamed as 1st (UK) Armoured Division. But the RAF suffered too, and tactical air power in Germany was reduced by half; RAF Wildenrath closed in April 1992, followed by RAF Gütersloh in March 1993, and six squadrons were withdrawn. Royal Air Force Germany was officially disbanded in a ceremony attended by Prince Philip at the Joint Headquarters, Rheindahlen on 20th April 1993.

On 2nd October 1992, 1 (BR) Corps was disbanded and became the Allied Rapid Reaction Corps, which was an international headquarters unit with a British commander. It remained in Bielefeld until 1994, when it moved to Rheindahlen. The same year, the British Army of the Rhine and Royal Air Force Germany were disbanded completely. The new formation in Germany would be known as UK Support Command (Germany). Across the old BAOR, barracks were closed and emptied; 3rd Armoured Division moved from Soest to Bulford in the UK, the 'Gunner Ghetto' of Dortmund was closed,

LEFT: The 1 (BR) Corps Flag lowered for the last time at the HQ in Bielefeld on 2nd October 1992, collected by General Sir Peter Inge, the Chief of the General Staff. The direct successor of 1 (BR) Corps was the Allied Rapid Reaction Corps (NAM)

CENTRE: The printed programme accompanying the military ceremony to close NORTHAG and the Second Allied Tactical Airforce. The last commander of NORTHAG was General Sir Charles Guthrie, and the last commander of the 2ATAF, and also RAF Germany, was Air Chief Marshal Sir Andrew Wilson (NAM)

RIGHT: Not all ceremonies marked closures or disbanding; there were some relocations. This programme accompanied the flag-lowering ceremony and transfer of title as 3rd (United Kingdom) Division moved from Körbecke to Bulford in the UK (Crown)

Two columns of British Army Chieftain tanks, in their distinctive urban camouflage design, drive along Strasse des 17 Juni during the Allied Forces Day parade on 18th June 1989. Those participating could not know it would be the last before the collapse of the Soviet Union (US Department of Defense)

and 11th Armoured Brigade in Minden and 12th Armoured Brigade in Osnabrück were both disbanded; 22nd Armoured Brigade was disbanded and merged with 7th Armoured, which moved from Soltau to Hohne, in 1993. The 6th and 33rd Armoured Brigades were also disbanded. Other units were retained but relocated under the new 1st (UK) Armoured Division structure; 4th Armoured Brigade moved from Münster to Osnabrück, and 20th Armoured Brigade moved from Detmold to Paderborn, with some units and its headquarters in Sennelager. The physical footprint that the British had occupied since the Second World War was changing irrevocably.

The most high-profile changes took place in Berlin, however, and were symbolic of the changing world order. After the Wall came down, the British retained a garrison in Berlin – at the request of the local government– until Russian forces were withdrawn. There were still 380,000 Russian soldiers in Germany in 1990, and so there was no rush for the British to leave entirely in a city where

their presence had been a symbolic bulwark for freedom and democracy. There were 5,000 British troops in Berlin in 1990, but they had all left by 1994. The 1st Battalion, The Queen's Lancashire Regiment was the last British unit to leave Berlin.

The Berlin Brigade HQ was disbanded on 1st January 1991, and the military hospital closed in May. On 7th February 1991, one of the icons of the Cold War ran for the last time. Since 1945, the Berliner train from Charlottenburg to Braunschweig had run every day apart from Christmas Day, and during the short interlude of the Berlin Blockade. Beginning in Berlin, the journey took about four hours to complete before returning in the afternoon. The operation and administration of the Berliner had been the responsibility of 62 Transport and Movement Squadron, Royal Corps of Transport, but the train guard staff were drawn from the Berlin garrison, giving many soldiers the opportunity to travel both as passengers and in a working capacity on the train.

OC Train, TCWO, Russian Interpreter of The British Military Train prepare to meet the Soviet Officer.

BERLIN FORM 18

FOR _____

AND _____ OTHERS

FROM **BERLIN** TO **HELMSTEDT/ BRAUNSCHWEIG**

DATE _____

AUTHORIZATION STAMP

CAR No. _____

COMP No. _____

PASSENGERS MUST READ THE INSTRUCTIONS OVERLEAF

BERLIN

BRITISH MILITARY TRAIN TICKET

FOR _____

AND _____ OTHERS

FROM **HELMSTEDT/ BRAUNSCHWEIG** TO **BERLIN**

DATE _____

AUTHORIZATION STAMP

CAR No. _____

COMP No. _____

ROUTE OF THE BRITISH MILITARY TRAIN (THE BERLINER)

TOP LEFT: A postcard of the Berliner train; the train and the journey, along with the associated ceremony and pageantry, were icons of Berlin and the Cold War (NAM)

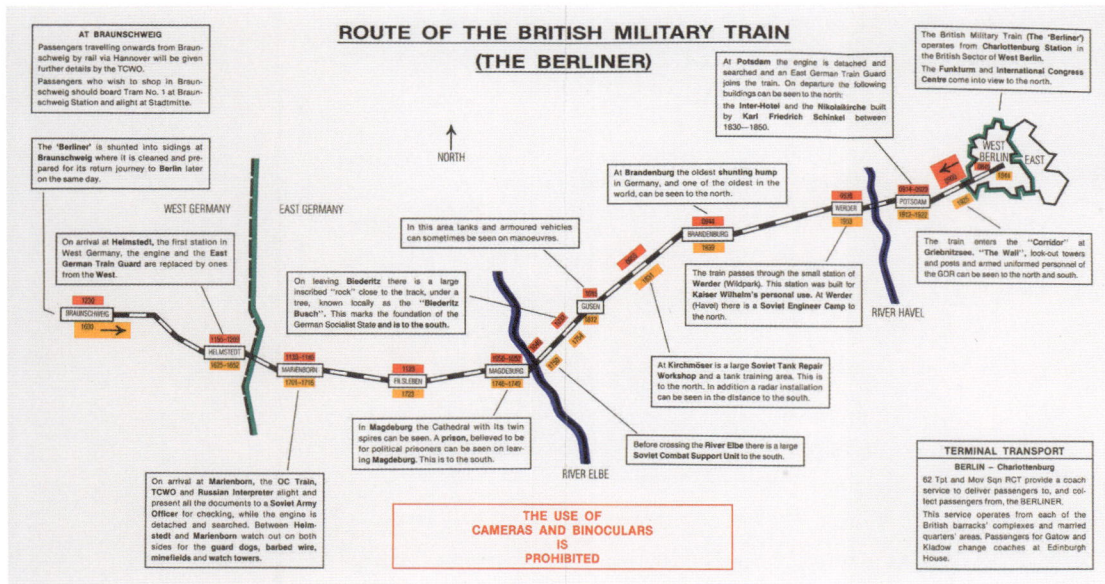

TOP RIGHT: An unused train ticket for the Berliner for a journey from Berlin to Helmstedt/Braunschweig from 1989 (NAM)

BOTTOM LEFT: A map of the Berliner's route, highlighting interesting sights for passengers (NAM)

BOTTOM RIGHT: The Berliner train's wine list was legendary among passengers, and also made excellent souvenirs (Private Collection)

BERLIN BULLETIN

PUBLISHED BY EDUCATION BRANCH, HQ BERLIN INFANTRY BRIGADE FOR BRITISH FORCES, BERLIN

FRIDAY 16 SEPTEMBER 1994   FINAL EDITION   VOLUME 45 – ISSUE 36

"WE LEAVE AS FRIENDS"

Photo: Michael Klinec

During his visit to Berlin to attend the Federal Farewell Ceremonies to the Western Allies on 8 September, the Prime Minister, The Rt Hon John Major MP, visited Brigade Headquarters to unveil a commemorative stone in front of London Block, Stadium Barracks. The stone commemorates the fact that the buildings accommodated the British Military Government in Berlin from 1945–1990, and until 1994 served as the Headquarters of the British Garrison. Also pictured above are Herr Eberhard Diepgen, Governing Mayor of Berlin, and Brigadier D de G Bromhead CBE LVO, Commander Berlin Infantry Brigade.

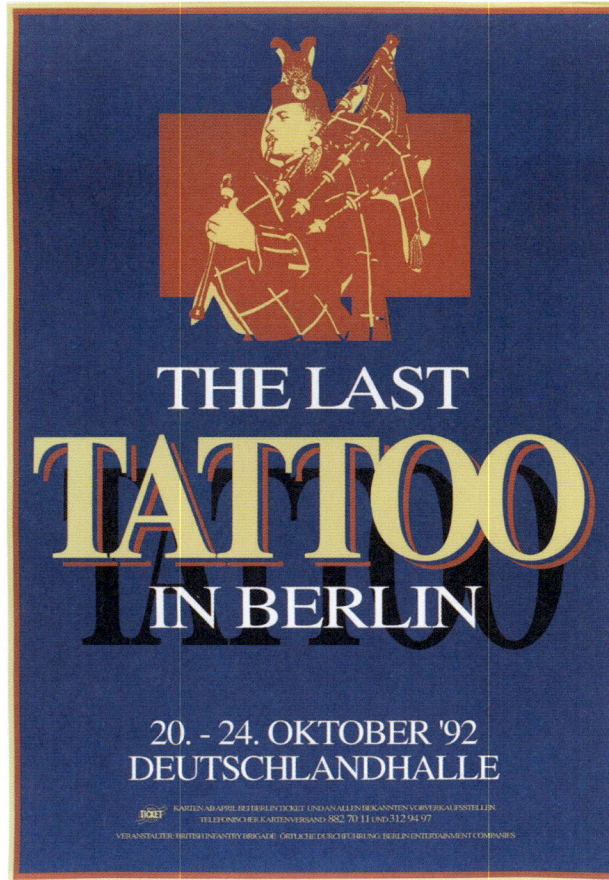

THE LAST TATTOO IN BERLIN

20. - 24. OKTOBER '92
DEUTSCHLANDHALLE

KARTEN AB APRIL BEI BERLIN TICKET UND AN ALLEN BEKANNTEN VORVERKAUFSSTELLEN
TELEFONISCHER KARTENVERSAND: 882 70 11 UND 312 94 97
VERANSTALTER: BRITISH INFANTRY BRIGADE. ÖRTLICHE DURCHFÜHRUNG BERLIN ENTERTAINMENT COMPANIES

LEFT: The final edition of the *Berlin Bulletin* illustrating the visit of the Prime Minister, John Major, to say farewell on 8th September 1994. The newspaper was published weekly for British Forces in Berlin by the Education Branch of HQ Berlin Infantry Brigade (Crown)

RIGHT: A poster for the last Berlin Tattoo, a much admired annual event organised by the Berlin Brigade, supported by the wider army, and seen as one of the highlights of the Berlin social events calendar (NAM)

The soldiers acting as guards were under strict instructions not to communicate with the Soviets – but they frequently did. Any journey began with the issuing of the BTD, the Berlin Travel Document, which needed to be completed in triplicate with utter accuracy. As Colonel Richard Spencer, who served in Berlin with the Army Legal Corps between 1983 and 1986, recalled, this needed to be done, 'because, we were told, the Soviet Red Army comparing your form with your ID card was an illiterate peasant who is just going to look at them, not read them, so therefore it had to be perfect'. This was handed to the train duty officer. The ritual of the engine being checked at Potsdam, the BTDs and identity documents for the passengers being checked at Marienborn as soldiers of opposing sides met on the platform, of the engine being changed at Helmstedt for the run up or down the corridor, and of passing through East Germany were unique aspects of the Cold War. The train journey of course had been another opportunity to wage the ideological Cold War – it was not a coincidence that when the train stopped at Potsdam Hauptbahnhof

in the rush hour, dinner was being served in the dining car, in full view of the East German citizens just across the tracks. Spencer recalls watching them, 'beavering around, trying not to catch your eye. There was the Iron Curtain, just the other side of the track. And one would either be finishing off the bottle of excellent Rhine wine, or enjoying a glass of port.' The opportunity to showcase the higher standard of living in the West was never missed.

A helpful information leaflet given to passengers on the train pointed out interesting sites that could be seen from the train – including Soviet military camps near the towns the train passed through, places where Soviet armour could occasionally be seen on manoeuvres, and the 'guard dogs, barbed wire, minefields and watch towers' that could be seen at Marienborn. Meals in the dining car, along with its impressive wine list – all of which were supplied by the NAAFI and branded to the Berliner – feature high in people's memories of the journey. The Berliner was an icon of the Cold War, but

The Berlin Travel Pack, issued to all personnel moving by car on the Helmstedt-Berlin autobahn and vice versa – the only official car route to the divided city. This was required paperwork for any vehicle until 29th September 1990, but after the collapse of the Soviet Union and the re-unification of first Berlin, and then Germany itself, it became another relic of the Cold War

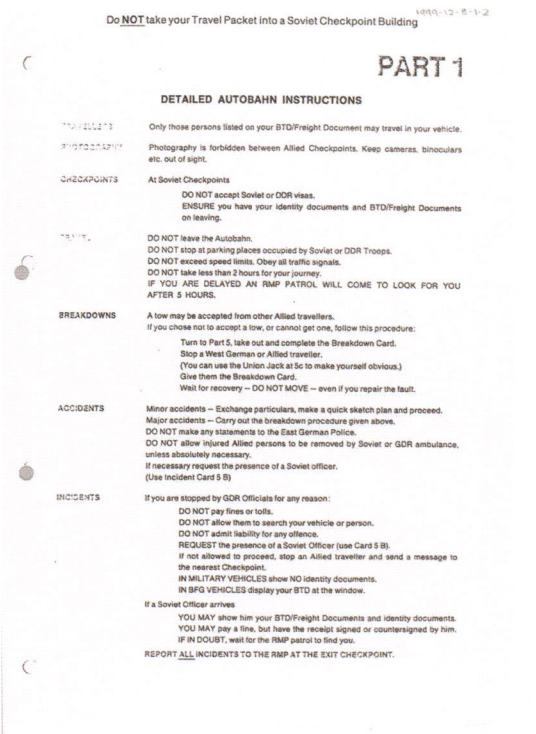

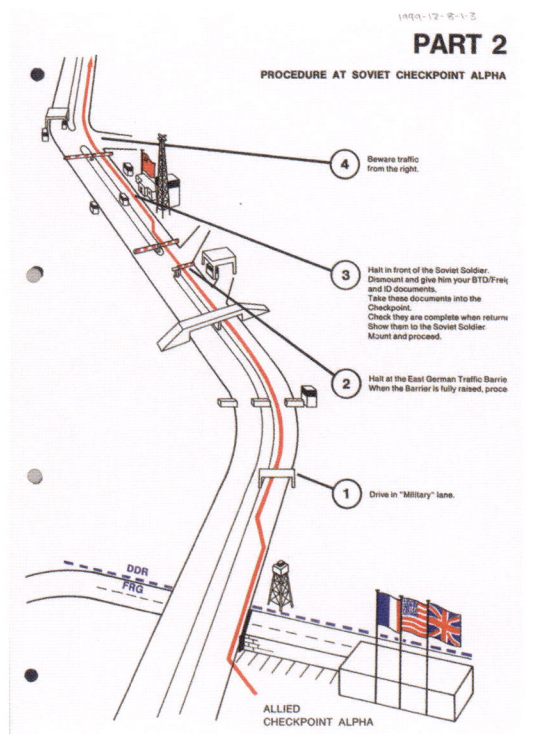

with the conflict over, Germany reunified, and greater air and car travel, it passed into history.

Other iconic events associated with the British presence in Berlin were also held for the last time. The final British Berlin Military Tattoo, for example, was held in October 1992. Scores of parades and festivals attracted more than one million Berliners, until the last round of events took place on 8th September 1994. In a round of speeches to British military personnel and their families at the old brigade HQ at the Olympic Stadium, and then at Berlin's Schauspielhaus theatre, the British Prime Minister, John Major, summarised how the relationship between the countries had changed: 'We came as adversaries, we stayed as allies, and we leave as friends.'

A NEW RELATIONSHIP

The British, having been a dominant power in their Zone for so long, were now undoubtedly faced with a new ally in the aftermath of the Cold War. Germany had been transformed by the fall of the Wall. Between its opening on 9th November 1989 and January 1990, 225,000 people crossed into the West. In October 1990, it became a single country again – though one still heavily divided in terms of culture and economic prosperity. It would take decades for this upheaval to fully level out. There were still heavy restrictions on where the British could go in the former East, but many took the opportunity to explore what had, until very recently, been an entirely separate country. General Walter Courage was one such soldier: 'I took myself off into East Germany to have a look, and that was fascinating.'

The 1990 Two Plus Four Agreement between East and West Germany and the four victorious powers from the Second World War had terminated the Allies' rights over Germany and Berlin, rights the British had certainly become accustomed to exercising. The British were entering into a new phase of their relationship with the Germans, and uncharted territory. The restructuring of the *Options for Change* allowed some high-profile handovers of flashpoints in the relations between the British and Germans, best exemplified by the Soltau-Lüneburg Area. What had been 'a running sore' in British-German relations, in the words of Mungo Melvin, could be remedied, even if it meant giving up 'one bit in the jewel of the crown' of British Forces Germany. A growing

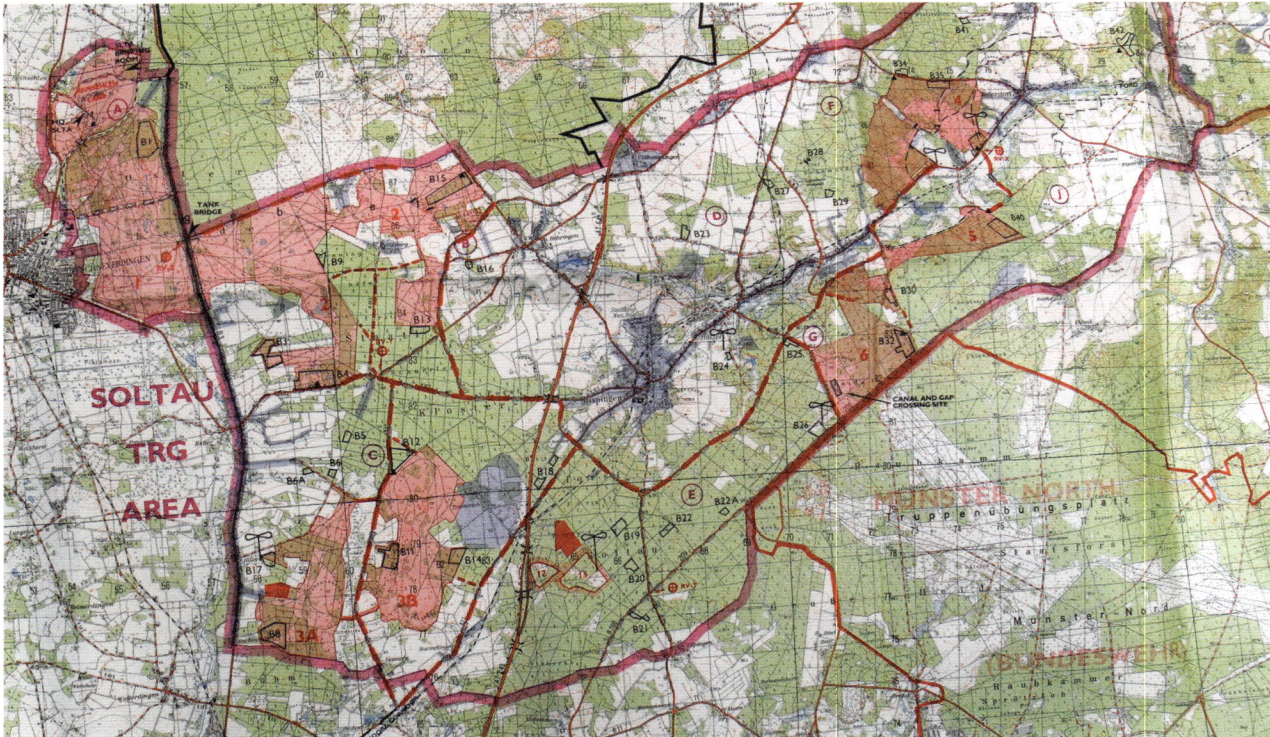

The Soltau-Lüneburg Training Area. The red areas were the manoeuvre areas for armoured vehicles (Crown)

environmental movement had been protesting about the military use of the heath area since the mid-1980s, which the British had made concessions to. In 1990, for example, a break in training of several weeks had been agreed during the time when the heath was in bloom during the peak tourist period between August and September. Increased urbanisation also meant that more and more people lived near the training area, and were having their lives disrupted. The political climate of *Options for Change*, combined with the effects of German reunification, meant that an agreement was reached in 1991 that all training would cease. The last training package there ran from 28th January to 11th February 1994, and the agreement between the British and German governments was not renewed when it ran out on 31st July 1994 and the area was formally handed back.

But first it needed to be repaired. Courage was head of the British Forces Liaison Organisation (Germany) at the time, and helped facilitate this process. As he recalls, the damage inflicted by such rigorous training was severe: 'We'd absolutely mashed it ... It had been devastated.' It was a cratered landscape, marked by ridges and rises created by the passage of hundreds of armoured vehicles over the decades. In winter it was covered by pools of icy mud,

and in summer it was thick with sand clouds. The British therefore had to put an enormous amount of work into stabilising, restoring and repairing what damage had been caused. An engineer plant squadron was put to use, filling ditches, rebuilding walls and doing anything else that might appease the local farmers and landowners. It took two years, and was as much a training exercise as it was a hearts and minds operation.

Soltau had been a major part of life for those who served in the British Army in Germany. It had been an area given over to battlegroup-size manoeuvre and while the main area was challenging to operate on, for those on recce vehicles the Lüneburg extension allowed unparalleled opportunities for freedom of movement, observation work and map-reading skills. Places that had become synonymous with serving in Germany, such as Reinsehlen Camp, the Tank Bridge, the Jerry Can, the Pylon Line and not forgetting the Schwindebeck River – the final resting place of one or more armoured vehicles that could not be recovered from the banks – were gone forever.

The handing back of Soltau saw the end of an era for British forces in another way. Since 1974, British soldiers on the training area had enjoyed supplements to their

rations when on exercise that had been provided by Wolfgang Meier and his fast food van. Meier had begun in 1974, taking over an existing food van business that had been run by a Brit and operated around the Bergen-Hohne area. He had heavily modified a blue Mercedes van to make it suitable for driving across country, meaning he could get into the hides and lager areas that the British troops were using, even during exercises. His ability to find troops who considered themselves concealed, and then get to them, was legendary – though on several occasions his van had to be towed out of difficulty by an armoured vehicle after bogging down. Wolfgang the Bratty Man quickly became an icon of the British Army of the Rhine, and part of the fabric of life on the training area – a 'legend in his own lifetime', in the words of Melvin. He sold Wittinger Beer, and his chips and mayonnaise were highly sought after. His van even played a special tune to alert everyone to his arrival. After the SLA closed, he ran a small campsite near his home in Heber.

However, the bluster of the politicians' public speeches about resolving decades-long disputes, or taking back ownership of real estate occupied by the British, often contrasted with views held privately by the officials of the towns they occupied. Privately there was considerable alarm over the potential impacts of the drawdown of British forces. Verden's Bürgermeister was shocked when Rupert Smith told him the British were leaving:

'The Bürgermeister's reaction was, "Who's going to play at the Schützenfest? Where are we going to get a band

from?" And then he said, "But we've always had a garrison." … We were so embedded in the society of Verden that there was a working assumption that it would be a British Army band that would play at the Schützenfest, and we were the extension of an historical trend that had started in the 1600s.'

Russell Law had arrived in Germany in 1993 with the REME, and found his preconceptions about the relationship between the Army and the local Germans didn't match the reality:

'I had it completely and utterly wrong … when we pulled out of Dortmund and closed the whole of Dortmund down, I had a chat with a few people and I said, "Oh, you'll be pleased once we move!" And they went, "Why would we be pleased when you've gone?" I said, "Well, it's known the squaddies cause a bit of trouble downtown." And they went, "Not bothered. Even slightly. It's life, we kind of grew up with it! But you've got to think about the other side: the massive amount of employment that we get out of here, the money, the income, the economy … All of that's gone!" … So I had a complete misconception of the relationship between us and German people, prior to obviously marrying a German and living more in a German community.'

Courage noted that in the nearly 30 years he had been in Germany the relationship with the local people had been transformed. The occupier mentality was completely gone. More importantly, this change had occurred 'right through the ranks'. Arguably it had been the

LEFT: **Part of the human landscape of Soltau was the legendary Wolfgang Meier, who provided hot food and liquid refreshment to the British troops exercising there. His van was a welcome sight for many** (Wolfgang Meier)

RIGHT: **Soldiers of the Coldstream Guards enjoying a break catered by Wolfgang, 1993** (John Henderson Collection)

ordinary soldiers, rather than officers, who had driven this over the previous decades, in particular with their relationships with German women, but also in their willingness to get out of their camps and into the local towns. Nina Smith, who served in the Women's Royal Army Corps and was based in Krefeld, saw this first-hand, and realised how much her life in Germany differed from that of her mother's when she was growing up as part of an Army family in Germany:

'I went to local pubs, I went to local eateries, I shopped in the local places ... For me, the only thing I really bought from the NAAFI was cigarettes, alcohol and teabags ... generally, I preferred the German food: paprika crisps ... their bratwurst. There was a lot of things in the local supermarkets I preferred ... I think after a period of time, wives would shop locally because it was better for them, and they would become more integrated into the local community. And I think it was easier for them than it was in my mother's day. Because my mum was a bit shy and introverted and wouldn't say boo to a goose, so for her to go over there and start speaking or trying to speak German ... she would have found this extremely hard.'

Links between the two communities were further driven by social and recreational activities. Sport had been the first and main area of British-Germany unity and friendship. Soldiers regularly took part in the sports teams of their local towns, or joined running clubs. Other sports, such as Enduro – cross-country motorcycling – had been introduced to Germany by the British, but enthusiastically taken up by the locals. Regular competitions brought the two together.

At a formal level, more towns had been twinned, and the Germans increasingly awarded their local units with a Fahnenband – an honour similar to the Freedom of the City. The British Army had become part of the fabric of the local area. As Melvin believes, 'we were regarded as friends', which meant that, when bases invariably closed throughout the 1990s, 'towns were sorry to see the Allies go'.

Despite the changing political climate, there were close links between the British and the local Germans, a real legacy of the previous 50 years. As Smith summarised best: 'You were there. You were part of this place ... And it wasn't you as you. It was us, the British Army, all their living memory.' The end of the Cold War had undoubtedly

removed the main imperative for the British forces to be in Germany, and Smith for one could not foresee the British presence lasting long into the 1990s:

'I had thought we'd all be out of there by the end of the decade. If you'd told me that we'd still be scrabbling around in 2018 I'd have laughed my socks off. The only reason we were staying was we had nowhere to put these people in the UK, it wasn't a question of that we needed to be there. That was my understanding.'

However, many others recognised the value of living and working in Germany, and retaining a British military footprint there.

THE LAUNCHPAD

Global events following the end of the Cold War would keep the British in Germany. The speed of change of the early 1980s and 1990s was rapid not only in Germany, but also across the world. The forces in Germany would be at the forefront of the British response. For them, change came quickly, and it was lasting. Hew Pike, who had commanded the 22nd Armoured Brigade until 1989, noted what life was like right up until the end of the Cold War:

'It was a very comfortable existence ... You might have had a six-week deployment to Suffield, Alberta and BATUS in Canada for a very demanding period of armoured

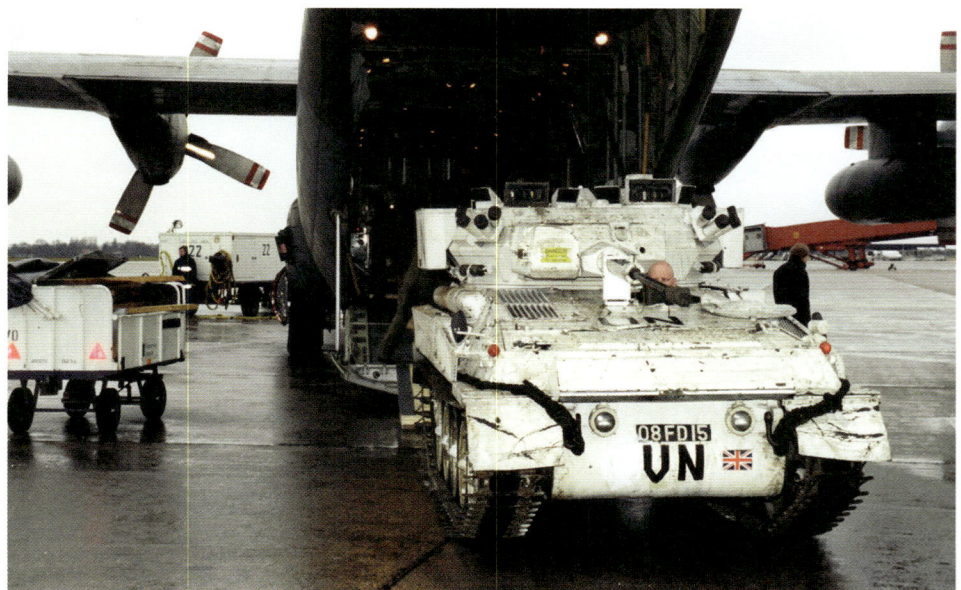

British forces prepare equipment for the UN deployment to the Balkans, mid-1990s [Crown]

LEFT: Challenger tanks of C Squadron Queen's Dragoon Guards in the 'mud park' in Bosanski Petrovac, Bosnia, during the Regiment's tour there between June and December 1996 (Crown)

RIGHT: Soldiers of the King's Royal Hussars on mounted patrol with pack horses, alongside their Challenger 1 main battle tanks, in the Mrkonjic Grad area of Bosnia, 1997. Three squadrons of The King's Royal Hussars, part of Multi-National Division (South West), were based at Mrkonjic Grad. They were equipped with Challenger I tanks, Warrior armoured infantry fighting vehicles and Scimitars light tanks (Crown)

training, but that was your only time out of the comfortable pattern of life in BAOR, where you had the Rhine Army Summer Show and lots of other wonderful things going on, lots of skilled horsemanship and so forth. Nothing against any of that, but it settled, rather like the Indian Army must have been ... into this routine pattern of life, which rather like the operation concept you started to assume exactly what it was going to be like ... It got complacent, too comfortable by half.'

Britain would play a major role in attempting to navigate the disorder that followed the collapse of Communism in Europe. Beginning in 1992, the deployment to Bosnia drew heavily on those units based in Germany, and the pace of these deployments would not slacken. Whereas previously soldiers had been kept occupied through training, now it would be pre-deployment training, and the deployments themselves, that would consume their time. The 2nd Battalion, Royal Anglian, for example, deployed from Trenchard Barracks in Celle to Split and onwards into Bosnia from April 1994.

For other soldiers involved in these deployments, like Pazcul Barton, who had arrived in BAOR in 1989 as a private soldier and then worked across Germany in various roles, there was a marked change from what the Army had been doing when he first joined:

'I was under no illusion what I was coming out here to do. We were briefed: going to Germany, you're there as a Cold War element. And that's what we trained. We were permanently in training. If we weren't downtown, we were on exercise. And that's how it rolled. But over the years, as that came to an end, our role changed; we had more peacekeeping duties to do all over the world, so all our Cold War training, we kind of retuned, rejigged and then went off on ops. We were permanently stationed in Germany, going away all the time. For the period after the Cold War, I was away a lot of the time, I was out of here ... That's actually a hard period to describe, going from the Cold War to non-Cold War times, because we went into a lull but we went on a lot more operations then.'

Fidelix Datson served with the Royal Artillery and was stationed in Bergen-Hohne from 1993 to 1996. For him, life in Germany was still good – though the removal of the threat of the Soviets meant that some of the disadvantages of some of the postings became more apparent, especially as the Army navigated the ramifications of *Options for Change* and re-established its sense of purpose. Even so, this could be turned into an advantage:

'I was based in Hohne and Hohne is in the middle of nowhere. I think one of the phrases people used to use was, 'Hohne is not a word, it's a sentence.' And therefore you're forced to socialise with everyone. And actually, it's quite good because we had a good bunch of officers there who got on quite well within the garrison itself and who got on quite well with other garrison units as well ... we'd have parties in our mess, we'd go to other messes for parties as well ... I enjoy playing sports so I was

LEFT: A Warrior, painted white for UN duties, navigates a bridge with some difficulty in Bosnia. Difficult road conditions were a major hazard for British soldiers deployed to the Balkans (NAM)

BELOW: Soldiers of the 2nd Battalion, Royal Anglian Regiment on their tour of Bosnia in 1994

playing rugby and football as well. So actually, time-wise it worked very well ... '

What Germany represented for the British had changed. The Army was no longer static there. It became a place from where the British would launch back into expeditionary warfare, a place from where they could move directly to the trouble spots and disorder that swept parts of Europe in the aftermath of the Cold War. Change came quickly and it was lasting. As Melvin noted, 'Now it was a launchpad. By the 1990s, Germany was just seen to be a firm base ... with good training areas, good accommodation, good welfare, good education, good value of life, etc. ... units could launch from there to anywhere in the world and be ready to go.'

The appeal of living in Germany remained for Service personnel, and it was still a draw. Jim Toms, for example, was not alone in trying to get a posting back into the country after being posted to the UK; in his words, 'I was desperate to go back to Germany; I just didn't want to be based in the UK.' But at the same time, service living in Germany had also changed – at both the professional and the social level. With the end of the Cold War, the need to maintain the 90 per cent manning levels that had so dominated life had gone. People were therefore far more able to spend their weekends at home in the UK if they wanted to. This had a noticeable effect on the social life on the bases. Squadron Leader Andrew Smith was a flight commander at RAF Brüggen in the immediate aftermath of the Cold War. He had served in Germany before, but four and a half years had passed between his postings, and the difference shocked him: 'The whole ethos of squadrons and the way they conducted themselves in Germany had changed ... I just couldn't believe how much the whole thing had changed.'

British society, from where the newest drafts of personnel were being drawn, had also changed from previous decades. With more and more partners of Service personnel having careers of their own, the attraction to 'follow the drum' was diminished. Spouses were less inclined to give up these careers and accompany their partners to Germany, which resulted in the nature of service changing. In this the RAF was certainly worse effected than the Army, but it was not a unique problem, and both services saw the impact of the changing attitudes. As Smith noted, 'I guess maybe there were more of the young guys who

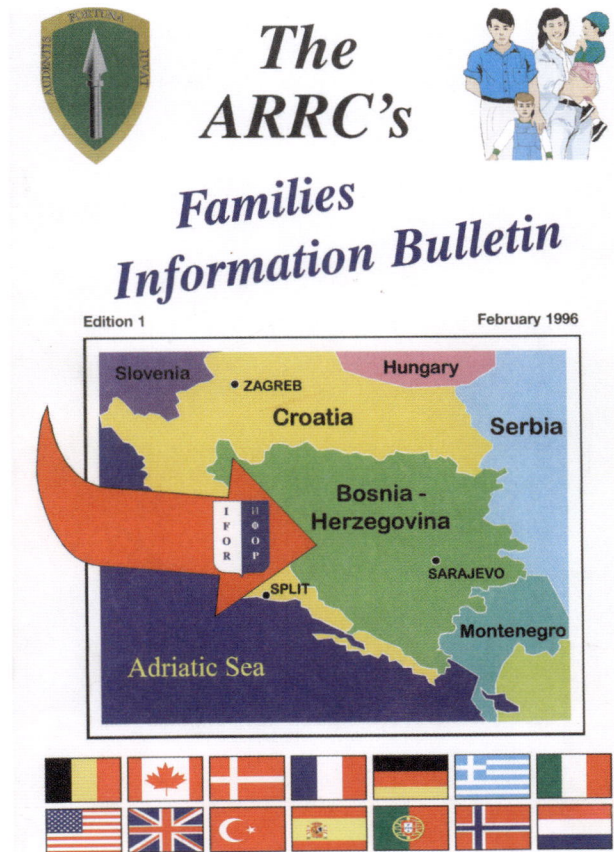

The first edition of the *The ARRC's Families Information Bulletin,* covering February and March 1996 [NAM]

were on squadron; there were more graduates than when I first joined, and of course they met future wives at university ... they had careers that were based in the UK.' Ultimately, this meant that:

'We had a lot of guys who wanted to do the job but didn't want to do it in Germany. Come Friday tea time they didn't go to happy hour, they got in their cars and drove back to the UK. And they were requesting not to do flying time on a Monday morning so they could come back Sunday night and get a few hours kip ... Things were changing. Whereas when I first joined, when I first got married, the squadron, the station basically ran your life; the rest of your life went around what was required of you by the job. It was a vocation, not a job. And we could see that that was changing. And it was quite uncomfortable to live with at times.'

The British military continued to make the most of living and working in Germany. It offered facilities unmatched by those available anywhere else. But as the 20th century came to an end, it was clear that a particular era of British Forces Germany had ended with it.

TURBULENCE

2000-2010

THE WORLD CONTINUES TO CHANGE

As Britain and NATO continued to react and adapt to the changing dynamics in Europe following the collapse of the Soviet Union and the end of the Cold War, further questions were asked as to what the British Armed Forces were actually for – and by implication how big they needed to be, and how they should be equipped. Was it a warfighting organisation or a force designed for interventionist, peacekeeping operations across the world? It had conducted both types of operation in the previous decade with considerable success.

Britain was prepared in the aftermath of the Cold War, and more than capable of deploying across the world. Its forces had been recast as expeditionary and interventionist, as seen in the deployments of the 1990s. Europe itself was also changing. Armies across the continent were being reduced in size – Britain's had reduced to around 100,000 by 2000, around 6,000 less than the target – and former adversaries who had been part of the Warsaw Pact were joining NATO. A new political outlook on Britain's place in the world resulted in huge changes for the British military.

The tone had been set by the government's Strategic Defence Review (SDR) of July 1998. The report had identified that the British Armed Forces should be able to mount expeditionary operations at a divisional level, and respond to international crises. One of these divisions would be the 1st (UK) Armoured Division in Germany, containing the majority of the Army's heavy armour and its Main Battle Tanks, and the other would be the 3rd (UK) Mechanised Division, which was based

in the UK and designed to fulfil a lighter role. The review also recommended that the Army should expect and be able to undertake a smaller operational deployment at the same time should it be necessary, carrying out something similar to what had taken place in the Balkans in the previous decade. However, it was made clear that it would not expect both deployments to involve warfighting or to maintain them longer than six months at the same time.

As for the RAF, the process of recalling the squadrons from Germany that had begun in the mid-1990s continued. With the ban on low-level flying in force in Germany, training now needed to be done in the UK anyway, which hastened the end of the relationship between the RAF and Germany. The view emanating from Whitehall was also that any requirement to send out aircraft could be better coordinated from the UK. In 2001, 56 years of flying from German airfields came to an end. At its peak in the 1950s, there had been 26,000 people serving with the RAF in Germany at 19 separate

PREVIOUS: Iraqi civilians seek the help of a soldier serving with Number 2 Company 1st Battalion The Irish Guards to locate their child caught up in the panic caused by incoming small arms fire from Iraqi positions in Basra on 20th March 2003. The Battalion had deployed for the invasion of Iraq from Oxford Barracks in Münster (Crown)

bases. But no longer. RAF Nordhorn, the aviation bombing and gunnery range close to the Dutch border in Lower Saxony, was handed back to the Germans in 2001 – though the RAF have retained a presence there and still operate alongside NATO partners. RAF Brüggen near Elmpt in North Rhine-Westphalia, the last remaining air station, was formally closed in a ceremony on 15th June 2001 and by September 2001, the last Tornado aircraft had relocated to RAF Marham in East Anglia. Brüggen was not given back to the German Luftwaffe, but to the Army, and it was renamed Javelin Barracks in 2002. It became home to soldiers of the Royal Signals and the Intelligence Corps. They would remain there until 2015. The 18-hole RAF Brüggen Golf Club became the West Rhine Golf Club.

The new strategic outlook and the operational requirements had also affected the Army. They had been forced to adapt in the 1990s to humanitarian operations in the Balkans, but by 2000 they were more practised and proficient, indeed they had settled into a routine. The Formation Readiness Cycle included preparation for a tour in the Balkans as part of the development of formation skills for the Army units. Northern Ireland deployments continued following the Good Friday Agreement of 10th April 1998 and the threat level on these from terrorism, while reduced, was still present, but ultimately, a new normal had been established for the soldiers in Germany. General Sir Richard Shirreff, had first arrived in West Germany in 1978 as a Troop Leader and saw this first hand when he returned to

Corporal Jonathan Duffy from Manchester, serving with the 1st Battalion, The Irish Guards, bathes his feet next to his Warrior during a break for personal admin in Iraq in March 2003. The Irish Guards had deployed to Iraq with 7th Armoured Brigade from Oxford Barracks in Münster (WO2 Giles Penfound/Crown)

143

Bergen-Hohne as the commander of 7th Armoured Brigade in 1999: 'Germany had effectively become a home base ... for expeditionary operations to the Balkans.'

British Forces Germany ended the 20th century and began the 21st with a commitment to the Balkans. The headquarters and elements from 102nd Logistic Brigade deployed to Kosovo in 1999, and they were followed by 7th Armoured Brigade who deployed there on Operation AGRICOLA III in February 2002 under Shirreff's command. Based in Pristina, Shirreff saw his troops' task as being very much in the same vein as those previous deployments to the Balkans, where peacekeeping and the prevention of further ethnic violence were the major requirements. In the mind of the British government, there was a clear moral imperative to the mission and the humanitarian dimension was clear, though as always the situation on the ground was more complicated. Despite being launched to protect Kosovo from Serb aggression, there was also a need to protect Serb communities inside Kosovo from retaliatory acts of violence, as Shirreff pointed out:

'We found our task was, number one, to ensure that there could be no embarrassing invasion by the Serbs. So we started on that premise, that we had a plan to ensure we could protect our bit of Kosovo. My main effort was to protect the remaining Serb communities in my area of operations against Albanian sectarian terrorism and killings.'

This mission was not about conventional warfighting; it was about operations within a civilian population that needed stabilising. One major obstacle the British had to overcome was the destruction of infrastructure, and they were able to build on their previous experience of working alongside international partners and civilian aid agencies in the previous decade to achieve their objectives. Stabilising fractured territories and communities and enabling the conditions for a peaceful return to eventual prosperity, backed by the potential use of force, was at the core of these missions. Shirreff again summarised the experience of operating in Kosovo:

'What was it like? It was pretty well trashed; there was no town or village which wasn't pretty much destroyed. The infrastructure was in a very bad way. Life [was] very

tough. And so the UN administration was working hard to try and rebuild the sinews of life.

This was where one really understood and learned on the job the importance of that comprehensive approach, the recognition that you have to protect the people, but you've also got to ensure reconstruction, development – and working with other stakeholders was critical to ultimately producing a degree of stability and protection.'

In the aftermath of the seismic changes arising from the end of the Cold War, and the cultural and practical results of the *Options for Change* restructure, by the end of 2000 the Army in Germany had seemingly found a routine. Yet events in the United States the following year were to result in a complete rethink of that routine.

TURBULENT TIMES

On 11th September 2001, the two towers of the World Trade Centre in New York and the Pentagon in Washington DC were attacked by al-Qaeda in an action that shocked the world. Soon, British forces were again being pushed to redefine their role and adapt to a new threat. This would set in motion a series of commitments that would transform the professional and domestic lives of the British Army in Germany. As Major General Mungo Melvin recalled, this was the beginning of a period of turbulence and intensive operations that continued the trend of the 1990s, but escalated it to a new level, one that completely transformed life for the British forces: 'By and large, apart from Northern Ireland, 1980s life in Germany was very stable. The 1990s, with the Gulf War and with the Balkans, where the Army was continuously deployed, it never finished operations. It went from the Balkans in Bosnia-Herzegovina, then to Kosovo, to Afghanistan, to Iraq, and then back to Afghanistan.'

The 9/11 attacks of 2001 convinced the UK government that fighting international terrorism required smaller, more precise forces that could be rapidly deployed in expeditionary operations. A *New Chapter to Strategic Defence Review* was prepared and published in 2002, which aimed to address the new strategic reality. It identified that, while asymmetric warfare had been

considered in 1998, it underestimated the scale of the threat. The UK Armed Forces needed to be recast: the greatest threat to Britain in the 21st century was international terrorism rather than conventional war, and the best place to fight this threat was overseas, rather than on the streets of Britain. As the report stated:

'The Armed Forces can play a role as part of a cross-Government and international effort to counter the threat from international terrorism at home and to engage it overseas. Much of the capacity needed for key operations – such as operations to stabilise, coerce or find-and-strike – will come from the new force structure the SDR put in train.

But new elements and capabilities are needed to seize what may be fleeting opportunities to engage terrorists, to deal with them in remote areas and cater for their possible acquisition of CBRN devices. We need to look further into how we should allocate the investment

which is needed, including, for example, to intelligence gathering, network-centric capability (including enhanced strike and Special Forces capabilities and unmanned air vehicles), improved mobility and fire power for more rapidly deployable lighter forces, temporary deployed accommodation for troops, and night operations.'

In 2003, a new Defence White Paper, *Delivering Security in a Changing World*, was launched. This highlighted how, since the previous Defence review, the world had changed so that the British Armed Forces faced 'an even broader range, frequency, and often duration of tasks than envisaged in 1998'. At the same time, NATO had also evolved as it had grown, moving through an 'evolution from large static forces to smaller response forces, able to undertake operations beyond the NATO area itself'. It was identified that there was no existential, conventional threat to NATO in 2003. Having been the frontline of NATO, the troops in Germany were

Soldiers serving in Basra were determined to enjoy the 2006 World Cup despite being in Iraq. While on a routine patrol in Basra city on his first operational tour of Iraq, Gunner Philip Peers serving with 17 Battery, 26 Regiment Royal Artillery, who had deployed from Mansergh Barracks in Gütersloh, found time to have a kick around with some soccer-mad Iraqi kids. 'They love football and all I did was a few kick ups and they were shouting "Beckham",' he said.

going to have to change how they operated to reflect the new strategic reality.

Ultimately the review made it clear that the British Armed Forces would continue to be used for strengthening international peace and security, and that they would act as 'a force for good in the world'.

Much as it had in the First Gulf War, the Army in Germany would play a major role in the deployment to Iraq in 2003, which became known as Operation TELIC. 1st (United Kingdom) Division took part, with the divisional headquarters deploying from Herford, and 7th Armoured Brigade deploying from Fallingbostel and Bergen-Hohne. The 2003 deployment had a major impact on those left behind. The spouses of British Forces Germany had become used to the ritual calendar of life in Germany, with exercises, training in Canada at BATUS and deployments to the Balkans. But Iraq in 2003 appeared different, as Wendy Faux, who had served in Germany as a regular officer in the Royal Artillery and a reservist, and was living in Herford as the division deployed, remembers:

'This was nothing that we had known before. Although the marker before it had obviously been 1991. But people were saying, "No, it's going to be different this time," but they couldn't tell us why it was going to be different and how it was going to be different. And it was very surreal, because certainly the plans, obviously, weren't being told to the families, so we didn't know what the contingency plans were at all …

And it was quite a long build-up. Because it was, "They're going before Christmas, they're going over Christmas." And then they went after; I think they deployed in January, February, something like that. It was a lot later. So there was lot of anticipation time. That's the worst bit.'

Invariably those personnel being deployed shared the feelings of excitement and trepidation that came from having the opportunity to do the job for which they had trained, but for the families left behind there were different challenges. In Britain, a million people had marched against the war in protest over the UK government's actions. Germany as a country was also a

Concrete blast wall sections decorated with murals of 7th Armoured Brigade's jerboa insignia, Allenby Lines, Basra Air Station, Iraq, 2009 (Crown)

vocal critic of the war in Iraq, and when war began to look likely in early 2003 there were protests on German streets as well that focused on the British Army garrisons. This had a major impact on those left behind by the deployment: the spouses. It was on a scale unlike anything previously seen in British deployments. Faux again relates the story:

'I think the difference … was that the Germans … didn't agree with the British decision to go to war or to deploy. And the fact that we were deploying from Germany, from their soil, meant that they … felt that they had a bigger voice … And there was the understanding that actually, they didn't consider how they made us feel, because we didn't want our husbands to go but they are trained soldiers. That's what they do. They do whatever the political masters require them to do …

And in Herford, it was quite easy to block off the main entrance of the headquarters. And generally speaking, because of the nature of the community, there were always lots of activities that were Anglo-German activities, there was the Anglo-German Club, and so it seemed very strange all of a sudden to have people protesting outside the camp. And, of course, the school was inside the camp, the nursery was inside the camp, I had to go into the camp to go to work … It was just very intimidating … But when I was talking to this other person, [a] German lady about it, she said, "I didn't even consider

A good-natured German protest about houses vacated by the British in Münster 2010/11 being left unoccupied in a town where there was a serious housing shortage (LWL-Mediaezentrum für Westfalen)

how it made you feel as a family member, that your spouse is going and how it would impact your family." '

The year 2003 and Operation TELIC marked only the beginning of a turbulent period for the Army in Germany. A new routine of pre-deployment training, an operational tour and then post-operational leave was established. All three brigades that were based in Germany (and 102 Logistic Brigade) were called upon in the subsequent TELIC operations. In 2004, 20th Armoured Brigade went to Iraq as part of TELIC III, and were based out of Basrah Palace as part of the Multinational Division. They were followed in 2005 by 4th Armoured Brigade from Osnabrück. In April 2006, 20th Armoured Brigade returned to southern Iraq again for TELIC VIII, and was deployed throughout Basra, Al Amarah and Al Muthanna Provinces. In 2005, 7th Armoured Brigade returned to Iraq, and then again between June and December 2008 for TELIC XII. In 2009, 20th Armoured Brigade carried out the last combat operations in Iraq as part of TELIC XIII. Overlapping, the British commitment to Afghanistan also increased, which as Iraq was wound down began drawing more soldiers from Germany, and would last well into the next decade.

This relentless cycle had an impact on the domestic lives of soldiers and their families. While troops may have been based in Germany, they were actively deployed elsewhere. This certainly blurred the lines between living and working, and it also added new pressures on the welfare system that looked after the spouses and families of those left behind. The frequency and intensity of operations, including the pre-deployment training, undoubtedly ramped up pressure on the families, especially for those living far away from their own support networks. There were also other challenges. It was announced that 4th Armoured Brigade, for example, was to move from Osnabrück to Catterick in the UK in 2006, and the drawdown would take place while it was in Iraq. By 31st March 2009, the Osnabrück garrison was to be closed. Those living in Germany suddenly had another major issue to worry about: they had to pack up their belongings and prepare to move back to an area very few of them had lived in before, and they had no idea what awaited them there.

The strength of the Army community in Germany was reinforced during this period of activity around the continued deployments on high-intensity operations, and it proved its resilience. The Army had well-practised formal welfare procedures in place, but the informal support provided by the unique Army community in Germany was a point of difference. Indeed, for all the questions asked in the aftermath of Iraq and Afghanistan about policy, doctrine and equipment, the years between 2000 and 2010 saw the community left behind in Germany perfect their roles and duties, and generate huge benefits to the fighting component. It was a grassroots movement, one that received enthusiastic support from the chain of command who recognised its value.

Building on the experience of the previous deployment to the Gulf in 1990, magazines for those left behind, like *4 Home*, were produced for when 4th Armoured Brigade went to Iraq for TELIC IX in 2007–08, which provided practical information. Simple activities like coffee mornings became more important, and other events were put on to fill the time. As Faux noted,

'All of a sudden there was this rise of the community and all those spaces were filled with community activities. The tanks maybe weren't going out and exercising, you didn't see armoured vehicles driving around, there's

no firing or less firing on the ranges, but there was more activity going on. And so you found yourself going into camp more.'

Steps were also taken to limit the potential impact of rumours that were coming back from Iraq, in particular. BFBS was used during the early TELICs as an opportunity for the senior command to speak directly to the families, to reassure them about what was happening in the Middle East. As in 1991, blueys were initially the main form of communication in 2003. But on subsequent tours these were gradually replaced by email – which became known as e-blueys – and other instant connectivity as the decade went on.

As the scale of commitment increased to Iraq, and later on Afghanistan, drawing in more and more of the British Army in Germany, the local community did more to look after and care for the families left behind. This included the local German community. As Pazcul Barton, who in 2018 was in the Staff and Personnel Support branch, noted: 'The interactions with the Germans that I had, they realised that the families were going away and there were strong friendships, so not only did the English families have the English support from the military community, they also had the support from their German friends as well.'

ABOVE LEFT: *4 Home* magazine, the garrison magazine for 4th Mechanised Brigade, which provided guidance to families relocating to Catterick from Germany [Crown]

ABOVE RIGHT: Major Spenlove-Brown and family on the return of the Royal Scots Dragoon Guards to Wessex Barracks in Fallingbostel from Afghanistan in 2008 [Crown]

OPPOSITE TOP: On 19th July 2008, 4th Mechanised Brigade – recently retitled – held their Farewell to Osnabrück. 500 soldiers were on parade, accompanied by the Band of the Scots Guards. The Honour Guard had been provided by 4 Regiment Royal Artillery, the longest serving unit in Osnabrück. The Mayor of Osnabrück, Boris Pistorius, took the salute [Crown]

OPPOSITE BOTTOM LEFT: The 4th Mechanised Brigade Farewell to Münster, with the 1st Battalion, Scots Guards and the Queen's Dragoon Guards on parade, took place on 18th July 2008 [Crown]

OPPOSITE BOTTOM RIGHT: The Osnabrück farewell parade took place in pouring rain, but was still well attended by locals eager to show their appreciation for the British [Crown]

LEFT: Major General Mungo Melvin and other guests at the Wreath-Laying Ceremony Commemorations to mark the 250th anniversary of the Battle of Minden, 1st August 2009. British Forces played a major role in helping the town – a major garrison for the British for decades – to stage a programme of mostly events for the enjoyment of the local German population (Crown)

BELOW: The Friendship Bridge, an M3 Bridge staged by 412 Amphibious Troop RE (Volunteers) and the Bundeswehr's Heavy Engineer Regiment 130, in commemorations to mark the 250th Anniversary of the Battle of Minden, 1st August 2009 (Crown)

While the Germans had not changed in their opposition to the war in Iraq, the protests of the initial deployment were a flashpoint, and were not repeated. A distinction was made between the decision to go to war and those who were doing the fighting, as well as those who were left behind during the deployments. During the first TELIC, Herford's town council brought a bus into camp and familiarised families with the practical questions of how to buy tickets, as well as how to use the train, in order to give greater confidence to spouses and families who were looking to get beyond the confines of camp – but had perhaps never done so before. Local towns and businesses arranged for discounts for service families, or special sessions, whether it was giving military families free tickets for the swimming pool; giving discounts and special sessions at the Paderbini Land softplay centre in Paderborn; or closing the local ice rink to the German public so that military families could go there together. The Herforder Brauerei threw a huge festival for 1st (United Kingdom) Division when they returned from Iraq. This made the departure of some units from Germany even more poignant. On 19th July 2008, on their return from operations in Iraq, 4th Mechanised Brigade held a Service of Thanksgiving in the Domkirche in Osnabrück, as well as the final parade to exercise the Freedom of the City that they had been awarded in 1980 – before they moved back to the UK for good.

The importance of local support for the families left behind was clear. But the community leaders also needed to be reminded what it was the British were doing, and be advocates for the people at home. Despite the political hostility to the deployment in Germany, a small group of local Mayors from the region of Bergen-Hohne were invited to visit 7th Armoured Brigade in Basrah in 2003, with the aim of seeing for themselves the situation on the ground and experiencing the work of the brigade in supporting the new Iraq after toppling the dictator Saddam Hussein. The escorted group were flown on a RAF flight via Cyprus to Kuwait, where they were met by members of 2nd Battalion REME, who had deployed to the Middle East from Bad Fallingbostel. As a

unit, they had one of the oldest partnerships with any town in Germany, having been established in the 1960s.

From there the German guests were escorted into Iraq and to an airfield on the outskirts of the city, where the rear echelon of 7th Armoured Brigade was set up. What followed was a tour of the brigade area, and visiting Basrah Palace to meet the headquarters staff. They also visited the outlying posts within the district of Basrah and units such as 1st Battalion, Royal Regiment of Fusiliers and the Royal Scots Dragoon Guards, who were based in their districts in Germany. Among the interesting stop-off points was the so-called 'Bread Basket', from which supplies, held centrally by Ba'athist party officials, were distributed on a rationing basis. The visit had the desired effect in that it was immediately apparent how severely controlled the Iraqi population had been, along with the shortages that they had been subjected to by the previous regime.

The Germans were also able to see how the Iraqi population viewed the British, and that initially it seemed that they were being welcomed as liberators after the oppression of Saddam. Later all three of the Mayors invited 'their' units to a reception on their return, and were able to report favourably in the local press about their experiences in Iraq. As the Oberbürgermeister of Celle said, having visited a company of Fusiliers in their outpost on the edge of Basrah, 'I would like to thank you for showing us the work you are doing here, and I shall invite you all to have a beer with me in the Town Hall when you return.' And he held true to his word when the Fusiliers returned to Germany a few weeks later as the first roulement of TELIC took place, and the battalion was also awarded the Freedom of the Town.

AWAY FROM OPERATIONS

Yet away from active operations, serving and living in Germany was still seen by most as being advantageous. This was not lost on Major General Mungo Melvin, who became General Officer Commanding United Kingdom Support Commmand (Germany) in 2006. As he said: 'Germany still had many, many advantages over service in Britain: better unit cohesion to some extent, better

training areas, better quality of life. That's why people in the 1990s and early 2000s wanted to serve in Germany.'

This was not an accident. Germany had become the launchpad for operations, and Melvin saw the value in securing the home front, of maintaining a base that would translate into greater operation effectiveness in the field. For Melvin, 'I saw my job very much as providing, for all my experience of Germany, that firm base, the best possible training areas, the best possible welfare, best housing, best education, best relations with the German community.'

Germany continued to offer the soldiers based there fantastic opportunities for those willing to embrace them, such as Lieutenant Colonel Billal Saddique of the Army Legal Service, who was stationed there between 1999 and 2009:

'Germany was great. I was single in the first few years and then married in the last few. It was great for travelling and so on. Beautiful part of the world, because you're bordered, I think, by nine countries, so great for travelling. I learnt some German, made some friends, did taekwondo, great singleton's posting. And then when I was married and had children, it was good on the exchange rate, you had tax-free status on certain goods, such as cars, so you could have a tax-free discounted car and sell it after a year and not make any real loss. So, it was enjoyable in that aspect.'

British Forces Germany helped to organise the annual swim along the part of the River Aller that ran through the town of Celle. The annual event, which first took place in 1966 and is the oldest of its kind in Germany, was organised as part of a training exercise for members for the German Life Guard Association (Crown)

Soldiers from 7th Armoured Brigade respond to a request to assist efforts to shore up the banks of the river Elbe during the floods in the Lüchow-Dannenberg area in 2002. Each of the 300 soldiers was awarded a High Water medal from the state of Lower Saxony for their participation in the relief effort (Crown/Private Collection)

The deployments and the steps both the British and the Germans had taken to integrate with each other were accelerated by the years of turbulence, but they were also part of the trend that saw the British and Germans living and socialising much closer together. Captain Daniel Wall of the Royal Signals noted that, unlike in previous eras, there was far greater interaction between the two groups:

'Interaction with the locals on an evening and a weekend was absolutely encouraged, and the locals enjoyed us being there. There was still a language barrier; a lot of British people when we go to Germany can't speak German, and they're not interested in speaking another language because we're British, we don't need to. So there's a language barrier there, but the locals, some of them try to speak English with you. If you try and speak German they try a little bit harder on their English.

There was a community feeling about a lot of Herford and it really was nice. We had our Signal Regiment, we had Divisional headquarters across the road, and then we had a couple of squadrons up in another camp, all around, obviously, within the town. So yeah, it was good. It was great to experience a completely different culture, a different way of life, a different style of cooking ... I was fortunate enough that I also played hockey out

there, for a civilian club called Arminia Bielefeld. So I got to experience the sporting side of life as well.'

Sport continued to be a major way of building bridges between the two communities. The Red and White Football Club on Hohne Camp was run by the British for the children of Service personnel and they would take part in local German competitions, for example. As the number of soldiers in Germany had reduced, opening up the regular events to the local German clubs served a dual purpose of both improving community relations, but also preserving the integrity of the competition.

It was not all smooth sailing and tireless friendship, however. There were occasional flashpoints, as Saddique noticed:

'There were some difficulties with Germany, because they have I think a five or six million Turkish immigrant population in the country, and there's most certainly tension between Turkish immigrants and Germans. And often I was thought to be Turkish, and when I explained that no I wasn't Turkish, but English, and they realised that I was English, that didn't really help my position much either. So, it did have some difficulties to it, being brown-skinned in Germany, I'm afraid to say.'

For those in the more isolated garrisons, such as Bergen-

Hohne or Fallingbostel, a strong sense of community pervaded that brought everyone together, both in times of crisis during deployments, but also in the times in between.

The British garrisons also served as good neighbours to the Germans. When they weren't on operations, they continued to host and support events for the local German community. They would help in the running of local sports events, such as the Aller Swim through Celle, a water-borne survival exercise in the middle of winter for thousands of participants. The Kiel Training Centre provided equipment for servicemen and their families to take part, but the Bergen-Hohne Garrison also helped with transport and facilities to help its smooth running. Soldiers would act as marshals at road races and marathons, or provide the necessary organisation and equipment for outdoor activities such as district orienteering competitions. The Queen's Birthday Reception, including a sunset ceremony and Beating Retreat, was also a formal event, whereby the garrisons would invite their local German dignitaries. The British also stepped up at times of crisis; soldiers turned out to help the Bundeswehr at the request of the local German government during the severe floods of 2002 in the Elbe Valley, delivering supplies and shoring up flood defences.

THE BEGINNING OF THE END

On 19th October 2010, the Conservative-Liberal Democrat coalition government published its plans for Defence reform: *Securing Britain in an Age of Uncertainty: The Strategic Defence and Security Review* (SDSR). The review was conducted in a climate of financial austerity, and its main aim was to reduce defence spending. It would see the Armed Forces cut its budget by 7.7 per cent over the next four years.

All three of Britain's Armed Forces would take cuts in manpower, and the new strategic reality was that any future overseas deployment would not be able to call on more than 30,000 personnel, including those elements from the Royal Navy and the Royal Air Force. In contrast, 46,000 personnel were deployed to the Gulf in 2003. For the Army, the plans laid out in the *Army 2020* plans were to reduce it in size to 82,000 regulars and 30,000 reservists, later upgraded to 35,000 in 2015. But most

significantly, the 20,000 troops (and their families) that were still based in Germany in 2010 were going to be recalled to the UK. As the SDSR stated, despite the rising threat from Russia and the important role played by the Army in showing solidarity with Britain's European partners, and not least the training and operational opportunities provided to its soldiers through being based in Germany, 'There is no longer any operational requirement for UK forces to be based there, and the current arrangements impose financial costs on the UK, disruption on personnel and their families and opportunity costs in terms of wider Army coherence. We therefore aim to withdraw all forces from Germany by 2020.'

The Army's permanent deployment to Germany was going to end. The long goodbye for the British in Germany was about to begin.

Brigadegeneral (Brigadier) Carsten Jacobson (later Lt Gen), Commander Panzerlehrbrigade 9, presents the Fahnenband to the Colour Party of 2nd Royal Tank Regiment on behalf of the German Federal Republic during the Queen's Birthday Reception at Schloss Bredebeck, Bergen-Hohne in 2008 (Crown)

OVERLEAF: Challenger 2 tanks of D Squadron, The Queen's Royal Hussars getting into position for a live firing battle run on Range 9 on the Bergen-Hohne training area in Northern Germany, 13th February 2019. This was the QRH's last firing camp when they – the last armoured regiment to be based in Germany – were based in Athlone Barracks in Sennelager; shortly after they began their relocation to Tidworth in the UK. QRH were the last armoured regiment to leave Germany (Tobias Wilkinson)

CHAPTER
IX

THE END OF AN ERA
2010-2019

RE-LOCATION, RE-LOCATION, RE-LOCATION

After the announcement in October 2010 that British Forces Germany would close, the Army began to reorganise and prepare. This was a well-trodden process, having begun really in the 1990s, with *Options for Change*. The immediate implications of the 2010 SDSR saw some units disbanded, such as 4 Regiment Royal Military Police and 8 and 24 Regiments Royal Logistic Corps, in Münster and Bielefeld respectively. Others were relocated as British Forces Germany centred on Bielefeld in North Rhine-Westphalia. The closure of British barracks was not a new phenomenon in Germany, and there had always been a sense of movement and flux across the British Zone. Yet those moves had been done in the greater context of BFG, and with a sense of continuity, but after 2010 there was undoubtedly a greater poignancy. A unique way of life was passing into history. The MFO boxes were not being packed up and sent to another garrison town in Lower Saxony or the North Rhine-Westphalia, but to the more unfamiliar Cottesmore and other barracks in the UK. Some soldiers' units that had never been stationed in the UK, and had been in Germany or further afield since 1945 were going home – yet home for them was Bergen-Hohne, Bad Fallingbostel or Gütersloh.

One of the more symbolic moves from Germany involved the Allied Rapid Reaction Corps, who left Rheindahlen in 2010. They relocated to Imjin Barracks, just outside Gloucester. The move was three years in the making, taking place in-between roles leading the International Security Assistance Force (ISAF) in Afghanistan in 2006 and 2011. General Sir Richard Shirreff was in command, and tasked with overseeing this move. He recalls the locals in Mönchengladbach and those serving with the ARRC greeted the occasion with similar feelings of sadness, from both a professional and a social sense. There were, he remembered, feelings of

'Deep, deep regret. Very, very strong regret ... because the thing that underpinned the ARRC's cohesion was the British as framework nation. And because the British were in Rheindahlen, and therefore, not in their own country ... There was a community and they were there.

ABOVE: How *Sixth Sense* covered news of the 2010 SDSR (Crown)

PREVIOUS SPREAD: 23 Amphibious Engineer Troop (part of 75 Engineer Regiment) and Schweres Pionierbattalion 130 of the Bundeswehr, both based in Minden, load their M3 Amphibious Rigs on to Deutschebahn trains to be transported to Poland for Exercise ANAKONDA

And the result of that was that there was such great integration with the, at that stage, 15 nations who provided staff to the ARRC, and a really, really terrific team effort.'

The relocation of the ARRC heralded the end for Joint Headquarters in Rheindahlen. What had survived the collapse of the Soviet Union and the remaking of the world in the aftermath of the Cold War could not escape the political imperative to reduce defence spending further. The headquarters of British Forces Germany moved from JHQ to Bielefeld in July 2013, and the military complex was handed back to German federal authorities on 13th December 2013.

It was a period of huge organisational and cultural change. Units were being rerolled, relocated or disbanded. Iconic sites of the British footprint in Germany were vacated and passed back into German ownership. Celle Station closed in 2012 when the 2nd Battalion, Royal Regiment of Fusiliers were the last to depart Trenchard Barracks, bringing to an end 66 years of British presence there. Celle had more than a long legacy as a military posting; it had also been the birthplace of the first BFBS television station in Germany in 1975.

The moves from 2010 onwards signalled the end of an era for the British forces. For so long, Germany had been the centre of Britain's armoured fighting component, but in 2015, 1st (United Kingdom) Division, the last British armoured division headquarters in Germany, moved from Herford to Imphal Barracks in York. The same year, 28 Engineer Regiment in Hameln was disbanded and Gordon Barracks closed, thereby ending the long and close relationship by the Royal Engineers with the famous 'Rat-Catcher' town on the River Weser. The unit's amphibious M3 bridging and ferrying vehicles were transferred to a German base in Minden. Javelin Barracks in Elmpt, having only been taken on from the RAF in 2002, also closed in 2015. Among the last occupants were 628 Signal Troop of the Royal Signals, who had only ever worked in Germany, having been specifically created to serve in 1st NATO Signal Battalion. The year 2016 saw Princess Royal Barracks in Gütersloh close, along with Alanbrooke Barracks in Paderborn and Tower Barracks in Dülmen – which was then taken over by the American forces in Germany, who were increasing

their footprint in the country at the same time as the British were drawing down. The scale of the change was unprecedented, and rapid. Within five years, more than 80 per cent of the troops stationed that had been stationed in Germany in 2010 had been relocated.

After 71 years, the Kiel Yacht Club was closed after a parade and formal ceremony in August 2016. These closures were the equivalent of entire towns moving away, and the impact this had influenced far more than just those in uniform. The spouses and families of the

TOP: A final Queen's Birthday Reception and Parade takes place at Villa Spiritus, the headquarters of the British Forces Liaison Organisation (Germany) in Bonn, before its closure in June 2011. Since 1945 it had been the home of the British Army's Liaison organisation with the German government (Crown)

ABOVE: Soldiers of 1 Royal Regiment of Fusiliers march through the historic town centre of Celle during their farewell parade in July 2012 (Crown)

soldiers being relocated were also affected, with the supporting infrastructure such as schools being closed down, too, as their pupils – and their parents – moved away. Shackleton, Slim, Montgomery, Gloucester and Heide Schools in the Bergen-Hohne Garrison, for example, all closed on 19th July 2015. The closure of Bergen-Hohne also saw the relocation of the BFBS studio that had been based there to Sennelager, as the British footprint contracted onto a mere handful of sites in Bielefeld, Gütersloh and Paderborn.

Running alongside all these changes were major active operations in which the Army in Germany continued to play a major role. While combat operations in Iraq had been formally ended in 2009, the Army dedicated its focus to Afghanistan. The launchpad of Germany simply prepared to send its shrinking number of soldiers to a different part of the world, and the two armoured brigades remaining in Germany would need to adapt yet again to a different operating environment; 20th Armoured Brigade took over command of Task Force Helmand on 9th October 2011, the start of Operation HERRICK XV. In October 2013, 7th Armoured Brigade deployed to Helmand, Kandahar and Kabul. Elements of 20th Armoured Brigade were also deployed on the last combat operations in Afghanistan before the final withdrawal of combat troops in October 2014 on HERRICK XX. The war in Afghanistan was not popular in the UK by 2014, but it still did not evoke as much public outcry as the war in Iraq had. Within Germany, the local community continued to support the soldiers of their garrisons who had been deployed. The fact that German soldiers were also deployed to Afghanistan was certainly significant in this. But it served to make the partings of the drawdown all the more poignant.

Each of the closures was marked by parades and acts of friendship between the Army and their German neighbours. On 14th November 2014, 7th Armoured Brigade, the famous Desert Rats, held their last parade as an armoured brigade ahead of their transformation into 7th Infantry Brigade, with 640 soldiers marching through the town of Bergen in Lower Saxony. The Headquarters was among the brigade units that was presented with a Fahnenband by the German Commander of the Regional Command for Lower Saxony, on behalf of the Federal Republic of Germany, to

mark their long period of friendship. It was an occasion, in the words of the 7th Armoured Brigade's commander at the time, Brigadier James Woodham, 'to celebrate a fantastic history that has been based here in Germany since the end of the Second World War and to thank our German hosts who have been so fantastic at looking after us whilst we've been here'. The Desert Rats left Germany the following year when Bergen-Hohne closed, moving back to Chilwell in the UK. It was the first time the brigade was headquartered outside of Germany since 1945.

For the Germans, the huge real estate being handed back was greeted with some enthusiasm. The opportunity to turn some of it into housing to help ease domestic pressures was welcomed, and there were plans to convert the accommodation blocks of the former Alanbrooke Barracks in Paderborn into new homes as part of a major residential development. Other barracks had been given over to universities, hospitals or businesses. In Celle, the enormous Taunton Barracks had already been handed back to the Germans in 1999, and had become the Neues Rathaus, or new town hall. Other barracks were swiftly repurposed too.

The reaction to the drawdown has been mixed. From a German perspective, it is part of a wider process of demilitarisation of Europe. For Carlo Dewe from Herford, it was inevitable that the British would leave eventually given that the Cold War has long been over:

'Many people in Herford regret that the British have left the town; they say the British were good customers,

LEFT: Soldiers of Royal Scots Dragoon Guards on parade in Bad Fallingbostel on 24th November 2011 to receive their campaign medals for their operational tour in Afghanistan from Andrew Robathan, the Parliamentary Undersecretary of State at the MoD and Minister for Veterans (Crown)

LEFT TOP: Marking the closure of the Joint Headquarters (JHQ) and the Rheindahlen Military Complex (RMC), a Farewell Parade was held on the Kapurinerplatz in Mönchengladbach's Altstadt, attended by the Oberbürgermeister Norbert Bude, Lord Mayor of Mönchengladbach, Major General John Henderson, GOC British Forces Germany and the Vice Chief of the Defence Staff, Air Chief Marshal Sir Stuart Peach (Crown)

RIGHT TOP: The final parade of 7th Armoured Brigade in Bergen-Hohne, November 2014 (Crown)

BOTTOM: 28 Engineer Regiment, based at Gordon Barracks, were disbanded in 2014. They held a final Freedom of Hameln Parade, marking the end of a British presence in the town dating back to 1945 (Crown)

1st Armoured Division Signal Regiment, which had been stationed in Germany since 1960, marching in their farewell parade on 24th April 2015 (Crown)

good friends and good neighbours – why must they leave? I think the good relations between the two countries will carry on, but the time of British Forces in Germany should be over ... I had relatives in East Germany, when it still existed. The Russian forces there were very unfriendly towards the local population. They were locked up in their barracks and had no contact to the locals, who were very hostile towards them because they were seen as an occupying force until the last day. And it was very different here in West Germany with the British, because we saw them as normal people, and we had a good relationship.'

Similarly for Frank Föste from Bielefeld, while he recognised the positive impact the British had on the local area – his own business included – this had not come without financial investment on behalf of the Germans.

'When the British leave Germany, I'm not sure if it's a good or a bad thing ... The good thing about the British people being here was, in the beginning, they made our lives more colourful. They were good for the local economy and employed Germans, such as my father-in-

law ... The British Army spent money here, but we also had to spend a lot of money on them, and I don't know which was more.'

Dagmar Railton lives in Sennelager. The town, and its infamous 'strip' outside the barracks, attracted a dubious reputation, but many residents still believe that the British have helped shape the local area for the better: 'The Army has given quite a lot to the local area, by way of friendships and the British culture. We'd like to see a museum in Sennelager, because there are lots of items that people have about the Brits that could be displayed.'

For some German observers, such as General Leutnant Carsten Jacobsen of the Bundeswehr, the sadness that has accompanied the drawdown and final closures has been somewhat of a surprise, and the fact that it always drew a bigger reaction than when units of the Bundeswehr closed bases or relocated has demonstrated just how the relationship between the British and Germans has transformed over the past 75 years. They have gone from, 'foe to friend ... The warmth and genuine sadness

Senne Training Area Open Day in 2014 showing the iconic Windmill, the location of many high profile parades on the area (Rhoda Wilson)

when the British left is difficult to explain.' Yet the transformation in that relationship, which was not instantaneous but instead a gradual process, is one of the legacies of the long deployment in Germany.

For many British veterans who had spent some of their formative years in Germany there was a real sadness at a personal level that this period of the Army's history was coming to an end. For Jim Toms, 'the soul of the British Army was in Germany'. Others found the idea that the Army would no longer be in Germany to be almost inconceivable, including former Royal Military Policeman Keith Bailey: 'Everyone I spoke to loved Germany; very few wanted to go back to the UK. The majority thought of Germany as a home posting ... so for a lot of people, including myself ... we always thought that Germany would be a home posting. So the drawdown is very sad.'

Nobody is quite sure how many British veterans there are living in Germany, or how many children or dual national citizens there are as a result of the British deployment, but it probably numbers in the tens of thousands. Quite what happens to them after the British leave – something

very few of them thought would happen – remains to be seen. Jim Griffiths is one such veteran. He completed multiple tours of BAOR between 1958 and 1983, and has seen the relationship between the Army and locals change a huge amount. He is disappointed that the Army are leaving, but recognises that it's not really their decision:

'Relations between the British troops and the Germans have changed so much for the better during my time here – things are very friendly and it has taken a long time to get there. When the British Army is gone, it's gone. I will miss it, as well as other people. But if they've got to go, they've got to go ... I know a lady who lives just over the road in Sennelager who asked me if I could stop the soldiers from going. A lot of the Germans are sorry that the troops are leaving and would like to see them stay.'

Ken Railton also stayed in Germany with his German wife once he left the Army, making a new life in a garrison town as a civilian. He says:

'I have mixed feelings about the British Army leaving Germany. The German population now suddenly realise

163

The Farewell Parade for 16th Signal Regiment and 1 Military Intelligence Battalion at Javelin Barracks in Elmpt in 2015. Both units were presented with a Fahnenband (Crown)

that the British Army wasn't so bad after all. In the very early days, the soldiers were sometimes a little bit rough, but the quality of soldiers has changed. They are more educated, more responsible and they take part in more activities these days. If you speak to many of the soldiers, they don't want to go back. Most of them have comfortable accommodation and nice surroundings and they don't want to go back to some old unused airfield or some place like that. So it's a bit sad for everybody.'

John Kellas also grew up in Germany, and then made a career working there serving the British forces with the NAAFI:

'It will be a very sad day when the British troops finally leave Germany, because for all the time I've lived here, I've seen Forces wherever I've gone. And I know from the various friends I have in towns in Germany where the British Forces are, that they will certainly miss them when they go. They've been part of the furniture in North

Rhine-Westphalia. I think the Army has given a very good insight into the British way of life, because wherever the British Forces are in Germany, they take a lot of icons of British life with them – British chip shops and garden fetes. A lot of British Servicemen have taken German wives, so the continuity will go on, even long after the British have left. Lots of local German businesses have built up their businesses over the years – restaurants, pubs, garages and all kinds of shops, and they are definitely going to miss the British forces when they leave.'

In 2019, the final formed units began moving back to the UK. On 13th May 2019, 26 Regiment Royal Artillery bid their final goodbye to Gütersloh, and the Headquarters of British Forces Germany received a Federal Fahnenband at a ceremony at the Landtag in Düsseldorf the following day. The salute was taken by the Landtagspräsident, such was the importance given to the event by the German authorities. Other British institutions closed their doors for the last time. Church

House in Lübbecke, which long provided a place of retreat for Service personnel and their families, will close. The Royal Army Chaplain's Department had moved its retreat and conference centre from Iserlohn to Lübbecke in 1983, into the building that Field Marshal Montgomery himself had used as his Headquarters between April and August 1945, before he moved to Bad Oeynhausen. With its community leaving, the call for its services, as a conference centre, as a place of retreat and reflection, was no longer needed.

The remaining British presence in Germany that endures beyond 2020, and the start of a new phase in the relationship between Britain and Germany, will centre on Sennelager. The Senne range complex and training area will continue under British control. A small number of detachments are set to remain following the drawdown to maintain and improve the close ties with Germany and the Bundeswehr, as well as other NATO partners, and to continue to fly the flag for the British Army in Germany. Also, 23 Amphibious Engineer Squadron of 75 Engineer Regiment will be based in Normandy Barracks in Sennelager. The Sappers will continue to work closely with their similarly equipped counterparts from the Bundeswehr, Panzerpionierbataillon 130, in Minden to operate the M3 amphibious bridging and ferrying vehicles. These capabilities and training facilities simply cannot be replicated in the UK. There will also be some munition logistic support based in Wulfen. The Stored Equipment Fleet will remain at Ayrshire Barracks in Mönchengladbach, housing around 2,000 vehicles. A Garrison Support Unit in Sennelager will provide the day-to-day support for those remaining, complete with health service support, welfare structures, and even BFBS.

While at the time of writing it had not been decided under what badge this group would operate, it is likely the crossed swords will be preserved for the Garrison Support Unit. The symbol that Montgomery's 21st Army Group first marched into Germany under, that survived the *Options for Change* revolution, and carried the British into the 21st century, will therefore live on into the next phase of the British military's relationship with Germany. A new chapter will be written – but a unique part of the Army's history will soon come to a close. It is the end of an era.

The Duke of Cambridge visited Düsseldorf on 23rd August 2016 to attend a series of events honouring the role of the British Forces in Germany, and celebrating the 70th anniversary of the state of North Rhine-Westphalia, and the role British Forces Germany had played since 1945 (Crown)

British and German M3 Amphibious Rigs on the River Elbe in 2017 celebrating forty years of partnership (Crown)

SOME REFLECTIONS

As the Army prepares to close one chapter on its life in Germany, there is much to take stock of and reflect on. What had the Army given Germany, and what had it taken from its long experience of being posted there?

Aside from the enormous economic boost the British provided to the former Zone and the garrison towns, particularly after the Second World War, there were many other successes of the long British deployment. From a military perspective, Lieutenant General Sir John Kiszely believes that the Army gave, 'a certain amount of deterrent protection, and increasingly ... there was much more interaction with the Bundeswehr, joint exercises, much more social interaction and professional interaction ... I found that hugely valuable.' The feelings of the closer professional ties were mutual.

Carsten Jacobsen noticed an increasing amount of interoperability developing between the British and the Germans from the start of his career in the Bundeswehr in 1978, when it never really happened apart from major exercises, to 2019, culminating in the maintaining of 23 Amphibious Engineer Squadron and their work with their Bundeswehr counterparts on the M3 rigs. Jacobsen describes this as the 'biggest win of all'.

From a German perspective, Jacobsen was not alone in identifying the value and cultural enrichment that came from having such large, English-speaking communities living in Germany. But as he acknowledged, 'there was always a price to that'. There had always been some trouble and fighting between British soldiers and German civilians in towns in the Zone on the weekends, normally fuelled by alcohol. Several areas had always needed to be placed out of bounds. However, most of the fighting had been between British soldiers.

There were undoubtedly some sacrifices made by the British to serve in Germany. Shirreff reflected on some of the drawbacks that came with a posting there, particularly during the Cold War:

'It's worth saying that there were penalties. There were penalties in terms of staying in touch with family. Phone calls were really expensive. Driving back was not easy, certainly from Hohne. There wasn't the network of motorways ... Flying back was damn expensive for a weekend. So the cheap flights, Internet, FaceTime, that didn't exist. And so that was tough ... And you definitely lose touch with friends as well in England.'

Even as new technology allowed more frequent and instantaneous contact with those in the UK, moving to a new country could still prove a challenging time for many, particularly in later decades. While those in uniform were occupied by their job – which was familiar, even if the environment they were working in was not – some of their spouses could find the move to Germany, and establishing a life there, more difficult. Tara Yarker moved to Gütersloh in February 2014 and found it very hard: 'The first time we were in Germany I really did not enjoy it. I was lonely, bored, stuck in a flat off the main patches, overwhelmed by the culture change; and we were only going to be there for eight months, which quickly became four, so never really settled.' Ann Crawford first came to Bergen-Hohne as a civilian teacher in 2010, married into the Army and later returned to Gütersloh on a subsequent posting with her husband. She also found that being away from the support network of one's family at a time of 'experiencing life's highs and lows and having to cope with being in a different country with different expectations' was a challenge, particularly at significant moments in life such as the birth of children or bereavements in the UK. Yet it was the military community that rallied around at times of crisis, and supported people through difficult times.

Helping people overcome these difficulties was a major task for the welfare organisations, but it was the military community that provided the essential practical and emotional support on which so many relied. The

The children of Colonel and Mrs Thorne on the final day of school at ARK School at JHQ. The amazing community within BFG, and the good service schools, are things that many people will miss when they move back to the UK (Courtesy of the Thorne family)

experience of garrisoning Germany pointed to the importance of allowing the military families to live and socialise together, to provide support to each other, on specific patches. This model meant that a unique community developed, one that was not replicated elsewhere within the British forces. For many, being able to take part in this and be immersed in it helped offset some of the apprehension about moving either to or within Germany, particularly when it came to moving from larger garrisons to those that were more isolated. Wendy Faux, for example, having been based in the small cities of Herford, Osnabrück and Paderborn, remembers the apprehension that came with moving to the far more isolated Fallingbostel, with its famously derogatory nickname of 'Effing B': 'I remember going from Paderborn, another university city with so much going on, going up to Fallingbostel and going into the camp. And I'm thinking, "I'm going to hate it. I hate it here, there is nothing here." ... And I thought, "Oh my God, this is just awful. This is just dreadful."'

But, because of the 'incredible', active community, Faux remembers how much she enjoyed it. She recalled, 'you're dragged into Fallingbostel, and you're dragged out.' Organisations like the Military Wives Choirs certainly helped bring spouses together, providing an

20th Armoured Brigade vehicles drawn up for Exercise BAVARIAN CHARGER, the first of three large contingency operation exercises undertaken by the brigade between May and October 2013. The training opportunities in Germany remain unparalleled anywhere in Europe (Crown)

opportunity to have great fun while also acting as a network to provide support in day-to-day life, as well as during the periods when their spouses might be deployed or on exercise. Being able to be immersed in an active community did make a massive difference for people, and helped overcome the isolation some undoubtedly felt by living in Germany, something Yarker noticed when she and her husband were posted back to Gütersloh: 'When we returned we were much happier, we lived on patch, had a two-year posting … and became part of the community. I had a one-year-old when we returned, so we were immediately into Tots groups, Funworld, etc., and he was a real conversation starter/ friend maker.' Yet this experience of living in close proximity to the rest of the military community is not something that will be replicated in the UK for those units and their families being relocated here as part of the rebasing programme.

Family undoubtedly had a big impact on people's experience of Germany, and could be a key mediator. Lieutenant General Richard Nugee reflected on this when discussing his own experience of living and working there:

'I did four postings in Germany; I lived there for nine years. They're very conflicting memories, or they're very various memories. I lived there as my first posting, as a very young officer, where I was bored in Dortmund … And so, my abiding memory was trying to get away from Dortmund. Then I went up to Paderborn, which I loved, and my abiding memory was going downtown … and enjoying myself. And then, when I went back to Hohne, north of Hannover, I had little children … So it was all

about what we could do with the children, allow them to enjoy Germany and enjoy being abroad and go skiing, you know, with three-year-olds at Garmisch and so on. And my final tour was in Rheindahlen … So, lots and lots of variety … I love Germany.'

But the central component and theme of the German experience was the professional reward that came from being there, the quality of the training and the soldiering. More than a million Service personnel and their families called Germany home between 1945 and 2019. It therefore had a major impact on many people's professional careers, and indeed made their careers. It was undoubtedly professionally and personally satisfying, as Sir Richard Shirreff believes: 'I think many people of my generation will [think] back to Germany as a pretty gilded period actually for the Army. It was professionally satisfying, challenging and interesting. As well as being enormous fun, later on … I got married and [had a] family – a great, great place to be with a family.'

For Stephen Blackshaw, who flew Puma helicopters with the RAF and lived in Gütersloh with his family between 1980 and 1983, service in Germany was professionally enormously rewarding: 'It was being in a different environment. You knew that Germany was different. You knew the Germans were different. You knew that the job was different because there was an identifiable threat.' For Blackshaw, it was only when he was posted to Northern Ireland that he realised how good life in Germany had been, and he frequently found himself thinking, '"I'd rather be back in Germany doing the day job."'

General Kiszely believed that being based in Germany had unparalleled benefits for the Army, that it, 'provided a focus for professionalism that would not necessarily have been the case if we had all been deployed in the United Kingdom'. The training in the UK could not have replicated what existed in Germany, the ability to exercise armoured divisions across huge swathes of land with very few limitations, as there was no tradition that allowed the widespread use of agricultural land for this purpose. As technology has improved, more can be done with simulation and there is a less pressing need for such widespread manoeuvre exercises, yet of course simulation can only achieve so much. In the Cold War in particular, the ability to put into practice the doctrine and the theory, and exercise over territory that they expected to fight over, 'contributed to the level of professionalism' in the British Army.

Major General Mungo Melvin certainly agreed, and thought that being based in Germany not only enhanced the professionalism of the Army, even after victory in the Cold War, but made it a better organisation overall.

This was worth the investment of being based in Germany:

'Serving in Germany maintained the Army's professional edge. I think it was important for its warfighting power. It was well equipped, well trained, well resourced. And because we were there people focused on it, we were in the public eye, we were alongside our NATO allies … It made sense economically … it was obviously cheaper for British units to be based in Britain than in Germany, but what did you get for the premium of being based in Germany? I think you got a better Army. It's as simple as that.'

Shirreff agreed, and the value of being based alongside European partners could not be overstated. It was a unique opportunity to operate with peers and allies:

'Germany, I think, in military terms, gave … some really good training areas, gunnery ranges, and very good accommodation and barracks. But more broadly, it opened the Army's eyes; it exposed the Army, not necessarily on a day-to-day basis but certainly on a

The sniper platoon, Princess of Wales's Royal Regiment (Queen's and Royal Hampshires), on the Bergen-Hohne Training Area in 2015. Bergen-Hohne remains a NATO training area, but the Sennelager Training Area will continue to be run by British Army Germany beyond 2020 (Crown)

regular basis, to regular multinational interaction and integration with Germans, with Americans, with Danes, with other allies certainly during the during the Cold War, and even after, and built relationships. And so it allowed the Army to, I think, learn from best practice – to realise that it didn't have all the answers, that other armies sometimes did things maybe differently but quite often better.'

Lieutenant General Sir Roderick Cordy-Simpson was disappointed from a personal and strategic perspective on the decision to close down the British bases in Germany:

'I'll be sad from an old-fashioned way in that it's part of our life and our history. I also think it's wrong that we do not keep a brigade in Germany ... In Germany you have all your kit ... Good equipment, and you can go in short time, you haven't got to go and draw the stuff up from somewhere. I personally think it's wrong, I think we should have kept a brigade in Germany ready to go. Good barracks, all paid for by the Federal Government ... I'm sentimental about it and I also think it's wrong not to keep a forward presence.'

Jim Toms offered an ordinary soldier's view on the value of Germany to the Army:

'It gave the Army a sense of purpose. It knew its job ... For all the joking about [how] we were there just to drink beer and harass the Fräuleins and all the rest of it, I think everybody really knew we were there for a purpose, to fight a war if it came to it. It gave a sense of purpose, and a sense of identity to the Army ... I think it will be a different Army when it comes back to the UK.'

Because of the value of being based in Germany, which was well-recognised by those who served there, the decision to withdraw virtually entirely from Germany and hand back some of the finest training areas available to it was greeted with surprise in many circles – not least in Germany itself. Jacobsen says that 'I personally always thought ... the British Army would never give up these training areas.' Since the original decision was made, the British have decided that they will hold on to Sennelager, and they will continue to use the Bergen-Hohne ranges under the NATO umbrella. But for Lieutenant Colonel Danny Wild of the King's Royal

British military vehicles moving through Emden Port in North-West Germany on their way back to the UK, 2015 [Crown]

RIGHT: On 29th June 2018, 1,400 soldiers from 20th Armoured Brigade marched through the Paderborn on their Freedom of the City Parade. In celebration of nearly seventy years of shared heritage between Paderborn and the Iron Fist, four units were awarded the Fahnenband, Germany's highest honour [Crown]

Hussars, the Army is still giving up an opportunity to develop professionally and personally:

'I think we've lost a fantastic training opportunity; the training areas here are far superior. We're well respected in our training with one of our most important NATO allies, and I just think that when soldiers come to Germany and they see a different culture, and how the Germans value things ... [To] give the Brits the opportunity to go into a running club, or a football club with the local Germans and all this sort of thing, it can only develop that person better.'

Being based in Germany undoubtedly helped develop soldiers individually. As Toms pointed out, 'it was a good place to be, and a good place to soldier'. Being based in a different country undoubtedly forced soldiers to grow up and mature, and for those who wanted to take the opportunity of being based in Europe to broaden their horizons, the possibilities were extensive, particularly after the fall of Communism. Nugee believed this was one of its major strengths:

'It's about being in a foreign country ... when you're young certainly that's exciting, there's so much more to explore. You can go abroad, literally – you can go away from your home and you can be in a foreign country in half an hour ... There was a lot of excitement and a lot of imagination, a lot of interesting things to do in Germany. And as I say, you weren't home. So you were away from your hinterland of family. I didn't get to see my parents

very often. And you learn independence, and you learn resilience, and you learn to get on with life and take opportunity. That's less easy if you're living with your mother just down the road, certainly for the soldiers.'

It also offered a wonderful family life for soldiers. Staff Sergeant Marc Collis of 35 Engineer Regiment, who marched out of Barker Barracks in 2018 and returned to the UK and rerolled from an Armoured Engineer Regiment to Explosive Ordinance Disposal and Search, believed that, 'Germany is the best place to be in the Army ... One of the reasons I came back, I opted for it. It's the best place to be. You're in the centre of Europe, the life for my family is much better here compared to the UK. I can't talk highly enough of Germany.' His colleague, Staff Sergeant Steven Evans, agreed: 'We all know how lucky we are to be here, and we all go that

Troops from 3 Armoured Close Support Battalion REME, some of the last troops based in Germany, close out their time with a parade that awarded a Fahnenband and saw them march through the castle of Schloss Neuhaus (Crown)

extra mile to enjoy it.' And despite the sadness at leaving, 'for me, to be able to close Germany, having been here for so long, having lived here as a child, it's especially poignant for me to see it out ... I'm really glad to be here to see it out and do the final stint.'

For many of the soldiers among the last units that are in Germany, there is sadness at moving back to the UK. There is a worry that the cohesion that came from all living in close proximity, without the easy ability for people to disappear at weekends, would slowly ebb away once based back in the UK, where barracks can empty by Friday evening as people return to wherever they live across the country. There is a real sense that soldiering in Germany is different. Lieutenant Colonel Victoria Moorhouse of 1st Armoured Medical Regiment, which was one of the last units to leave Germany when they moved out of Dempsey Barracks in 2019, recognised this as a risk: 'We're a very close-knit unit, and I think it's because we spend a lot of time together. We live together, we train together, we socialise together, we've a lot of shared experiences ... We are very much a family,

and I think that might change slightly when we move back to the UK.'

THE FUTURE

The preservation of the spirit of the Germany experience will be a major challenge moving forward for the British Armed Forces. How all the benefits of the past 74 years can be harnessed and adapted to the future challenges the Army will face remains to be seen. Once all the emotion of the final farewells has subsided, what lives on will be very different. But the Army and the RAF will adapt to the new strategic outlook, wherever they are posted – just as they have always done throughout history.

How will the British forces look back on their time in Germany? With fondness for all it gave the organisation and its people, with satisfaction for a job well done in the Cold War, and with some sadness for opportunities no longer available. Shirreff recognised the value

A fireworks display for officers, soldiers and guests of 20th Armoured after Beating the Retreat at Schloss Neuhaus on the outskirts of Paderborn in 2012 (Corporal Wes Calder RLC/Crown)

Germany had for the soldiers who were lucky enough to be stationed there: 'On a cultural level, I've always benefited from living in Germany and understanding Germany, culturally and socially and historically and artistically. It's not just me, but it's generations of soldiers who've come from growing up in Rochdale and been exposed to a world which they'd never otherwise have.'

A new generation will soon step into uniform, one that has no experience of the Zone of BFG. In many ways, this has already happened with the RAF, but in the Army it will take a few years yet. Germany will live long in the memories of those who were there, but a new generation will make their own memories of where they are deployed. The British forces have always moved through such moments of change and generational transformation. As Richard Spencer noted,

'Through most of my service, we in officers' messes used to have curry lunches from time to time, which I think harks back to the good old days in India. I think quite soon that you're going to find officers' messes having bratty and kartoffelsalat lunches, and getting in some decent beer to remember what life was like in BAOR.'

The world has changed since the British first arrived in Germany in 1945. With the retention of the training areas, and the legacy of multinational cooperation, this will not be the end of British forces operating in Germany, though they will only come as temporary visitors in future. The military case for maintaining these links, and making use of this capability, is clear. But there will not be another generation of Service personnel that calls Germany home. A unique era for the British Army and the Royal Air Force has come to an end. But the memories will live on for a long time yet. Whilst this is the end of another chapter of life in Germany it is not the end of our presence or deep and special relationship.

AUTHOR'S ACKNOWLEDGEMENTS

There are many people to acknowledge for their help in bringing this book to publication. Firstly, I am indebted to British Forces Germany for the opportunity to tell this unique story at this poignant time; in particular, to Brigadiers Ian Bell and Richard Clements. Thanks are also owed to Lieutenant Colonel Danny Wild and the staff at HQ BFG, who always provided such a warm welcome on my frequent visits. But most significantly, thank you to Hugh Pierson, whose advice, tireless work, hospitality and friendship have been invaluable and key to the success of this book. Herzlichen Dank!

I must thank the Council of Trustees of the National Army Museum. The Chairman of the Council, General Sir Richard Shirreff, has been kind with his time and generous with his enthusiasm and his contacts to help me tell this story. The staff of the Museum, in particular the Museum Director, Brigadier Justin Maciejewski, Ian Maine, Terri Dendy and Kirsty Parsons, who have been supportive every step of the way. My sincere thanks also go to Ewan Burnet and the Trustees of the Royal Air Force Museum for their generous help and support, and kind permissions to reproduce material from their archive in this book.

I am grateful to all the BAOR Cold War warriors and veterans of British Forces Germany who shared their experiences with me, and who showed great generosity in giving up their time to indulge my questions. You are the soul of this book. Major General Mungo Melvin kindly reviewed the script, sharing his memories, time and knowledge as a historian, which only improved my work.

Finally, and most importantly, I am forever grateful and fortunate to have been able to rely unconditionally on the unwavering support of my wife, Hannah, and my daughter, Matilda. They have followed every step of the journey, and kept me going through the tough times. Thank you for your help, your patience and kindness, and your tolerance of the long hours and research trips to Germany that the last two years have required. Without you, I could not have written this book, and it's dedicated to you both.

BFG ACKNOWLEDGEMENTS

We are indebted to the many contributors who have made this book possible. We have had help from present and past staff in HQ BFG; we have had anecdotal notes, some in the form of scruffy letters with fading photographs attached, to electronic copies and high-resolution images; and we've conducted dozens of interviews, oral and visual, with a wide range of servicemen and women, families, civilians and those associated with the British Forces in Germany. In particular we would like to thank the following for their written submissions through the BFG Legacy Project: Keith Bailey, Jim Boyle, Dietmar Brandt, Arndt Brannolte, Robert Brignell, Terry Bryne, Sir Mike Carleton-Smith, Samuel Carter, Alastair Clark, Graeme Cooper, Gavin Dickson, Günter Düe, Peter Elgar, John Emersen, Frank Föste, Paul French, Peter French, Diana Goldsworthy, Stephen Griffiths, Peter Harrison, Peter Howson, Michael Kahlbow, Bill Kenney, John Leggett, Stephen Lewis, Walter Lewis, Nigel Lillywhite, Valerie Major, Neil Mapp, John McCormick, John, McGuiggan, Roy McIntosh, Paul Middlemiss, Daniel Millan, Bert Pautz, Kim Payne, Alan Peacock, Nicola Reid, David Ronald, Charles Roskelly, Jeff Short, Nigel Stafford, Tony Skipper, Paul Smart, Gordon Smith, Howard Gater-Smith, Pat Springford, Isabel Taylor, Linda Thompson, Debs Thorne, Daniel Torschläger, Gerard Vines, Mavis Vines, Jan-Dirk von Merveldt.

Much of the legacy of BFG is contained in local museums found throughout northern Germany, and we are particularly grateful to the following for their contributions: Colin Albert – Hohne Museum; Kevin Greenhalgh – Oerbke Museum; Rod Hawkings – RAF Laarbruch Museum; Paul Hicks – Luftbrücke Museum Fassberg; Heiko Wolff – Garrison Museum Celle; Andreas Gaidt – Stadtund Kreisarchiv Paderborn; Christoph Gockel-Böhner – Kulturamt Paderborn and Dr Andreas Neuwöhner; Bernd Koska and Florian Pauls – Allied Museum Berlin; and Stefanie Hillebrand – Archiv Bad Oeynhausen. From the UK we would especially like to thank the following: Marjolijn Verbrugge – AAC Museum; Peter Williamson – Royal Anglian Museum; Sarah Paterson – IWM. Many of the contributions have come from the Army's Museum in Chelsea – the National Army Museum, and for this we have had regular contact with the home team, and are very grateful for the support of NAM's Director, Justin Maciejewski.

Some of the more unusual contributions have come from far and wide. Although we have not been able to include all items in the book, we would like to thank the following: Nick Barnard for contributions from Berlin; Heinrich Baumann – historian in Oerbke; Dr Bettina Blum and her project 'Briten in Westfalen', Paderborn; Hans-Joachim Bold – photographer; Barry Davies – last Deputy Director of the British Forces Liaison Organisation Germany; Jan Effinger – German War Graves Commission Lüneburg; Andreas Ege – Commissionar Oerbke; Ulrike Gutzmann – VW Heritage; Karl-Heinz Heineke – History of Hildesheim Garrison; John Henderson image collection; David Hercus – BLO FüAk Hamburg; Pim Hogben – RBL Photographer; Kenrick Jones – BFES / SCE Association secretary; Dr Christopher Knowles – author, for his valuable ideas on research; Sir Charles Macready – grandson of the Regional Commissioner Lower Saxony 1946; Steve Muncey, Becky Clark, Peter Davies and Tudor Morgan – *Soldier Magazine*; Wolfgang Meier – for his culinary contribution over decades to starving troops exercising on Soltau; Chris Pearson, Rob Olver and Andy Asprey – BFBS Germany; Laurence Roche – Media Ops ARRC; Carl Schulze – photographer; Fam. Von Vincke and Sabine Gräfin von Perponcher-Sedlintzky – owners of Gut Ostenwalde; Hajo Boldt – photographer; Chris Atkins – photographer.

The seeds for this book were sewn by the last GOC of BFG, Maj. Gen. John Henderson and his successor, Brig. Ian Bell, who formed the initial Legacy Steering Group and our thanks go to those members – Brig. Richard Clements, Col Andy Reynolds COS, Col Andy Thorne DCOS and Mr Peter Godwin Civil Secretary, ably supported by Sue Berry, for their contributions to editing. Our thanks must also go to Mr James Neely, who contributed to the early procurement of a publisher and author, and did much work on securing early contact to the NAM and documentary film companies. Within the headquarters a number of contributors should be mentioned: Pete Modley for his insight into Russia in the Cold War, Danny Wild for his insight into all aspects of Germany and serving there; Steve Graham for saving some of BFG for posterity; Gez Hills for accounts of broken engines and other oily rag stories, Ritson Harrison for his contribution from the British Army Sports Board, Bill Buckley for his engagement with the sport of Moto Cross in BFG, Paul Janes and Dave Smith from the TSU in Paderborn. The chief lawyer in BFG, Finbar Leahy, for his insight into the legal background to the founding of BFG, Nick Henthorn to his invaluable assistance with procurement procedures, to Helen Ross and her IT skills in bringing the project to the face of BFG, Natalie Deacon and the Comms team, and to Wendy Brune in supporting the team with her wand of clerical magic. In particular we would like to thank Phil Welsh, the last editor of *Sixth Sense*, for his journalistic research work in interviewing Veterans and assembling the legacy image collection.

From outside the headquarters we have had support from Army Media and Communications, and thanks go in particular to Charles Heath-Saunders in Andover, Mike Whitehurst and his media team in Bielefeld, Dominic King as the resident Army Photographer who has contributed so much to the book, to Army Historical Branch and Air Historical Branch for their advice. In support of the project from Paderborn station, our thanks go especially to Lindsay McCran from 41 AEC for her support generally and in particular to her project to capture the families story of their time in Germany and to Kim Fox – John Buchan School for her project on school-life in Germany, and Carl Griffiths from King's School, Gütersloh, for his help with life and times of the school interviews. We are also very grateful for the helpful comments and critique covering the text from two external BFG warriors, Maj. Gen. Mungo Melvin and Col Andrew Cuthbert. All of this work would not have been possible without the specialist support and endless patience shown by the Profile team led by Peter Jones, with Neil Burkey, Caroline Clark, Jon Allan, Russel Bell and Graeme Hall.

No research these days would be possible without using the Internet. Within this web lies a multiple number of separate and varied sites that contain information covering the British Forces in Germany. It would be impossible to list all those we have seen, including the social network sites, but some of the better known and long established include *BAOR Locations* and the *British Army in Germany*. Our thanks to these sites, and in particular to Mike Graham and Steve Wright and various anonymous contributors scattered across the world of the Internet. Another contributor from America with a passion for BAOR is Louis Vieuxbill, now living in Florida, who has completed extensive work on the organisation of BAOR at the end of the Cold War. For those on Facebook, BAOR Photos and a number of other sites provide a steady stream of images, mixed in with anecdotes about service life in Germany over these last 75 years.

The Legacy of this project belongs to the National Army Museum, and it is to them, and in particular to Dr Peter Johnston, that a great amount of this work will be saved for the future. The story we have told in this book just scratches the surface, and for every unit, every corps and formation that existed in BFG there is an extensive tale to tell. Some of this might remain on the Internet, but the ephemera, stories, images and personal memories that abound in publications and albums, in diaries and scrap books will be well looked after in the National Army Museum for generations to come.

SUBSCRIBERS

Christopher Adair
Robert Adams
William Adedze
Colin Agius
Iain Aird
Rosemary Alder
Jim Alger
Angela Anderson
Barry and Sheila Andrews RE
Dennis Appleyard
Edward Arnold
Thomas Arnold
Nigel Ashcroft
EX Sergeant Paul D Atkinson (QDG)
Simon Attwater

Steven Bagnall
Amanda Bailey
Anthony Bainbridge
Andrew Baker
Paul Baker TD VR
Terry Banks
Brian Barkworth
John Barkworth
Mat Barnes
Charles Barnett
Graham Barnett
Michael Barnett
Margaret Baron
Adam Barrett
Christopher Barry
James Bartlett
Jay Bartlett
Bob Bazley
Adrian Beak
Richard Beale
Roland Beard
Donald Bearon
Amy Beasley
Judith Beauchamp
Jim Beazley
Andrew and Susan Bedford
Martin 'Lofty' Beech
Benjamin Behrens
Kevin Belam
Gary Bell
Alexander Bennett
Jon Best
John Beuzeval
Matthew Bilous
Lieutenant Charles Bird
Andrew Blackledge
Hugh Blackman
Gary Blain
Richard Blythe
Ted Body
Martin Boesch
James Bond
Dick Boorman 17th/21st

Spencer Booth
Steven Booth
Aaron Bower
Ethan Bower
Isla Bower
Jack Bower
Kevin Bower
Leanne Bower
David Bowers
Bert Bowes
John Bowie
Colonel Mike Bradley
Arnd Brannolte
Christopher Breen
Christopher John Brightman
Duncan Broad
John Brook-Smith
Chris Barrington Brown
David Brown
Jason Edward Brown
Bill Buckley
Mike Buckley
Jochen Büddecker
Andreas Bühler
Mat Burch
Ian Burden
John Burgess
Lieutenant Max Burgin
Janet Burke
Corporal Foster Burt
Lee Burton
Ron Bygate
Terence Byrne

Liz Cable
Christopher Callow
Stephen Cameron
Gemma Campbell
Mark Campbell RA
Peter Campbell
Hugh Campbell-Smith
Stephen Cannon
Paolo Capanni
John Cargill
Roderick Carpenter
Erica Carr
Gary Carswell
Rob Carter
Stewart Carter
The Cattermoles
Shelley Chalmers
John Chandler
Nicholas Channer
Patricia Chapman
Richard Charrington
Christopher Charter
Kevin Chatfield
Alan W Chatt
Rene Cheema

Don Chester
Paul Chilcott
Simon Childs
Mark Churchman
John Edward Clare
Donald S Clark
Graeme Clark
Daniel Clarke
Lieutenant Colonel I R S Clarke
Jason A Clarke
Richard Clarke
Mark Clegg
Rowan Clelland
Finn Clement
Floraidh Clement
Jonathan Clement
Lynne Clement
Brigadier Richard Clements
Robin Clifford
Keith Clowes
Lance Corporal Cocker REME
Angie Coleman
Christopher Coles
Andrew Robert Colton
Martin Common
Darryl Roy Cone
Alan Connolly
Stephen Cook
John Colins Cooper
Roy Cooper
Clive and Julie Cope
Michael E W Cope
I P Gordon Corbett
Robert Cosgrove
Stephen Coughlan
Corporal and Mrs M Couzins
Hugh Cowan
Adam and Alexandra Cowle
A J Cox
C A F T Cox
J C Cox
S J Cox
Shona Croly
Philip Crook
Michael Crosbie
Andrew Cross
John Crouch
Stacey Crump
Mark Cubitt
Michael and Anna Culver
Alasdair Cuthbert

Douglas Dales
Major Christal Dalley
Major M J Dalley
Barry Davenport
Rob Davie
Barry and Ilona Davies
Grant Davies

Jeff Davies
M F Davies
Catherine and Tim Davis
Andrew Davison
Lance Corporal Ian Robert Dawson
Shaun Edward Dawson
Christopher Day
Philip Day
Stephen Day
Troy Day
Christopher Deacon
Barbara-Ann Deakin
Lieutenant Colonel G A Deakin
Timothy Denman
Adrian Denyer
Kevin Diton
Julien Dixon
Simon Dixon
Brigadier W I C Dobbie
Cathy Dobson
David Dolan
Leo Domeisen
Suzie and Tony Domeisen
Toby Domeisen
Stephen Donovan
Philip Douthwaite
Brendan Downey
Marie Downton
Frank Duncan
Jason Durkin

Andy Edington
Fiona Edington (née Rider)
Keith Eddie Edmonds
Geraldine Edwards
Brigadier Clive Elderton CBE
Phil Eley
Jessica Elkington
Phil Ellis
Robert Ellis
Jeffery Elson
John Elthick
Amelia Essam
Sarah Essam
Sophia Essam
Tobie Essam
Dieter Esser
Amber Evans
Amy Evans
Iain Evans
Ian Evans
Paige Evans
Martin Exner
Chris Eyre

Wayne Farrier
Wendy Faux
Major (Retd) John Feast
Robin Featherstone

Lieutenant Colonel (Retd) Jim Ferrier
Peter Ffitch
Brigadier Colin Findlay
Kim Findlay-Cooper
Christoph Fink
Donald 'Mickey' Finn
James Fisher
Arthur F Flinn
Pam Flitcroft
Steve Flockhart
Jeremy 'Jez' Fordham
Keith Forsey
K J Foster
S J Foster
Lieutenant Colonel Ian Foulkes RE
Corporal Matthew Frankham
Paul Franks
Ivan Freeburn
Stephen Freeman-Pannett
Leslie French
Paul French
Peter French
Ron French
Derrick Frost
Richard Fry
Doris and Geoff Fryatt
Ian Gordon Fudge
Adrian Fulton
Eva Fulton
Lisa Fulton
Joe Furey
Wayne Fury
Simon Fynn (ex-BFBS presenter)

Matilda Gaal
Thomas Gaal
Anne Gardner
Frederick Gardner
Lee Gardner
Grace Garry
Laura Garry
Michael Garry
Howard Gater-Smith
Marc Raymond Gavin
Corporal Daniel Gelabert-Smart
Michelle Gierke
Jerry Glazier
David Glen
Alan Goddard
John Goddard
Peter Godwin
Leslie Gooch
Colin and Maggie Gordon
Diaana Graham
John Francis Grange
Ian Grant
Marlies Grant
Robyn Grant
Jennifer Grant

Jim Grant
Lissa Grant-Nichols
Brian Charles Gray
Hugh Gray-Wallis
Brian Greatorex
John Greatrix
Philip Greatrix
Rupert Greatrix
David Green
Andrea Greenwood
Nick Griffiths
Graham Groom
Major Thomas Groome
Jan Guenther
Peter Gutberlet

Andy Hadfield
Jez Hair
S A Hairst
T C Hairst
Martin Hajduk
Andrew Haldane
Michelle Hall
David Hambidge
Shona Hamlin
Peter Hampton
Hank Hancock
T W Hancock
Craig and Phillipa Hanson
Keith and Angela Hanson REME
Steven and Claire Hanson-Church RLC
Alan Haresign
Kevin Haresign
Mark Harney
Christopher Harris
David Harris
Dennis Harris
Richard Harris
Paul Harrison
Ritson Harrison
Tim Harrison
Susan Hartley
Reverend Dr Desmond Harvey
John Harvey
Stephen Haskins
Clare Haworth-Maden
Alec Hayton
Hazel Hebden
John Hedges
Captain J Heffernan BEM
Alfred Hellberg
Steven Henderson
Shirley Hendricks
David Hercus
Geoffrey Hetherington
David Hewson
Stephan Hey
Bill Hickey
Kayleigh Higgins

A Higton
Lieutenant Colonel (Retd) J F Higton
Eric Hillman
Lieutenant Colonel (Retd) Gez Hills
    REME
Beville Hilton
Mark Hitch
Andy Hobbs
Kathleen Hockley
Gary Hodge
Gary Holden
James Hollas
Martina Hollmann
John Hopkins
Ray Hopkins
Lisa Horder BEM
Stuart Horder
Chris Horton
Ashley Howard
David Howe
Joleem Hoyes
Stephen Huddlestone
D and J Hughes
David Hughes
Ian Hughes
Margaret and Brian Hughes
Paul Hughes
Peter Hughes
Richard Hughes
Helen Hunt
John Gray Huntly
Malcolm Hurrell
Jonathan Hurst
Niall Hutchison
Brian Hynds

Lisa Illingworth
Philip Inman
Glynn Ireland
Richard Ives

Karen Jackson
Stephen James
Liz Jay
Colonel Richard Jeffrey
Christopher Jenkins
Alcuin Johnson
Marc Johnson
Angus Johnston
Frank Johnstone
Dennis Jolly
Gary Jones
Marlene Jones
Stewart Jones
Captain C W Jordan

Jan Philipp Kaeselau
M K P Kahlbow
Nicolas Kasch

Jonathan Kay
Brian Keeffe
Robin Kemp
John Kerce
Terry Killelay
Mike Kinrade
Peter Kinsman
Joshua Kirkham
Martyn Kirkham
Nicola Kirkham
Jack Kitchener
Dr Wilhelm Knicker
Clive Knightley
Gerda Kohrmann
Jens Korte
S A Krstic
Sav Kyriakou MBE

John Lambert
Clive Lane
Sylvia Lane
Grant Laney
Walter Langer
Colin Langford
Major John Langhorne
Toby Lankester
Warrant Officer class 2 Adrian Larsen
Robert Laurie
Russell Law
Louise Lawless
Terry Lay
Finbarr Leahy
Walter ('Wally') and Margaret Legg
André Lennartz
Caroline Leonard
Kenneth Bradbury Little
Steve Little
Barrie Lloyd-Williams
Kim Logan-Basham
Dieter Lohmeyer
James Loney
Michael Louden
Jane Loy
Susanne Luhmann
Owain Luke
Fiona Lytham

Anthony Macey
Jim Macken
Christopher Mackey
Danny Mackness
Robin Maddison
George Magnus
Kenneth Maher
Stephen Major
Tony Mann
Mark Mans
David James Marr
Peter Marshallsay

Alan P Marsland
David E Martin
Graham Martin
Stuart Martin
Charles Mather
Brian P Matthews
Richard Matthews
Andrew Maude
Sergeant Shane Maughan
Arthur Maxfield
Peter May
Alex McAllister
Chris McCarthy
Samantha McComb
Lieutenant Colonel Andrew McCran
Julian McDonnell
Ross McDuff
Gerry McGachy
Robert McGilvray
Adrian McGivern
The McGowan Family
Mac McKillop
Kevin McLelland
Corporal Sean McLoughlin
Simon McLoughlin
Simon Alexander McMahon
Nickie Sara McMullan
William McNab
Joe and Jean McSorley
Graham Meacher
Tom Meade
Sue Meader (née Bailey)
Dr Udo Meier
Jordan Mellor
Major General Mungo Melvin
Lieutenant General Robert Menzies
Dominik von Wolff Metternich
Gary Middleton
Eldon Millar
David Miller
Andrew Milton
Allan Mitchell
Lee Mitchell
Robert John Mitchell
Corporal Mark Mobsby
Peter Modley
Davie Moir
Major Hugh Montgomerie
Howard Moore
David Moreton
Jon Moreton
John Morley-Clarke VR
Ian Munro
Stuart Munro
Richard Murphy
Marilyn J M Murray
Stephanie Myers

Genevieve Alice Crawford Nasse

Tom Neal
Roderick Neilson
Stuart Neilson
Christopher Nelson
Jackie Newman
Stephen Nobbs
Reverend and Mrs Noetzel
Darren Nolan
Debbie North
Group Captain Mark Northover

James O'Hagan
Frauke O'Keeffe
Pauline G O'Keeffe
Philip Odling
Michael O'Donnell
Seay O'Neill
Tom Ormiston
Keith Orton
Elke O'Sullivan
Titch O'Sullivan
Clwyd Owen
Michael Owens

Captain I K Page
Kay Page
Neill Page
Catherine Cecilia Parker (née Reed)
David Parkin
Claire and Ron Parnell
Colin Parr
Paul M Parrott
Glen Passant
Major Matthew Paterson
Arthur Paton
Ray Patrickson
Dale Patterson
Monika Pawson-Rumney
Ian Payne
Rex Pearson
Ingo Peikert
John Peile
Angela Penfold
Cory Pennicott
James Pettifer
Anthony Phillips
Hugh Phillips
Jason Phillips
Steve Piddell
Stephen Pim
Rosemary Pitchener
Brian and Yvette Pitchforth
Philip Plant
Michael Pleszak
John Pluckwell
Chris Plumb
Wilfred Pole
Carl S Portman
Major Al Prescott RE

Rainer Preuss
Duncan Price
Phillip Price
Tim Pringuer
Staff Sargeant K S Proctor
Captain Martin Proctor
Petko Protopopov
Ian Puddy
Owen Punter
Carole Purdy

Florian Raebel
Graham Ramsey
Richard Ravenscroft
John Read
John Redfern
Joe Redhead
Martin Reed
James Reid
William Reid
Andrew Relf
Michael Remm
Verena Katrin Reusch
Jim Revell
Andrew Reynolds
Group Captain Mark Richardson
Paul and Cheryl Rickard
Gus Rider
Ingrid Rider (née Lenger)
Rob Rider
Colin Ridley
Lieutenant Colonel (Retd) Nick Ridout
Ian Ritchie
Andi Rivers
Neil and Sarah Roberts
Peter Roberts
George Robertson
Alan Robinson RAF
Anthony Robinson
Bianca Robinson
Chantal Robinson
Gary Robinson
Kimberley Robinson
Neal Robinson
Joji Robo
Laurence Roche
Patrick Roche
Peter Rogers
Jacqui and Jonathan Rollason
Alistair Ross
Dominic Rossi
Wendy Rothwell (née Martin)
John Rowan
Guy Rowland
The Royal Military Police Museum
Dona and Roger Rudd
Martin Rushton
Kevin Russell
Jane Ryan (née Hope)

Mark Salmon
Peter Sass
Stuart Saunders
Corporal Hubert Savarin
Maggie Sawade
Donna Scaife
Thomas Schmidt
Ulrike Schmidt
Jorrit Schrauwers
Carl Schulze
Dr Marli Schütze
Ailsa Scotland
Crispin Scott
Pat and Ken Scott
Sharon Scott
Julie Sears
Stephen Senft
Thomas Senier
Richard Shackleton
Audrey Shalders (née Grandison)
Warwick Shaw
Colour Sergeant Carl Sheehan
Marc J Sherriff
Alex Shimmings
Billie Simpson
Kestrel Simson
Deb Sinderberry
Wolff van Sintern
Paul Sinderberry
Andreas Skala
Anthony Skipper
Thomas Slavicek
Malcolm Sleight
Chloe Smith
Dave Smith
Dave Smith
Gavin and Mairéad Smith
Gordon D Smith
Graham and Avril Smith
Mike Smith
Colonel Paul Smith
Stacie Smith
Querida Smith
Brendan Snodden
Antony Snowden
Andrew Snowdon
Russell Somerville
John Sougherland
Richard Spencer
Owen Spure
Major Lawrence Stacey (Lancs Fus.)
Robert Stearn
The Steele Family
Patrick Steen
C R Stephens
Yvonne Stevens
Mark Stewart
Uwe Stichnothe
Barrie Stink

David Stockton
David Stone
Alan Storey
Donald Storey
John William Storey MBE
Richard Strachan
Alan Stringer
Tom Stringer
Brian Stubbington
Kerry Stylianou
Guy Sudron
Alan Sullivan
Victor Surridge
John Sutton
Daisy Swann
John W Swann
Alan Swanwick
Phil Swarbrick
John Syme
James Symon

Robert Tarr
Mike Tasker
Maurice Taylor
Paul Taylor
Tom Taylor
Andrew Teeton
Ian Tennent
Andi Test
Christopher Thain
Mark Theobald
Franziska Thiede
Frederick Thiede
Miriam Thiede
Emily Thiede-Nelson
Ian Thirlwell
June Thomas
Kay Thomas
Peter Thomas
Mike Thomason
Paul Thomson
Andrew Thorne
Darren Thornhill
John Tillstone
Lieutenant Colonel Mike Tizard
Karen Tolladay
Brigadier Ian Townsend
Seymour Townsend
Colin Treby
Chi Hang Tsang
Mike and Cherry Tugby
Tuivonovono
Stephen Turpin
David Twigg
Lee Paul Tyrrell
Alan Tyson-Carter

Margarita Underwood
Simon Upton

Derek Vanstone
Nigel Vause
Neil Villiers MBE
Mavis Vines
Michael Wade
Anja Wainwright
Neil Walker
Steve and Marina Wall
Charlotte Ward
John Ward
Rosie Warne
Jonathan Perry Warnes
Gavin Watkins
John Watkins
Damian Watson
Mike Watson
Paul and Joan Watson
Helga Wawra
Martin Weatherley
Derek Webster
Julian Webster
William Webster
Anthony Wells
Caroline West
Tom Wharton
Bill Wheeler
Michael Whelan
David White
Martin Whittle
Terence Wilkes
Bob Wilkie
Stephen Wilkinson
Lieutenant Taylor Wilkinson
Andrew Willett
Barbara Williams ('Nicki')
Dai and Michelle Williams
David Williams
Ian Williams
Ian Williams
John Williams
John 'Andy' Williams
Martin Williams
Bill Wilson
David Wilson
Mark Wilson
Paul Wilson
Richard Wilson
Mick Winslade
Alan K Wint
Fred Winter
Major (Retd) Derek Wood MBE
Shirley and Mike Woodburn
J R Wooddisse
Stephen Wright
Geordie Wright-Rivers
Bettina Wuttke

Noel Yates
David Yexley

Mike Yolland
Clive Young
James Young

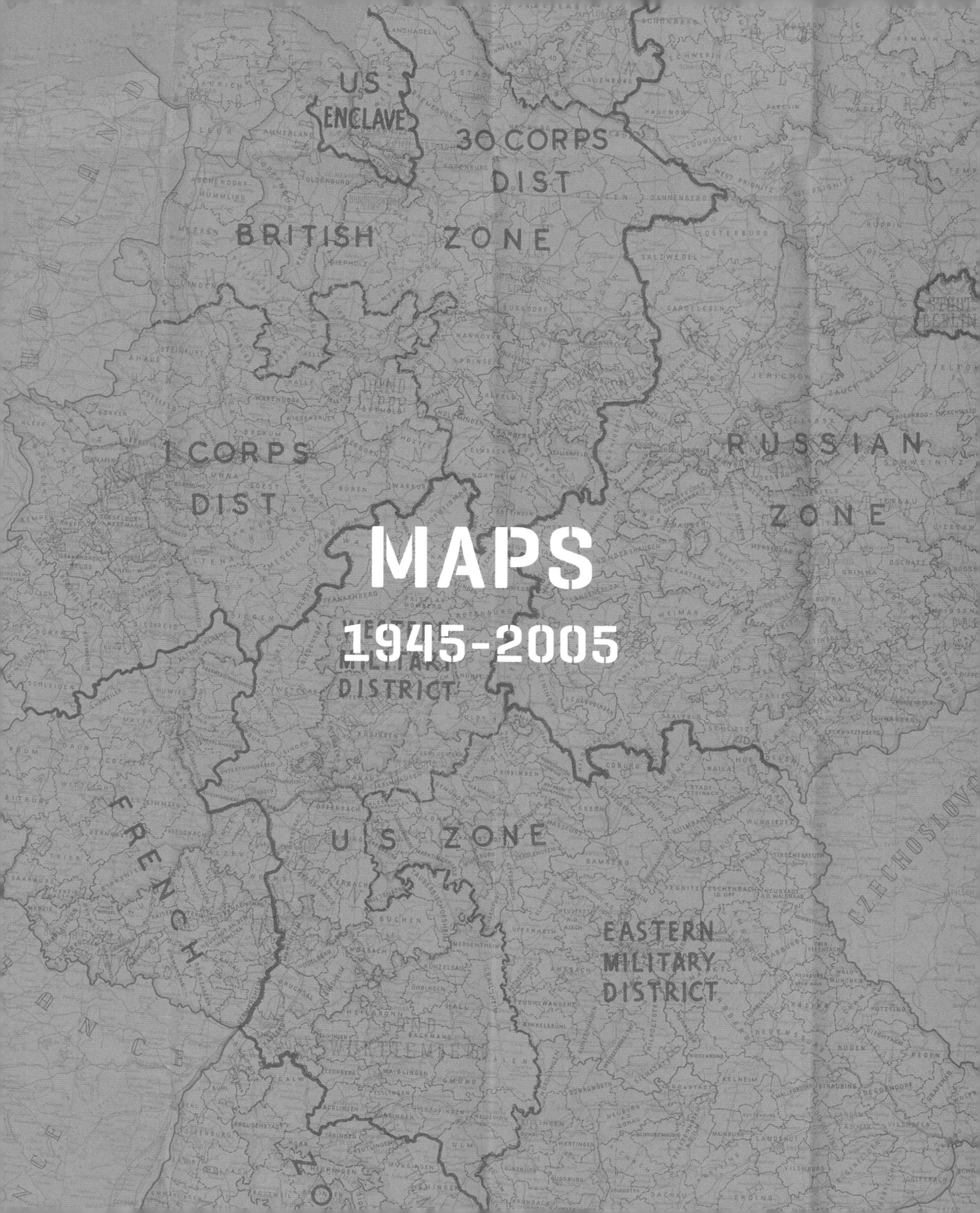

MAPS
1945-2005

FORMATION LOCATIONS ANNEX

This annex shows the locations of the main UK Army formations, from Army Group / Corps down to Division and Independent Brigade level, in snapshots of four periods between 1945 and 2005. It does not include all the many support Corps and Units that were so vital to keeping the fighting element supplied. The period 1945 relates to the earliest position after the Lüneburg surrender with effect 5th May, and does not include the many Allied Forces under command 21 AG, including in particular the Canadian 1st Army and the Dutch, Belgian, Czech and Polish troops. Some Formations are not included in this annex, such as 59 Inf Div, which had already left the orbat of 2nd Army by May 1945, some Royal Marine and Airborne formations, and 56 Ind Bde, which was under command 1st Canadian Army. The Line of Communication (LOC) troops are represented by 162 Ind Bde.

LOCATIONS OF 21ST ARMY GROUP FORMATIONS, 5TH MAY 1945

1. **21 Army Group** *Wendisch Evern / Lüneburg*

1. **2nd (British) Army** *Wendisch Evern*

1. **33 Armoured Brigade** *Lüneburg*

2. **Line of Communication Troops**

2. **162 Independent Brigade** *(LoC – around about Rotenburg)*

3. **1 Corps** *Oldenburg*

4. **49 (West Riding) Infantry Division** *Ibbenbüren*

5. **3 Infantry Division** *Bocholt (Wesel)*

5. **115 (Independent) Infantry Brigade*** *Bochholt (Wesel)*

6. **34 Armoured Brigade** *Schloß Burgsteinfurt (north of Münster)*

7. **6 (Guards) Armoured Brigade** *Plön*

7. **8 Corps** *Schloß Plön*

8. **11 Armoured Division** *Schloß Louisenlund*

9. **5 Infantry Division** *Lübeck*

10. **15 (Scottish) Infantry Division** *Schloß Ahrensburg*

11. **12 Corps** *Hamburg*

11. **53 (Welsh) Infantry Division** *Hamburg (Hotel Atlantic)*

12. **7 Armoured Division** *Itzehoe*

13. **4 Armoured Brigade** *Pinneberg*

14. **30 Corps** *Nienburg*

14. **31 Tank Brigade** *Nienburg area*

15. **Guards Armoured Division** *Delmenhorst*

16. **51 (Highland) Infantry Division** *Bremervörde*

17. **52 (Lowland) Infantry Division** *Villa Waldreise, Bremen*

18. **43 (Wessex) Infantry Division** *Celle*

19. **8 Armoured Brigade** *Rittergut Poggemühlen*

20. **116 Independent Infantry Brigade RM** *Buxtehude*

21. **50 (Northumbrian) Infantry Division** *Nijmegan Salient*

x. **79 Armoured Division** *Disbanded all but in badge by May 45*

x. **27 Armoured Brigade** *Disbanded all but in badge by May 45*

GERMANY
COLOGNE — BERLIN

10 0 10 20 30 40 50 60 70 MILES

North Sea

WEST AND EAST FRISIAN ISLANDS

DENMARK

Westerland

Flensburg

⑧ Schleswig

Husum

Sehestedt

Kiel

Rendsburg

KIEL CANAL

⑦

Preetz
Plön

Putlos

Neumünster

Eutin

Stralsund

Greifswald

Rostock

⑫ Itzehoe

SCHLESWIG-HOLSTEIN

Brunsbüttel

Glückstadt

Lübeck

⑨

Wismar

Güstrow

Schweriner See

Cuxhaven

Uetersen ⑪

⑬ Pinneberg

Todendorf

Ratzeburg

Schwerin

Neubrandenburg

Brake

Bremerhaven

⑲

Buxtehude

⑳ Harburg

HAMBURG

Glinde

⑩

Lauenburg

MECKLENBURG-VORPOMMERN

Müritz

Neustrelitz

Norden

Jever

Wilhelmshaven

③

Leer

Emden

Aurich

⑯

①

Lüneburg

ELBE

Dömitz

Ludwigslust

Pritzwalk

Wittstock

Oldenburg

⑮

⑰ Bremen

②

Rotenburg

Verden

Soltau

Munster

Ebstorf

Danneberg

Wittenberge

Kyritz

BRANDENBURG

Papenburg

Delmenhorst

Ahlhorn

Walsrode

Fallingbostel

Fassberg

Uelzen

Salzwedel

Cloppenburg

Essen

Vechta

NIEDERSACHSEN-LOWER SAXONY

Rethem

Bergen-Hohne

Belsen

BERLIN

Meppen

Diepholz

Liebenau

Nienburg

⑭

Steinhuder Meer

Celle

⑱

Wesendorf

Gardelegen

Stendal

Rathenow

Nauen

Lingen

Dümmersee

Wunstorf

Wolfsburg

SAXON-ANHALT

Potsdam

Nordhorn

Osterkappen

Lübbecke

Obernkirchen

Bad Eilsen

Hanover

Brunswick

Helmstedt

Burg

Magdeburg

Bad Bentheim

Osnabrück

④

Rheine

Minden

Rinteln

Springe

Hildesheim

Langeleben

Wolfenbüttel

Gronau

Bünde

Bad Oeynhausen

Herford

Bad Salzuflen

Hamelin

LEINE

Zerbst

Wittenburg

Arnhem

⑥

Münster

Bad Rothenfelde

Lemgo

Detmold

Scharfoldendorf

Alfeld

Delligsen

Einbeck

Goslar

Bad Harzburg

Torfhaus-Harz

Halberstadt

Bernburg

Dessau-Roßlau

Nijmegen

㉑

Dülmen

Warendorf

Gütersloh

Bielefeld

Nieheim

Höxter

Clausthal-Zellerfeld

Silberhütte in Harz

Goch

Wulfen

Sennelager

Bad Lippspringe

Northeim

Nordhausen

Halle (Saale)

Laarbruch

Wesel

Xanten

Recklinghausen

Hamm

Lippstadt

Paderborn

Borgentreich

Warburg

Göttingen

Munden

Heiligenstadt

Ebeleben

Merseburg

Leipzig

Venlo

Wankum

Duisburg

Bochum

Witten-Annen

Werl

Soest

Körbecke

Möhnesee

Brilon

Kassel

Mühlhausen

Bracht

St Tonis

Krefeld

Mülheim

Essen

⑤

Dortmund

Hemer

Menden

Iserlohn

Deilinghofen

Meschede

Viersen

Willich

Ratingen

Wetter

Sundern

Winterberg

Erfurt

Altenburg

Brüggen

Wildenrath

Düsseldorf

Wuppertal

Hubbelrath

Hilden

NORDRHEIN-WESTFALEN

(North Rhine-Westphalia)

Bad Berleburg

Eisenach

Gotha

Jena

Glauchau

Chemnitz

Birgelen

Mönchengladbach

Wegberg

Geilenkirchen

Norvenich

COLOGNE

Wahn

Morsbach

Sieburg

Siegen

HESSEN

Bad Hersfeld

Arnstadt

THÜRINGEN

Zwickau

Greiz

Aachen

Düren

Bonn

Bad Godesberg

RHINE

Hünfeld

Meiningen

Suhl

Plauen

Koblenz

Limburg

Bad Neustadt

Coburg

Hof

RHEINLAND-PFALZ

Wiesbaden

FRANKFURT

Gelnhausen

Fulda

FULDA

Gersfeld

Bayreuth

Bamberg

Mainz

RHINE

MAIN

Lohr

Euerdorf

Schweinfurt

Würzburg

Iphofen

BAVARIA

Weiden

Trier

LUXEMBOURG

Mannheim

Heidelberg

Uffenheim

Erlangen

Fürth

Nuremberg

Schwandorf

FRANCE

Rothenburg ob der Tauber

Ansbach

Neumarkt in der Oberpfalz

CZECHOSLOVAKIA

By 1955, the new Joint Headquarters had been completed near Mönchengladbach, and HQ BAOR moved from Bad Oeynhausen in 1954, where it formed the HQ of Northern Army Group in time of war. 2nd Tactical Airforce also moved west from its HQ at Bad Eilsen to JHQ in Mönchengladbach, and in 1959 was renamed RAF Germany, later forming the HQ of 2nd Allied Tactical Air Force in its war role. 1 (BR) Corps, having been disbanded in 1947, was reformed in 1951 at its HQ in Ripon Barracks in Bielefeld, with four divisions under command.

LOCATIONS OF THE MAIN UK FORMATIONS, 1955

(1) **HQ BAOR**
Mönchengladbach

(1) **NORTHAG**
Mönchengladbach

(1) **2TAF**
Mönchengladbach

(2) **1 (BR) Corps**
Bielefeld

(3) **5 Artillery Group RA**
Delmenhorst

(4) **11 Army Engineer Group**
Osnabrück

(5) **2 Infantry Division**
Hilden

(6) **4th Guards Brigade**
Hubbelrath

(7) **5th Infantry Brigade**
Iserlohn

(8) **6th Infantry Brigade**
Wuppertal

(9) **6th Armoured Division**
Bünde

(10) **20th Armoured Brigade**
Münster

(11) **61st Lorried Infantry Brigade***
Minden

(12) **7th Armoured Division**
Verden

(13) **7th Armoured Brigade**
Soltau

(14) **31st Lorried Infantry Brigade***
Lüneburg

(15) **11th Armoured Division**
Herford

(16) **33 Armoured Brigade**
Bad Lippspringe

(17) **91st Lorried Infantry Brigade***
Hildesheim

(18) **Ist Canadian Infantry Brigade Group*** *Möhnesee*

GERMANY
COLOGNE — BERLIN

10 0 10 20 30 40 50 60 70 MILES

North Sea

WEST AND EAST FRISIAN ISLANDS

Westerland
Flensburg
Schleswig
Husum
Sehestedt
KIEL CANAL
Kiel
Rendsburg
Preetz
Plön
Putlos
Eutin
Neumünster
Itzehoe
Brunsbüttel
Glückstadt
SCHLESWIG-HOLSTEIN
Lübeck
Wismar
Stralsund
Rostock
Greifswald
Güstrow
Schweriner See
Schwerin
Neubrandenburg
Neustrelitz
MECKLENBURG-VORPOMMERN
Müritz
Cuxhaven
Uetersen
Pinneberg
HAMBURG
Todendorf
Ratzeburg
Buxtehude
Glinde
Harburg
Lauenburg
Ludwigslust
Dömitz
Pritzwalk Wittstock
14 Lüneburg
ELBE
Danneberg
Wittenberge
Kyritz
Bremerhaven
Brake
Rotenburg
3 Bremen
12 Verden
13
Soltau
Ebstorf
Uelzen
Salzwedel
BRANDENBURG
Stendal
Rathenow
Nauen
BERLIN
Norden
Jever
Wilhelmshaven
Aurich
Emden
Leer
Oldenburg
Papenburg
Delmenhorst
Ahlhorn
Walsrode
Fallingbostel Fassberg
Bergen-Hohne
Belsen
NIEDERSACHSEN-LOWER SAXONY
Celle
Wesendorf
Wolfsburg
Gardelegen
Burg
Potsdam
Meppen
Cloppenburg
Essen
Vechta
Diepholz
Liebenau
Nienburg
Rethem
Steinhuder Meer
Wunstorf
Hanover
Helmstedt
Langeleben
Magdeburg
Lingen
Dümmersee
4
Osterkappen
Lübbecke
Obernkirchen
Springe
Brunswick
Wolfenbüttel
Nordhorn
Bad Bentheim
Osnabrück
11 Minden
Bad Eilsen
17
Hildesheim
Wolfenbüttel
Zerbst
Wittenburg
Rheine
9
Bünde
Rinteln
Hamelin
LEINE
Dessau-Roßlau
Arnhem
Gronau
15 Herford
Bad Oeynhausen
Bad Salzüfeln
Lemgo
Alfeld
Goslar
Bad Harzburg
Halberstadt
Silberhütte in Harz
Nijmegen
10
Münster
Bad Rothenfelde
2 Bielefeld
Detmold
Scharfoldendorf
Delligsen
Einbeck
Torfhaus-Harz
Bernburg
Halle (Saale)
Wesel
Warendorf
Gütersloh
Nieheim
Höxter
Clausthal-Zellerfeld
Northeim
Nordhausen
Wittenberg
Dülmen
Sennelager
16 Bad Lippspringe
Goch
Wulfen
Lippstadt
Paderborn
Borgentreich
Warburg
Göttingen
Heiligenstadt
Ebeleben
Merseburg
Leipzig
Laarbruch
Xanten
Recklinghausen
Hamm
Werl
Soest
Körbecke
Brilon
Munden
Kassel
Duisburg
Bochum
Witten-Annen
18 Möhnesee
Mühlhausen
Bracht St Tönis
Essen
Hemer Menden
Meschede
Altenburg
Venlo
Krefeld
Mülheim
Wetter Iserlohn
Deilinghofen
Sundern
Winterberg
Eisenach
Gotha
Erfurt
Jena
Glauchau
Chemnitz
Wankum
Viersen
Willich
Ratingen
8 Wuppertal
Hubbelrath
7
NORDRHEIN-WESTFALEN
(North Rhine-Westphalia)
Bad Berleburg
HESSEN
Bad Hersfeld
THÜRINGEN
Arnstadt
Zwickau
Greiz
Brüggen
1
Mönchengladbach
Hilden
5
6
Bad Berleburg
Siegen
Gersfeld
Bad Neustadt
Hof
Wildenrath
Birgelen
Wegberg
Geilenkirchen
COLOGNE
Wahn Morsbach
Siegen
Aachen
Norvenich
Düren
Sieburg
Bonn
Bad Godesberg
RHINE
Hünfeld
Fulda
Meiningen
Suhl
Coburg
Plauen
Bamberg
Bayreuth
Koblenz
Limburg
RHINE
FULDA
FRANKFURT
Wiesbaden
Mainz
MAIN
Würzburg
Iphofen
Bamberg
Weiden
RHEINLAND-PFALZ
Trier
LUXEMBOURG
Gelnhausen
Euerdorf
Schweinfurt
Lohr
Gersfeld
Schwandorf
BAVARIA
Mannheim
Heidelberg
Rothenburg ob der Tauber
Ansbach
Fürth
Nuremberg
Neumarkt in der Oberpfalz
Uffenheim
Erlangen
FRANCE
BELGIUM
CZECHOSLOVAKIA
SAXON-ANHALT
EMS
WESER
ALLER
SAALE
ELBE

By 1985, at the height of the Cold War, 1 (BR) Corps had again been reorganised to consist of three armoured divisions based in Germany, with 2nd Infantry Division based in York, England. By now, technological developments underlined the high manoeuvrability of the divisions and brigades as part of the British Army in Germany, and this effect was put to good use on OP TELIC in 1990. 1(BR) Corps was disbanded in 1992, but its successor organisation, the Ace Rapid Reaction Force, was formed as NATO's new rapid reaction force HQ, with its new HQ in JHQ Mönchengladbach.

LOCATIONS OF THE MAIN UK FORMATIONS, 1985

1 HQ BAOR
Mönchengladbach

1 NORTHAG
Mönchengladbach

1 HQ RAF Germany
Mönchengladbach

2 1 (BR) Corps
Bielefeld

2 2 Infantry Division *York – with Fwd HQ in Germany – the rest UK Based)*

3 I Artillery Division
Dortmund

4 HQ 4 Signal Group
Rhinedahlen

5 1 Armoured Division
Verden

6 7 Armoured Brigade
Soltau

7 12 Armoured Brigade
Osnabrück

8 22 Armoured Brigade
Bergen-Hohne

9 3 Armoured Division
Soest

9 6 Armoured Brigade
Soest

10 4 Armoured Brigade
Münster

11 4 Armoured Division
Herford

12 11 Armoured Brigade
Minden

13 20 Armoured Brigade
Detmold

14 33 Armoured Brigade
Paderborn

x (24 Infantry Brigade)
Catterick

x (15 (NE) Infantry Brigade)
Topcliffe

x (49 (E) Infantry Brigade)
Chilwell

GERMANY
COLOGNE – BERLIN

10 0 10 20 30 40 50 60 70 MILES

North Sea

WEST AND EAST FRISIAN ISLANDS

NIEDERSACHSEN – LOWER SAXONY

NORDRHEIN-WESTFALEN (North Rhine-Westphalia)

SCHLESWIG-HOLSTEIN

MECKLENBURG-VORPOMMERN

BRANDENBURG

SAXON-ANHALT

HESSEN

THÜRINGEN

RHEINLAND-PFALZ

BAVARIA

BELGIUM · LUXEMBOURG · FRANCE · CZECHOSLOVAKIA

Major cities: Kiel, Lübeck, HAMBURG, BERLIN, Bremen, Hanover, Brunswick, Leipzig, Münster, Osnabrück, Duisburg, Essen, Dortmund, Düsseldorf, COLOGNE, FRANKFURT, Nuremberg

Numbered locations: 1 Wildenrath, 2 Bielefeld, 3 Dortmund, 4 Wegberg, 5 Verden, 6 Munster, 7 Osnabrück, 8 Bergen-Hohne / Belsen, 9 Soest, 10 Münster, 11 Herford, 12 Minden, 13 Detmold, 14 Paderborn

Other place names on map: Westerland, Flensburg, Schleswig, Husum, Rendsburg, Sehestedt, Preetz, Plön, Putlos, Neumünster, Itzehoe, Eutin, Todendorf, Ratzeburg, Schwerin, Güstrow, Rostock, Wismar, Stralsund, Greifswald, Neubrandenburg, Neustrelit, Müritz, Kyritz, Wittstock, Pritzwalk, Wittenberge, Dömitz, Danneberg, Uelzen, Salzwedel, Gardelegen, Stendal, Rathenow, Nauen, Potsdam, Burg, Magdeburg, Helmstedt, Wolfenbüttel, Wolfsburg, Langeleben, Torfhaus-Harz, Bad Harzburg, Goslar, Clausthal-Zellerfeld, Halberstadt, Zerbst, Wittenburg, Dessau-Roßlau, Bernburg, Bernburg, Halle (Saale), Merseburg, Altenburg, Glauchau, Chemnitz, Zwickau, Greiz, Plauen, Hof, Bayreuth, Weiden, Erlangen, Fürth, Schwandorf, Neumarkt in der Oberpfalz, Ansbach, Rothenburg ob der Tauber, Heidelberg, Mannheim, Trier, Aachen, Düren, Norvenich, Bonn, Bad Godesberg, Siegburg, Morsbach, Siegen, Bad Berleburg, Limburg, Koblenz, Mainz, Wiesbaden, Gelnhausen, Euerdorf, Lohr, Würzburg, Iphofen, Schweinfurt, Bad Neustadt, Coburg, Bamberg, Suhl, Meiningen, Gersfeld, Fulda, Hünfeld, Bad Hersfeld, Eisenach, Gotha, Erfurt, Jena, Arnstadt, Mühlhausen, Heiligenstadt, Ebeleben, Nordhausen, Silberhütte in Harz, Northeim, Göttingen, Münden, Kassel, Warburg, Borgentreich, Höxter, Einbeck, Northeim, Hildesheim, Alfeld, Delligsen, Scharfoldendorf, Nieheim, Bad Lippspringe, Sennelager, Gütersloh, Warendorf, Dülmen, Wulfen, Recklinghausen, Hamm, Lippstadt, Werl, Körbecke, Möhnesee, Soest, Brilon, Meschede, Sundern, Winterberg, Bad Berleburg, Deilinghofen, Menden, Hemer, Iserlohn, Wetter, Witten-Annen, Bochum, Wankum, Krefeld, Mülheim, Ratingen, Wuppertal, Hilden, Hubbelrath, Mönchengladbach, Willich, St Tonis, Vierson, Bracht, Brüggen, Birgelen, Geilenkirchen, Venlo, Goch, Xanten, Wesel, Laarbruch, Nijmegan, Arnhem, Nordhorn, Bad Bentheim, Gronau, Rheine, Lengerich, Bad Rothenfelde, Osterkappen, Diepholz, Liebenau, Vechta, Essen, Cloppenburg, Meppen, Lingen, Papenburg, Oldenburg, Delmenhorst, Ahlhorn, Dümmersee, Steinhuder Meer, Wunstorf, Obernkirchen, Bad Eilsen, Rinteln, Hamelin, Springe, Bad Salzüfeln, Lemgo, Lübbecke, Bünde, Bad Oeynhausen, Rethem, Walsrode, Soltau, Fallingbostel, Fassberg, Bergen-Hohne, Celle, Wesendorf, Ebstorf, Lüneburg, Lauenburg, Ludwigslust, Schweriner See, Glinde, Harburg, Buxtehude, Bremerhaven, Brake, Emden, Leer, Aurich, Norden, Wilhelmshaven, Jever, Cuxhaven, Brunsbüttel, Glückstadt, Pinneberg, Uetersen, KIEL CANAL

Rivers: EMS, WESER, ALLER, LEINE, ELBE, SAALE, RHINE, MAIN, FULDA

After the end of the Cold War, a major drawdown of units and bases took place in Germany from 1992 onwards. The resulting structure was based on 1 (UK) Armoured Division, with its HQ now in Wentworth Barracks, Herford, having moved to amalgamate with HQ 4 Armoured Division. The three armoured brigades were re-located, with 7th Armoured Brigade moving from Soltau to Bergen-Hohne, Campbell Barracks on the edge of NATO's largest tank-firing ranges in Europe. 4th Armoured Brigade moved to replace 12th Armoured Brigade in Quebeck Barracks, Osnabrück, and 20th Armoured Brigade moved from Detmold to a new HQ in Normandy Barracks, Sennelager, with direct access to the Sennelager Training Area. 102 Logistic Brigade was formed from HQ Combat Service Support Group at Princess Royal Barracks, Gütersloh (the old RAF Gütersloh air-base) in 1999. The structure of this command would be the last divisional command on the mainland of Europe.

LOCATIONS OF THE MAIN UK FORMATIONS, 2005

1   **HQ United Kingdom Support Command (Germany)**
Mönchengladbach

2   **I Armoured Division**
Herford

3   **4 Armoured Brigade**
Osnabrück

4   **7 Armoured Brigade**
Bergen-Hohne

5   **20 Armoured Brigade**
Sennelager

6   **102 Logistic Brigade**
Gütersloh

GERMANY
COLOGNE — BERLIN

0 0   10   20   30   40   50   60   70 MILES

North Sea

WEST AND EAST FRISIAN ISLANDS

DENMARK

Westerland

Flensburg

Schleswig
Husum
Sehestedt
Kiel
KIEL CANAL
Rendsburg
Preetz
Plön
Putlos
Eutin
Neumünster
Itzehoe
Brunsbüttel
Glückstadt
Uetersen
Pinneberg
HAMBURG
Harburg
Buxtehude
Glinde
Todendorf
Ratzeburg
Lauenburg
Schweriner See
Schwerin
SCHLESWIG-HOLSTEIN
Lübeck
Wismar
Rostock
Greifswald
Stralsund
Güstrow
Neubrandenburg
Neustrelitz
MECKLENBURG-VORPOMMERN
Müritz

Cuxhaven
Bremerhaven
Brake
Norden
Jever
Wilhelmshaven
Aurich
Emden
Leer
Oldenburg
Papenburg
Delmenhorst
Bremen
Rotenburg
Verden
Walsrode
Rethem
Soltau
Fallingbostel
Fassberg
Munster
Ebstorf
Uelzen
Lüneburg
ELBE
Danneberg
Dömitz
Ludwigslust
Pritzwalk
Wittstock
Kyritz
Wittenberge
Salzwedel
BRANDENBURG
Rathenow
Nauen
BERLIN
Potsdam

Ahlhorn
Cloppenburg
Essen
Vechta
NIEDERSACHSEN-LOWER SAXONY
Meppen
Diepholz
Liebenau
Nienburg
Steinhuder Meer
Dümmersee
Lingen
Nordhorn
Osterkappen
Wunstorf
Bergen-Hohne 4
Belsen
Celle
Wesendorf
Wolfsburg
ALLER
Gardelegen
Stendal
SAXON-ANHALT
Burg
Magdeburg
Zerbst
Wittenberg
Dessau-Roßlau
Bernburg
Halberstadt

Bad Bentheim
Rheine
Osnabrück 3
Bünde
Lübbecke
Minden
Obernkirchen
Bad Eilsen
Wolfenbüttel
Langeleben
Helmstedt
Gronau
Bad Oeynhausen
Herford
Bad Salzuflen
Rinteln
Hameln
Springe
Hildesheim
Brunswick
Arnhem
Nijmegen
Warendorf 6
Gütersloh 2
Bielefeld
Lemgo
Detmold
Scharfoldendorf
Alfeld
Delligsen
Einbeck
Goslar
Bad Harzburg
Torfhaus-Harz
Clausthal-Zellerfeld
Münster
Bad Rothenfelde
Sennelager 5
Nieheim
Höxter
Dülmen
Wulfen
Bad Lippspringe
Paderborn
Northeim
Göttingen
Silberhütte in Harz
Nordhausen
Halle (Saale)
Wittenberg

Goch
Wesel
Xanten
Hamm
Lippstadt
Soest
Körbecke
Borgentreich
Warburg
Munden
Kassel
Heiligenstadt
Ebeleben
Merseburg
Leipzig
Laarbruch
Recklinghausen
Werl
Möhnesee
Brilon
Mühlhausen
Winterberg
Dortmund
Witten-Annen
Hemer
Menden
Iserlohn
Deilinghofen
Meschede
Sundern
Duisburg
Bochum
Essen
Mülheim
Ratingen
Wuppertal
Hubbelrath
NORDRHEIN-WESTFALEN (North Rhine-Westphalia)
Bad Berleburg
HESSEN
Eisenach
Gotha
Erfurt
Jena
Altenburg
Venlo
Wankum
Krefeld
St Tonis
Brüggen
Düsseldorf 1
Wildenrath
Birgelen
Wegberg
Mönchengladbach
Hilden
Siegen
Bad Hersfeld
Arnstadt
THÜRINGEN
Zwickau
Greiz
Glauchau
Chemnitz
Geilenkirchen
Norvenich
Morsbach
Siegburg
Bonn
Bad Godesberg
COLOGNE
Wahn
Aachen
Düren
Hünfeld
Eisenach
Meiningen
Suhl
Plauen
RHINE
Koblenz
Limburg
FULDA
Fulda
Gersfeld
Bad Neustadt
Coburg
Hof
Trier
Wiesbaden
Mainz
FRANKFURT
Lohr
MAIN
Schweinfurt
Bamberg
Bayreuth
RHEINLAND-PFALZ
RHINE
Gelnhausen
Euerdorf
Würzburg
Iphofen
BAVARIA
Weiden
LUXEMBOURG
Mannheim
Heidelberg
Rothenburg ob der Tauber
Uffenheim
Ansbach
Fürth
Nuremberg
Erlangen
Schwandorf
Neumarkt in der Oberpfalz
BELGIUM
FRANCE
CZECH REPUBLIC
EMS
WESER
LEINE
SAALE
ELBE

INDEX

Page references in *italics* indicate images.

PICTURE CREDITS

Every effort has been made to trace copyright holders and to obtain their permission for the use of copyright material. The publisher apologises for any errors or omissions, and would be grateful to be notified of any corrections that should be incorporated in future reprints or editions of this book.

We are enormously grateful to the many individuals who have submitted their own photographs and images for the book, and we regret that we have only been able to use a fraction of those available. From Army Press Office, we are indebted to Dominic King for his help in securing many Crown images, as well as a number of fine photographs he has taken in his official capacity as the last BFG Army photographer. Images from the National Army Museum are courtesy of their Council of Trustees. The following photographers have images within the book:

Chris Atkins: p.109; Sgt Simon Butcher RAF: pp.148 (all images), 150 (top and bottom); Terry Bryne: p.102; Cpl Wes Calder RLC: pp.168, 173; Kaspar Coward: pp.77, 80; Barry Davies: p.89; Cpl Adrian Harlen: p.146; Dominic King: pp.6, 7, 89, 134, 154, 155 (centre left), 156–157, 158, 159 (top), 161 (all), 162, 164, 166, 171 (top and bottom), 172; Pete Modley: pp.66, 67, 71; WOII Giles Penfound: pp.140–141, 143; Carl Schulze: p.107; Debs Thorne: p.167; Cpl Mark Webster RLC: p.169; Phil Welsh: pp.93, 114, 117–118, 129, 131, 132, 134, 149 (top left), 152 (top left), 158; Tobias Wilkinson: pp.154–5; Rhoda Wilson: p.163; Detlef Wittig: p.98; Bernd Witzmann: p.155 (bottom left).

The map appearing on pp.179–87 was created by Russell Bell.

A map of XXX Corps District, from a guidebook produced by the corps in 1945 (Crown)

I CORPS

L of C HQ's

7 ARMD DIV

3 CDN INF DIV

50

I CDN CORPS

G.H.O. & L of C TPS

II ARMD DIV

3 INF DIV

51

2 CDN CORPS

GDS ARMD DIV

79 ARMD DIV

5 INF DIV

MO

52

8 CORPS

I POLISH ARMD DIV

AIRBORNE TPS

15 (S) INF DIV

53

12 CORPS

4 CDN ARMD DIV

I CDN INF DIV

43 (W) INF DIV

59 (
(

30 CORPS

5 CDN ARMD DIV

2 CDN INF DIV

49 (W.R) INF DIV